D1085061

ONE SURGEON'S
PRIVATE WAR

SURGEON WILLIAM WARREN POTTER
57TH NEW YORK
(Three Years With the Army of the Potomac)

ONE SURGEON'S PRIVATE WAR

Doctor William W. Potter
■of the 57th New York ■

Editor-in-Chief, John Michael Priest
Researchers and Co-editors:
Brian Spry, Daryl Earnest, Matthew Swope,
Diane Grove, Megan Stoner, Melissa Henderson,
Jennifer Shank, Janice Hickey

BREVET LIEUTENANT-COLONEL,

U.S. VOL'S. SURGEON IN CHARGE OF

FIRST DIVISION FIELD HOSPITAL

SECOND ARMY CORPS;

SURGEON 57TH REG'T N.Y.V.;

ASSISTANT-SURGEON 49TH REG'T N.Y. VOL'S;

SIXTH ARMY CORPS; ETC., ETC.

BUFFALO.
1888.

 White Mane Publishing Company, Inc.

Copyright © 1996 by John Michael Priest

All rights reserved — no part of this book may be reproduced in any form without permission in writing from the publisher, except by a reviewer who wishes to quote brief passages in connection with a review.

This White Mane Publishing Co., Inc. publication was printed by:

Beidel Printing House, Inc.
63 West Burd Street
Shippensburg, PA 17257 USA

In respect for the scholarship contained herein, the acid-free paper used in this book meets the guidelines for permanence and durability of the Committee on Production Guidelines for Book Longevity of the Council on Library Resources.

For a complete list of available publications please write:

White Mane Publishing Co.., Inc.
P.O. Box 152
Shippensburg, PA 17257-0152

Library of Congress Cataloging-in-Publication Data

Potter, William W. (William Warren), 1837-1911.
    One surgeon's private war : doctor William H. Potter of the 57th
New York / edited by John Michael Priest et al.
        p.   cm.
    Originally published: Buffalo. 1888.
    Includes bibliographical references and index.
    ISBN 1-57249-021-7 (alk. paper)
    1. Potter, William W. (William Warren), 1837-1911. 2. United
States--History--Civil War, 1861-1865--Personal narratives.
3. United States. Army. New York Infantry Regiment, 57th
(1861-1864) 4. New York (State)--History--Civil War, 1861-1865-
-Medical care. 5. United States. Army--Surgeons--Correspondence.
6. United States--History--Civil War, 1861-1865--Medical care.
7. Surgeons--New York (State)--Biography. I. Priest, John M.,
1949-   . II. Title.
E523.5 57th.P68   1996
973.7'447--dc20   96-19886
                                                        CIP

PRINTED IN THE UNITED STATES OF AMERICA

TABLE OF CONTENTS

PREFACE

THE FOLLOWING PAGES are, as their title indicates, a personal history of my military service in the Civil War of 1861–5, during which time I served three years as a medical officer with the Army of the Potomac. That army, as is well known, was one of the two chief armies in that great struggle; it had, as equally well known, the most difficult field of operations, and, as a consequence, the most trying duties to perform of any of the Union forces. It was always required to protect Washington, while, at the same time, it was expected to destroy the most formidable army of the Confederacy, led by its greatest captain.

How well that mighty creation of the patriotism of a free people performed its duties, or how satisfactorily it accomplished its tasks, is not for me to say—these will be determined by that most impartial tribunal, history—but it is expedient that every man who can do so, should record what he did, and what he saw done, during his military service. Acting upon this conviction, I have attempted to carry out this purpose in my own case in a truthful manner, without any attempt at self-praise, or to embellish the pages with anecdote or eulogy.

It has, on the other hand, simply been my aim to bring together in a connected way the various scenes through which I passed, believing that possibly in future years if not now, my children, or theirs, will be interested to know just what part their paternal ancestor played in the great drama of war—that war waged for a mightier principle than any other in the history of the world.

The account is made up from letters which I wrote to my wife from the field that were always in the nature of bulletins, from memoranda made at the time, and from undimmed recollection of every event narrated. The dates are believed to be absolutely accurate, and the impressions [where any are given] are such as obtained at the time. It is probable that, in light of subsequent history, some of them may appear erroneous, or ill-conceived; but I prefer to let them stand as recorded at the time, as simply a reflex of the then accepted opinions of passing events.

In such a purely personal narrative the constant employment of the first person is unavoidable; yet, as it is not intended for publication, but merely for the eyes of relatives, or intimate friends, this will, I trust, be considered pardonable.

Finally, the consciousness of having performed my duty faithfully and to the utmost of my ability, even though humbly, during the period embraced in this record, has always been to me a comforting reflection, compensating in a full measure for all "the dangers I had passed," and if any one should, perchance, enjoy a moiety of pleasure in the perusal of these pages that I did in preparing them, I shall be more than gratified.

W.W.P.

March 23rd, 1888.

ACKNOWLEDGEMENTS

AS WITH ANY project of this nature it is very difficult to express adequate appreciation to everyone who made its completion possible. We are indebted to the following individuals for freely contributing their time and resources: the staff of the research library at USAMHI; Dr. Richard Sommers; Michael Winey, and Randy Hackenburg (USAMHI); Paul Chiles and Ted Alexander (Antietam National Battlefield); Dr. Anne Curran (South Hagerstown High School), who provided us with an IBM computer; the maintenance personnel at the Washington County Board of Education, who repaired the computer; the parents and guardians of the eight high school students for allowing their children to stay after school for many afternoons to work on this book; Dr. Martin Gordon, Harold Collier, and Duaine Collier of White Mane Publishing for accepting our proposal to publish; Ben Maryniak, Tim Shaw, and Daniel Wilcoz of Buffalo, New York, who provided us with photographs and a regimental history; my daughter, Kimberly, who typed the manuscript onto a disc from a photo copy of the original; and the Buffalo and Erie County Historical Society for granting us permission to start this work.

My special thanks go to the eight wonderful students who did most of the editing, research, and typing. Janice Hickey, who started this project with us as a 9th grader in 1992, moved out of our district and was not able to take part in the second year of work. Brian Spry, Daryl Earnest, Matt Swope, Melissa Henderson, Jennifer Shank, Megan Stoner, and Diane Grove began this project in 1992 as 9th graders. We took two field trips: one to USAMHI and the other to the resource center at Antietam National Battlefield. The students worked in the book stacks and took most of the photographs. We then met after school from 3:30 P.M. to 4:30 P.M. as often as three to four times a week to edit the manuscript.

The students generally worked in pairs with one reading the manuscript and supplying note material while the other typed the endnotes into the computer. They all decided to leave Potter's verb tenses as he had them in the memoirs. They also made the decision to eliminate as many of his "run on" sentences as possible to make the book more readable. Despite the many long hours, we genuinely enjoyed the work. With the exception of sports season I never had any difficulty in getting them to put in their time. They often competed to see which pairs could come in more often than the others. There were times when too many of them showed up and we did not have enough work for them to do. We laughed a great deal.

What did we learn from this project? Typing skills, keyboarding, punctuation, footnoting, bibliographic techniques, research techniques, grammar, military history, and medical history were all part of this exercise. It was a genuinely interdisciplinary course which, because of scheduling, we could not incorporate into the regular school day. I learned that there are eight special young men and women who were willing to sacrifice their time for an accomplishment from which they will not reap monetary rewards. They will probably never garner any fame but they have preserved for the future memories from the most crucial four years in United States history. The royalties from this work are going to the Buffalo and Erie County Historical Society and to South Hagerstown High School.

"I'd like to thank Mr. Priest for bringing this project to our attention. I enjoyed it immensely. The trip to Carlisle for research was great. I liked the editing because I'm quite the typist. Footnoting was the best and Mr. Priest knew exactly how to confuse me with the end parentheses, hyphens, and abbreviations for the ranks of the soldiers. The only thing that I didn't like was that I wasn't allowed to use the pretty parentheses, so here is my chance. {...}, etc.

"Thanks again for giving me the opportunity to participate in such a great, not to mention fun, project."

Megan E. Stoner

"The project was a totally new learning experience for me. I really enjoyed editing this book and I'm really grateful to Mr. Priest who gave me this opportunity. I enjoyed reading through the manuscript because it made me feel like I was back in time and right in the middle of the action. I also liked looking up the people listed in the book and finding out what regiments they were in, their rank, and what happened to them in battle. I even learned to type—a little bit. The only thing I didn't like was that Mr. Priest wouldn't let us use the pretty parentheses {...}. I loved every minute that I helped to work on the book and I thank Mr. Priest for everything he did."

Diane Grove

INTRODUCTION

WILLIAM WARREN POTTER was born in Strykesville, Genesee (now Wyoming) County, New York, December 31, 1837. His father, Dr. Lindorf Potter, a native of the town of Sheldon, Genesee (Wyoming) County, was a son of Dr. Benjamin Potter. The latter married Phebe, daughter of Dr. Eastman, of Connecticut, and came hence to Western New York in 1808, and was one of the earliest physicians in the Holland Purchase. Of four sons, two (Lindorf and Milton E.) became physicians and settled in the same county of their birth, where they became distinguished in their profession. Dr. Lindorf Potter, father of the subject of this sketch, married Mary G., daughter of the Rev. Abijah Blanchard, D. D., a prominent clergyman in the Episcopal Church, February 12, 1837, and settled in Strykesville, New York. He removed to Warsaw, in 1842; thence to Varysburg in 1844, where he practiced medicine until his death, which occurred March 27, 1857.

Dr. Milton E. Potter, uncle of William W., settled in Bennington Centre, whence he removed to Cowlesville, and thence to Attica, New York where he died in 1875, in the ripeness of years and the full enjoyment of a busy practice up to the last days of his life. He was the father of Dr. Milton Grosvenor Potter, late Professor of Anatomy in the Buffalo Medical College, who died in Buffalo January 28, 1878.

The early life of William W. Potter was passed in the vicinity of his birth, and his lay education was in the private schools at Arcade Seminary, and at Genesee Seminary and College at Lima, New York. He came to Buffalo in 1854, receiving his medical education at Buffalo Medical College, where he graduated February 23, 1859. Soon after graduating he was offered a partnership in the practice of his uncle, Dr. Milton E. Potter, of Cowlesville, New York, where he located in the

xi

spring of 1859. Upon the breaking out of the Civil War he made haste to offer his services in a professional capacity to the Government and passed the examination of the Army Medical Examining Board at Albany, New York, April 25, 1861. He became interested in the organization of the Second Buffalo Regiment (the Forty-ninth New York Volunteers) in the summer of 1861 and was commissioned its Assistant Surgeon by Governor [Edwin D.] Morgan, September 16, 1861, at the insistence of the Union Defense Committee, which was composed of Mayor F. A. Alberger, Dr. Edward Storck, James Adams, Isaac Holloway, Alderman A. A. Howard and others. Colonel D. [Daniel] D. Bidwell was selected to command the regiment and, under his experienced and able leadership, it bore its part honorably and well in the great contest which so sorely tried the metal of American soldiers. The history of the Forty-ninth Regiment has become a part of the History of Erie County and need not be recounted here.

Dr. Potter served as its junior medical officer during all of its earlier career from the date of its organization; was with it when it joined the Army of the Potomac; followed its fortunes during the Peninsular Campaign; then, when it was temporarily under [Major General John] Pope; again when it was under [Major General George B.] McClellan in the Maryland Campaign; and finally when under [Major General Ambrose] Burnside in the Fredericksburg disaster.

He was left with the wounded of [Brigadier General William F.] Smith's division on the night of the 29th of June, 1862 by order of [Major] General [William B.] Franklin, commanding the Sixth Corps, when the army was retreating by the flank to Harrison's Landing, and [the] next morning fell into the hands of the enemy, when he had an interesting interview with the redoubtable [Brigadier General Thomas J.] "Stonewall" Jackson. In a few days he was removed to Richmond and given quarters in Libby prison, then under command of the celebrated Lieutenant Turner. He was released among the first exchanges under the cartel arranged between the hostile powers and delivered to the hospital ship "Louisiana", July 18, 1862 and immediately thereafter rejoined his regiment at Harrison's Landing, Virginia. On December 16, 1862, just after the battle of Fredericksburg, he was promoted surgeon of the Fifty-seventh Regiment New York Volunteers, in [Major General Winfield Scott] Hancock's division of the Second Corps. He served with his regiment during the Chancellorsville and Gettysburg campaigns, and, in August, 1863, was assigned to the charge of the First Division Hospital, Second Corps, continuing upon that duty until his muster-out of service with his regiment near the close of the war. He was breveted Lieutenant-Colonel United States Volunteers for faithful and meritorious service by the President of the United States and of New York Volunteers by the Governor of the State of New York, for like reasons.

After the war he performed service for the Government in connection with the Pension Office as General Examining Surgeon, and was appointed Coroner of the District of Columbia. He resigned the latter office to return to the more congenial field of private practice, and located temporarily in Mount Morris, Livingston County. For several years he resided in Batavia, Genesee County, where he was physician to the New York State Institution for the Blind; he was a member of the Genesee County Medical Society, which his grandfather, Dr. Benjamin Potter, joined in 1813; which his father, Dr. Lindorf Potter, joined in 1833; and which his uncle, Dr. Milton E. Potter, joined in 1838. Finally he returned to Buffalo in 1881, where he has since resided pursuing the practice of his profession.

He is a curator of the Medical Department of the University of Buffalo; permanent member of the American Medical Association (1878); permanent member of the Medical Society of the State of New York (1883); member of the Erie County Medical Society; member of the Buffalo Medical and Surgical Association; member of the Buffalo Medical Union; and life member of Alumni Association of Buffalo Medical College. He was one of the founders of the latter association, and its president in 1877. His professional tastes, largely cultivated by association with his father, led him early into the field of surgery and he has performed many of the more important operations, both in military and civil practice.

Of late he has turned his attention quite largely to diseases of women, having performed many important operations in this department of medicine. He has been a frequent contributor to medical literature, and has, likewise, written many unpublished papers for medical societies and other bodies. Among his published writings may be mentioned the following: "Umbilical Hernia in the Adult, with the report of a successful operation," *Buffalo Medical Journal,* 1879; "Rectal Alimentation for the Relief of the Obstinate Vomiting of Pregnancy," *American Journal of Obstetrics,* New York, 1880; "Remarks on Rectal Feeding in Disease," *New York Medical Record,* 1880; "Epithelioma of the Cervix Uteri," *Transactions of the Medical Society of the State of New York,* 1881; "The Genu-Pectoral Posture in Uterine and Ovarian Displacements," *Transactions of the Medical Society of the State of New York,* 1882; "The Gynecic Uses and Value of the Genu-Pectoral Posture," *Transactions of the American Medical Association,* 1882; "Induction of Premature Labor in Puerperal Eclampsia," *Transactions of the Medical Society of the State of New York,* 1883; "Address to the Alumni of Buffalo Medical College," delivered in St. James Hall, February 23rd, 1875. He is a contributor to the *Army Medical Museum*, and to the *Medical and Surgical History of the War.*

Dr. Potter was married March 23rd, 1859 to Emily A., daughter of William S. Bostwick, Esq., of Lancaster, Erie County. His wife, a native of Erie county, is a lineal descendant of Ethan Allen, of Revolutionary fame, and her family came from Vermont to Erie County in an early day. He has three children, viz: Dr. Frank Hamilton Potter, born January 8, 1860; Helen Blanchard, born February 13, 1868; and Alice F. born November 22, 1870; all living in Buffalo. His son, Dr. Frank H. Potter, is engaged in the practice of his profession and is clinical assistant to the Chair of Surgery in the Medical Department of Niagara University.

[William W. Potter died at age 72 in Buffalo New York on March 14, 1911, - *Buffalo Enquirer,* March 14, 1911.]

CHAPTER ONE — 1861

THE START

ON THE 15TH day of April 1861, three days after the fall of Fort Sumter, the President called for 75,000 men and, in apportioning the number for each state, New York's quota under this call and a subsequent one made May 3rd, was fixed at 38 regiments of infantry. To raise, arm, equip, officer and get this force ready for the field became the duty of the Governor [Edwin D. Morgan] and his military staff. His surgeon-general, Dr. S. Oakley Vanderpoel, at once issued a notice to medical men throughout the state who might desire to serve as surgeons and assistant-surgeons, to assemble in Albany on the 25th and 26th days of April 1861, for examination as to their fitness for these positions in the volunteer forces then raising.

At this time I was residing in Cowlesville, Wyoming County, where I had been practicing medicine in partnership with my uncle, Dr. M. E. Potter, for about two years. I went to Albany on [Thursday] April 25th, presented myself for examination before the board of examiners in the assembly chamber [the] next morning, completed my duties at 2 o'clock P.M. and left for home that night. In about two weeks I received notice that I had passed the examination, and would be appointed an assistant-surgeon upon my nomination as such by the colonel of a regiment. It appears that under an old militia law rule this function was vested in the colonels of regiments, and this practice prevailed during the organization of the first 38 (two years' regiments) that the State of New York furnished. In all regiments subsequently raised the appointment of the regimental staff was made by the governor direct, without the intervention of any preliminary nomination.

1

During the few weeks following my successful examination, I made energetic, though futile endeavors, to obtain an appointment; but the numbers seeking places were so great, and the openings so few, that I soon began to despair of success. Most of these early appointments were obtained by men of influence with the several colonels, men much older and more experienced in affairs than I. (I was at this time but 22 years of age.)

Finally came the Bull Run disaster of July 21st 1861 and immediately thereafter followed a requisition upon our governor for 25,000 men for three years, under the authority of Congress [which] vested power in the President to accept the services of 500,000 men. Buffalo had already, under the first call, sent out the 21st regiment for two years, and soon after the second call authority was vested in a coterie of patriotic citizens, under the name of the Union Defense Committee, to raise another regiment. This committee numbered among its members Mayor F. [Franklin] A. Alberger, James Adams, Dr. Edward Storck, Alderman A. A. Howard, Isaac Holloway, and others whose names I do not now recall.

Recruiting for the new regiment began on [Tuesday] July 30th under the direction of this energetic committee. Fort Porter was selected as the rendezvous, and Major. D. [Daniel] D. Bidwell appointed to command the post and superintend the recruiting.[1] Major Bidwell was at the time an experienced officer in the state militia, and, as commandant of Company "D" [74th New York State Militia] had attained a reputation as an efficient drillmaster, as well as a disciplinarian of an unusual order in civil life, and it was expected that he would be chosen to command the regiment whenever it should take the field. He selected for his assistant George W. Johnson to act as Major, with Henry D. Tillinghast as Quartermaster, William Bullymore as Adjutant, and the usual non-commissioned staff.[2]

FORT PORTER

Early in August I sought Major Bidwell's acquaintance, through his brother Charles, whom I knew very well, and was authorized to obtain recruits for the command.[3] I visited a number of the villages of Wyoming County where war meetings were held, and succeeded in the course of a month in enlisting 10 or 12 men altogether, who were assigned to Company D which William F. Wheeler, then a lieutenant in the 21st Regiment was expected to command.[4] On [Monday] September 9th Dr. James A. Hall of Brocton, Chautauqua County, New York, was appointed surgeon of the regiment.[5] By this time the command had begun to assume the dignity of that title, being designated for the

Colonel Daniel D. Bidwell
of the 49th New York
(MOLLUS, USAMHI)

Major George W. Johnson
of the 49th New York
(NYSAG, USAMHI)

sake of convenience, the Second Buffalo Regiment.[6] I had already visited the post several times with recruits, and on [Monday] morning September 16th, I left home with 2 or 3 more men. Arriving in the camp, to my astonishment, I found the regiment under orders to proceed to New York [City] at once. The remainder of the day was spent in making hasty preparations for the journey. 6 o'clock P.M. had been fixed as the hour for our departure.

Up to this time none of the field or staff officers had been appointed, with the single exception of Dr. [James A.] Hall. All determined to go to New York [City], myself among the number, in the expectation that we would there receive our commissions. During the day I visited several of the Buffalo physicians and obtained from them recommendations to the governor, hoping they might have influence in securing for me the appointment as assistant-surgeon. I had already forwarded to the governor letters from Judge J. B. Skinner, Judge J. G. Hoyt, Hon. Augustus Frank, Albert Sawin and others, strongly recommending me for the place. I sought to still further fortify my case in the manner described, believing that "thrice is he armed" who hath plenty of endorsements from prominent public men.

We took up our march from Fort Porter about 4 o'clock P.M. on the day in question, which was Monday of the week, passing down Niagara [Street] to Main [Street], thence to Exchange Street and the Erie depot, where a special train was waiting to convey us on our mission. All the way from the fort to the station the streets were crowded with people cheering us as we marched along. The houses and other buildings along the whole route [were] filled with interested spectators. Flags and other emblems were displayed. Shouts of encouragement went up, and a hearty god-speed came from thousands of throats. It was truly an ovation and a scene never to be forgotten. So we were off for the seat of war. This indeed was the first stage of our journey with that objective, amidst the booming of cannon, strains of patriotic music, and the huzzahs and tears of our friends—the good citizens of Buffalo.

Our train was a heavy one and moved slowly, but we reached New York [City] on the morning of [Wednesday] September 18th without accident or mishap. We were accompanied by some of the members of the Union Defense Committee. Others went direct to Albany to confer with the governor, and finally met us in New York [City]. Those who went to Albany reached New York [City] on the evening of [Tuesday] the 17th and met us at the Ferry in Jersey City [the] next morning. In New York [City] the company officers and men were quartered in Park Barracks and the prospective field and staff at the Astor House, which was directly opposite the barracks. On our arrival at Jersey City Dr. [Edward] Storck of the Union Defense Committee, who had gone via Albany, met me with the information that my letter of appointment as assistant-surgeon had been sent to Cowlesville by the surgeon-general, that on reaching New York [City] I was to report to that officer at 51 Walker Street, the New York headquarters for the organization of troops and there write my letter of acceptance. After getting breakfast I so reported, and met Dr. [S. Oakley] Vanderpoel for the second time who received me with the utmost kindness and informed me that as soon as he discovered the regiment had been ordered to New York [City] he, finding my credentials of first class order, immediately wrote my letter of appointment and sent it to Cowlesville. He further said he was glad I had come on with the troops instead of waiting for the letter, and, as they would be sent to the seat of the war soon, I could not be permitted to return home for a few days as I [had] desired. I thus found myself suddenly taken from civil life and placed in the medical staff of the volunteer army, to which work I was to devote the next three years of my life.

My affairs at home were necessarily left in a somewhat chaotic state, due to the suddenness of my departure, but thanks to my good wife, they were straightened out in due time, reflecting great credit upon her business sagacity, as well as patriotic devotion to [her] husband, country and duty. For the next few days the state officials and the Union Defense Committee were busily engaged in organizing and equipping the regiment, and by Saturday night, September 21st, we were on our way to Washington.

THE FORTY-NINTH

I purchased a uniform in New York [City] with money kindly loaned me by my good friend Alderman A. A. Howard of the Union Defense Committee, and I repaid him from the first money I received from the United States sometime in November. The regiment was designated the 49th New York Volunteers, and was officered as follows: D. [Daniel] D. Bidwell, Colonel; W. [William] C. Alberger, Lieutenant Colonel; George W. Johnson, Major; William Bullymore, Adjutant; Henry D. Tillinghast, Quartermaster; James A. Hall, Surgeon; and William W. Potter, Assistant Surgeon.[7]

Lieutenant Colonel
William C. Alberger
of the 49th New York
(NYSAG, USAMHI)

We reached Philadelphia about 2 o'clock A.M. Sunday [September 22], via the Camden & Amboy route, and were fed, even at that late hour, at the celebrated "Cooper Shop"—a refreshment establishment voluntarily maintained by the patriotic men and women of the "City of Brotherly Love". The tables were served by fair maidens and good young men, whose praises have been sounded by thousands of weary soldier-travelers on their way to the front. In the early morning air we marched across the city to the Baltimore depot and near 8 o'clock A.M. were off for Baltimore to the Calvert [Street] Station. My mind was filled with the recollection of the "plug uglies" who had so murderously assaulted the 6th Massachusetts on April 19th, 1861. However, we passed through the city very quietly, and were soon on our way to Washington, reaching the capital about 7 o'clock P.M.

The men were quartered for the night in the "Soldiers Rest" adjoining the Baltimore & Ohio R. R. Depot, but the officers were obliged to remain in the waiting room of the station all night, without blankets or other articles of comfort. Here was begun the soldiers' experience of "roughing it," for it was truly a most uncomfortable night. We were here joined by Lt. Col. Alberger, late captain in the 21st regiment who, with Dr. [Charles H.] Wilcox, the surgeon of the 21st, was waiting

for us at the depot on our arrival.[8] The sight of one familiar face—
someone to meet us at the train—was truly a refreshing circumstance,
after a week of such experience as we had passed through. The next
morning, Monday, September 23rd, we received orders to proceed
out to Meridian Hill north of Washington and there take up our camp.
I strolled around the streets of Washington for an hour in company
with Lieutenant Colonel Alberger, who pointed out the various objects
of interest, after which I accepted his invitation to ride out to camp in
a carriage with him—a luxurious mode of travel not usually enjoyed
by a soldier. We arrived in camp about 11 o'clock A.M., and at noon
had our first meal, such as it was, cooked in the field. We had not yet
reached that degree of perfection in our culinary arrangements, which
would enable us to rival Delmonico's. In the afternoon I went with
some of the other officers across Seventh Street Road, on which our
camp fronted, and engaged board at Mr. Benjamin Summy's, an old
resident of Lancaster (New York). We fared well while we remained at
Meridian Hill. This family knew my wife's relations well, and inquired
after them. Our comfort was destined to be of short duration, lasting
only from Monday [September 23] to Friday [September 27] when
"Camp Leslie"—for such it was called—was broken up.

At noon September 27th an order came for the regiment to report to Camp Lyon, located on the Maryland side of the Potomac about
5 miles above Georgetown. I was detailed to accompany the sick which
were carried in two ambulances and I set out about 4 o'clock P.M. by
another route to overtake the regiment. The driver lost his way. It was
after dark and in the midst of a pouring rain when we reached Camp
Lyon. Here I learned the regiment had been ordered across the Potomac.
Owing to the lateness of the hour, it was considered unwise to follow
with the ambulances, so I sought quarters for the night with the 6th
Wisconsin regiment whose surgeon [Chandler B. Chapman], good Sa-
maritan that he was, kindly "took me in."[9] After breakfast next morning [Saturday, September 28] we started once more in search of the
49th, which we soon found near Fort Ethan Allen, about half a mile
above Chain Bridge in Virginia. The roads were all filled with troops
pouring into Virginia: but soon everything was straightened out and
the 49th was joined at first to General W. [William] F. Smith's brigade,
[and] afterwards to General Isaac I. Stevens' brigade which formed a
part of Smith's command. [Smith became the commandant of a division.] At last, after much fatigue of body and tribulation of spirit, I
found myself on the "sacred soil of Virginia". Our regiment [was] in a
division that was destined to make itself famous on the field of honor
in defense of the security of the Republic.

The regiment was put into camp south of the fort under its guns,
and daily furnished a large detail of men to work upon its unfinished

walls. Here we had daily drills and frequent night alarms, during [which] we would go inside the fort. Sometimes [we stayed] for a few hours only and [at other times we] remained all night, expecting the enemy to attack. He never came. One night, however, very soon after we came here, there was some firing in our front that occasioned great anxiety. [The] next morning we learned that the 72nd Pennsylvania had fired into its own ranks by mistake, killing and wounding several men.[10]

On the morning of [Wednesday] October 2nd at 3 o'clock, I started out with a picket detail from our regiment of 280 men under the command of Captain [William F.] Wheeler [Company D], who had already seen service of this kind in the 21st [New York]. As this was the [first] experience of the 49th of this sort, it was naturally an event of much moment to us. I went along because it was customary to send an assistant surgeon with the picket detail, to look after any who might fall sick or be wounded. The picket headquarters were near Langley Church on the Leesburg Turnpike. We remained on this duty 24 hours. I visited the whole line on foot. (Our horses had not yet arrived.) [The line] was about two miles long [and] I was very tired when night came. During the day W. [William] H. [Howard] Russell, the celebrated correspondent of the London *Times* who had written a sensational account of the Battle of Bull Run for his paper, visited Langley and I saw him for the first and only time.[11] Governor Patterson of Chautauqua County had visited us the day before [Tuesday] at our camp and complimented the regiment upon its soldierly appearance. We returned to camp Thursday morning, October 3rd, much fatigued after our tour of picket duty, for our march was some 5 miles after we were relieved. The experience was, however, wholesome and served to give us confidence in ourselves.

[Saturday] October 12. The regiment, excepting two companies [A and I], moved forward from Fort Ethan Allen about 5 miles to "Camp of the Big Chestnut," the object being to straighten out the lines of the division and thus shorten the distance to the picket line.[12] The two companies were left behind to care for the fort, and I was detailed to remain with them. (We lost one officer, Captain [Raselas] Dickinson, of Chautauqua County, who was seized with an apoplectic fit in camp on October [9th]. I took him to Georgetown and placed him in the Seminary Hospital, where he died [on Saturday] October 12th. He was, I believe, the oldest officer in the regiment, a genial gentleman, and we all felt saddened by his sudden and untimely death.)[13] We did not join the main body for ten days and when I reached the regiment again I found our horses had arrived, which relieved me of the further necessity of doing duty on foot.

[Memorandum] My horse arrived [Tuesday] October 15th with the other horses, and was taken to "Camp of the Big Chestnut." He was sent to me at Fort Ethan Allen the next day. The citizens of Buffalo [and Company D, 74th New York State Militia] presented Colonel Bidwell his horse, which was a fine solid fellow just suited to his master's wants.[14] Mine was purchased of Bridges & Millar, of Cowlesville and was bred by Sargeant. He was a pure black, six years old. I rode him all through the service, fetching him home with me when I returned. Our horses were all sent to us without cost of transportation, the citizens of Buffalo looking after that; and we presented the man who brought them [with] a gold headed cane, as he would accept no compensation in money for his services. I regret that I have forgotten his name.

On [Monday] October 21st we were mustered into the U.S. service by Captain R. [Romeyn] B. Ayres, U.S. Army.[15] The muster was, however, to date back to the regular dates of our respective enlistments.

On [Thursday] October 24th the division was reviewed by General [William F.] Smith on a large field near his headquarters, which was the first review I had yet seen. General [Isaac I.] Stevens was ordered to South Carolina about this time, which left Col R. [Robert] P. Taylor, of the 33rd New York Volunteers temporarily in command of the 2nd brigade, by virtue of his seniority of rank.[16] General J. [John] M. Brannan was, however, soon assigned to its command.

On [Saturday] October 26th General [Winfield S.] Hancock, of the First Brigade, reviewed the command, which consisted of 14 regiments, 2 batteries, and a troop of cavalry. A sham battle followed the review, and the 49th [New York] was complimented by the general on its good appearance and discipline.

About this time the name of the camp was changed in [the] general orders, from "Camp Big Chestnut" [so named from a tree] to "Camp Griffin", in honor of Captain [Charles] Griffin whose battery had shelled Lewinsville a few weeks before from a point near where General [William F.] Smith's headquarters now were and drove the enemy out.[17] The object of the change was to make the name of the camp uniform throughout the whole division, a division being considered a unit so far as the present organization of the Army of the Potomac was concerned. On [Monday] October 28th the 21st [New York] Regiment paid us a visit with its entire field and staff, headed by the Union Cornet Band. We were all very glad to see the "boys," with many of whom I had a personal acquaintance. The surgeon, Dr. [Charles H.] Wilcox, was one of the prominent Buffalo physicians and I was particularly glad to meet him again, as well as many other officers and men of the command. After remaining with us about an hour and a half, they started back to their own camp of Munson's Hill amidst the huzzahs of a thousand friendly voices.

On [Thursday] October 31st we were inspected and mustered for pay—the first time we were put through this ordeal but which was hereafter to occur at the end of every second month. The inspecting officer had to, at this time, call every man's name, check those present, inspect the arms, accoutrements, clothing and quarters. The rolls with his certificate attached were the paymaster's voucher. After the muster Colonel [William C.] Alberger, Captain [William F.] Wheeler and myself went to Falls Church for a ride, and enjoyed the scenery very much. The old church was built of red brick imported from England, the same as Pohick Church at Mount Vernon and other churches in Virginia.

During these days I frequently visited Washington, which was about 10 miles from our camp, sometimes remaining all night with friends in the city but generally returning the same day with stores, medicines, and camp equipage for the hospital. The requisitions for these articles were made by the surgeon [and] approved by the colonel and the brigade commander, when they were ready to be taken by somebody to Washington to be filled. This duty fell to me as I have just hinted. I usually enjoyed going to the city very much indeed. While it afforded diversion from its variety, it was often very fatiguing, not to say sometimes perplexing, and I generally returned in the evening tired and hungry, but getting a sound sleep. The regular monthly return of [the] sick was also to be made up at this time, the first we had made, and this duty fell to my lot as junior medical officer. It was a perplexing thing to do at first, but I soon "got the hang of it", and didn't mind it as much afterwards.

[Friday] November 1st 1861 saw us fairly established in the full humdrum ways of camp life. I do not mean by this that we were idle,— far from it. By this time we had gone through those very necessary early experiences of marching, drilling, inspecting and reviews; of requisitions, reports, musters, and picketing. We were now sufficiently acclimated and habituated to the military service to make us an effective factor in the autonomy of the division. We had a good hospital in excellent working order. Ours was reputed the healthiest regiment in the division. The men were happy in the confidence of their officers and realized the fact that they would be well cared for if sick or otherwise disabled.

The Rev. John Bowman, of Niagara County, who had been appointed chaplain, reported on Sunday, November 3rd and preached to the regiment for the first time the same afternoon. He was a stranger to most of us but a man of some ability. He did fairly well while he remained with the regiment. (He resigned [on Sunday] April 13th 1862, while we were before Yorktown.)

We received our first pay on [Friday] November 8th—it being for [the time] from September 16th to October 31st inclusive. It required 38,000 dollars to pay the regiment. My own pay for the same period amounted [to] $196.24, and it was given to me in gold. Out of this sum I paid all the expenses I had incurred on account of entry into the service, including the cost of horse equipments, retained $25.00 for current expenses, and sent $40.00 to my wife. (When everything was considered in regard to the matter of [the] high cost of living, as well as of all articles needed by an officer, this was regarded as a pretty good reckoning.)

All the indications now pointed to the fact that we would probably pass the winter in our present position and everybody began to prepare for a greater degree of comfort. I received another tent that I pitched in the rear of the first one and was thus afforded two comfortable communicating rooms, each 9 x 9 feet—the ordinary wall tent size. Our officers' mess was established under one roof, i.e., we built a large log house, roofed it with canvas, and the officers all took their meals together in that building, each paying a pro rata share that was determined by a committee, as in an ordinary club. We were thus enabled to have a greater variety of food at much less expense, than if we had broken up into several smaller messes.

THE GRAND REVIEW

On [Wednesday] November 20th General [George B.] McClellan reviewed the larger part of the Army of the Potomac at Bailey's Cross Roads, where there was a suitable field, [which was] centrally situated as to be within easy reach of both the right and left wings of the army. The troops, artillery, and 10,000 or 12,000 cavalry [numbered], in all, about 60,000 men. The President, Secretary of War and other distinguished public men were present and participated officially in the ceremony. Besides these there were 7 major-generals and 21 brigadiers, with their large and imposing staffs, together with a superb cavalry escort and innumerable bands of music. All contributed to the grandeur and [the] magnificence of the occasion. When to these are added the thousands of civilians, many of whom were ladies, who crowded the available space as spectators, it will be readily understood what an interesting picture the scene presented to the eye. The roar of cannon, too, added to its imposing splendor. Finally, when all was ready, the trumpets pealed forth the signal for the start, and this mass of living humanity moved forward at the beck of one man, constituting a pageant of magnificent splendor. This was the largest review of troops ever held on this continent up to this time. The 49th [New York] did not participate, but was left in charge of the camps of the division, and to support the pickets if necessary. I went, however, and secured a position opposite the reviewing officers, so I had a good opportunity to see them all. This was the first time I had ever seen

President [Abraham] Lincoln. He rode in [the] review in a tall hat, and seemed to take kindly to the self-imposed task, though I fancied he was glad when it was over. Two days afterward General [William F.] Smith again reviewed our division, which again ended in a sham battle. The general's wife, a beautiful young woman, rode gracefully at his side, entering with great zest into all the details of the parade.

Dr. [Charles] Wilcox, Captain [Jeremiah P.] Washburn [Company C], Lieutenant [Allen M.] Adams [Company C], and other officers of the 21st [New York] visited us on [Sunday, November] 24th, and we entertained them at dinner, serving to them roast beef [and] roast lamb.[18] They seemed highly pleased with our hospitality, and invited us to visit them in return, that they might reciprocate.

[Lieutenant] Colonel [William C.] Alberger and I dined in Washington on Thanksgiving Day, November 28th, at Mr. Wells's of 5th Street. This family were friends of the colonel. I [was] invited as his friend. The 9th New York Cavalry, from Chautauqua County, arrived in Washington Thanksgiving night, and I visited the regiment at [the] Soldier's Rest [the] next morning.[19] I had many friends and acquaintances in that regiment, among them [Corporal] E. [Erastus] H. Wilder [Company A], and [Private] H. [Harrison] G. Parker [Company G], of Varysburg.[20] I escorted some of them through the Capitol and other places of interest.

The 49th [New York] had two men wounded on picket [on Monday] December 2nd, which was our first taste of blood from the enemy.[21] On [Thursday, December] 5th, Alderman A. A. Howard, of Buffalo, visited us and spent some time with me. His visits had relations to the settlement of the accounts growing out of the expenses of raising the regiment and we had to supply the necessary vouchers. About this time we became pretty well convinced that we would remain in Camp Griffin during the winter. Some of us, therefore, commenced to consider the propriety of fetching our wives after the holidays to visit us for a few weeks. I wrote to mine to make herself ready to come, and that I should send for her by Mr. Harry Harbeck, our sutler, who was a very genial gentleman, an agreeable companion and the personal friend of many of us. He intended to start about [Sunday] the 15th and return near January 1st.

On [Friday] December 6th the whole division, consisting of 13 regiments of infantry, 2 batteries and one cavalry regiment, went out near Vienna foraging, and brought in 200 wagon loads of different kinds of forage. [We] started at daylight and returned at 7 o'clock P.M.

Our regimental hospital had been established at a deserted house, half a mile in our rear on the road to Chain Bridge, since the first of the month, previous to which time it had been a part of the regimental camp. Our first death in camp occurred on [Saturday] December

7th. One of the men of Company B [Private August Schweckendick], who had suffered with measles, died from its secondary effects.[22] On this day the Honorable Burt Van Horn and wife, of Niagara County, visited us and dined at our mess. On Sunday, December 8th, General [John M.] Brannan inspected the hospital in its new quarters, approved of the general plan but directed that the assistant surgeon be required to reside with it; accordingly, I took up my abode there on the 9th. (I have an India ink sketch of this hospital, made at the time by one of the soldiers—I don't recall his name—which is an excellent picture.)[23]

On [Tuesday] the 10th Lieutenant Colonel [William C.] Alberger received a telegram from his wife who was one of the first ladies to move toward paying us a visit, announcing that she had started for Washington. On [Thursday] the 12th, during one of my incursions to Washington, I visited both houses of Congress in session. As this was the first view I had taken of the National Legislature at work, the scene impressed me greatly. (As I became more familiar with Congress in after years, this early impression of the members and the grandeur of their work was removed or very much modified.) During these days the weather was most charming by day, and the nights even so mild that I did not need a fire. The bands of the several regiments gave evening concerts, filling the air with lively strains of patriotic and other martial tunes, which served to enliven the otherwise dull life that the officers led. The evening, as a rule, wore heavily on our hands at this time.

The good ladies of Cowlesville N.Y., through Mrs. Bruce Millar and Mrs. Gilman, sent our regiment a very nice box of hospital stores that we received on [Friday] the 13th. The goods and fruits were turned over to me and I distributed them among the sick. The officers met, passed appropriate resolutions and forwarded them to the ladies. (I was one of the members of the committee to do this.)

Mr. [Harry] Harbeck left for the north on the 15th and was instructed to fetch Mrs. Bidwell, Mrs. Tillinghast, and Mrs. Potter back with himself and Mrs. Harbeck when he returned, which he said would be in about two weeks. A number of the officers of the 9th New York cavalry dined with us by invitation the day of Harbeck's departure, and expressed much delight with their entertainment, as well as [their] envy that we were to have our wives with us. Mayor [Franklin A.] Alberger & Isaac Holloway, of Buffalo, visited us on [Tuesday] the 17th, and the mayor spent an hour in my tent, where a number of officers called and paid their respects to him.

Rumors of an impending battle filled the camp during these days. Finally, on [Friday] the 20th the long roll was sounded throughout the camp while we were at dinner. The regiment turned out and was speedily under arms when orders came for it to march with the other troops of the division toward Drainesville. After first paying the sick a visit, I started which delayed me about half an hour. When near Lewinsville I overtook the brigade surgeon, Dr. [Sydney] Herrick, who ordered me back to look after the camps and to be ready to receive the wounded, should there be any.[24] McCall's Division, on our right, had a skirmish with the enemy at Hunter's Mill, killing a number—rumor said 60 bodies were found on the field—and losing a few killed and wounded. Our division went as a support, but was not needed, so it returned to camp in the evening.

Lieutenant Colonel Alberger's wife arrived in camp while he was away on this expedition, so it fell to my lot to entertain her until his return. She expressed the hope that my wife would soon come, that she might, by the presence of other ladies, be enabled to spend more time in camp herself. On [Saturday] the 21st, [First] Lieutenant [Marcus] Carson [Company G], of North Java and the 9th N.Y. Cavalry, visited me and remained all night in my quarters.[25] He gave me some interesting news of Dr. Adams [and] of the gossip at his home.[26] General Brannan and his staff of six officers, by invitation of Colonel Alberger, dined with us on the 21st also. The general escorted Mrs. Alberger to the table. Our dinner was especially prepared for the occasion, and all seemed to enjoy the event, as it lent a little variety to the social part of our life.

On Christmas Day [Wednesday] the sick in hospital were furnished a special dinner by Dr. [James A.] Hall and myself, consisting of oysters, turkeys, chickens, and such other delicacies as were thought suitable to the occasion and to their stomachs. From this time until the end of the year I was busy, during all [of my] spare time, with the quarterly return of medical and hospital property, and stores. The return was a complicated and a perplexing one to make up at first, but I finally mastered it, finishing it on [Tuesday] December 31st in the afternoon. That evening my wife arrived, and as Colonel [Daniel D.] Bidwell had gone to Washington to meet his own wife, we occupied his quarters that night and during his absence.

CHAPTER TWO —1862

THE PENINSULA

[WEDNESDAY] NEW YEAR'S Day, 1862, was a warm, delightful day—so much so that we spent nearly the whole of it out of doors, without either overcoats or wraps. It was dusty, too, and reminded one of early October at the north. We had a special dinner in observance of the custom as in all well-regulated households. The day was generally observed as a holiday throughout the army, [with] only the necessary duty being required of the troops.

During the first two or three weeks of my wife's visit we were quartered at the hospital. After the middle of January the rains were so constant, that I moved back to the camp again, to avoid walking back and forth to meals in the mud. Dr. [James A.] Hall took my place at the hospital. The presence of so many ladies in camp made it quite interesting to the officers and soldiers, who seemed to enjoy this little infusion of home life into [the] ordinary military routine. The ladies, themselves, enjoyed it greatly. The troubles and inconveniences resultant from such restricted quarters they made light of. They readily took advantage of everything which contributed to the general good or amusement [of everyone] no matter how slight or trifling in character it might ordinarily have seemed to be. Evenings were spent in visiting each other, generally one of them inviting all the others, where conversation, singing, and eating, with some card playing served to while away many [of] a delightful hour. In this way the months of January and February slipped away, all too rapidly.

The latter part of January brought Dr. McCray to visit us and we enjoyed the week of his sojourn very much indeed. He, likewise, fell into our easy going ways with alacrity, and departed with regret. We were really a very jolly lot, skimming the cream of the hours as they flew by, and I now look back upon this winter at Camp Griffin as among the [most] pleasant of my life. We occasionally visited Washington staying for a night and a day but not often, for we all preferred the novelty of our camp life to the attractions of the capital.

Thus affairs went on day by day until the Ides of March. Then came certain premonitions of a probable early move in the way of preparatory orders, but nothing definite until, suddenly, in the middle of the night of Sunday, March 9th, an orderly galloped into camp, his horse's hoofs ringing crisp over the hardened ground, with orders to get ready to move immediately. (A little later in the campaign such an order, even in the dead of night, would not have disconcerted us in the least, but now, with all our comforts around us, and our wives still with us, we were startled as out of a dream, and everybody flew around without method or purpose, doing the most unnecessary things, and saying the most disagreeable things imaginable.) However, the regiment was aroused, breakfast cooked, and we were under arms at daylight, waiting for the final order which should send us forth. The ladies were left in care of Mr. [Harry] Harbeck, our good and trusted coadjutor and friend, who took them all to Washington during the day [Monday], while the division marched out as far as Flint's Hill, near Fairfax Court House, and bivouacked for the night, our first day's march covering about 12 miles through the mud. So we bade this hasty and unceremonious adieu to Camp Griffin, the dear old spot, where we had so many pleasant experiences, and where we had gone through so much of that tutelage so necessary to make us efficient soldiers.

Our first night at Flint's Hill was a pretty severe trial to me. I slept in a D'abri tent for the first time, pitched on a hillside. [It was] just large enough to permit me to lie down in [it]. I did not take off my clothing that night. I slept in my overcoat, hat, and spurs. The night was windy and trying, and I got but little sleep, fearing all the time we might be roused by orders to move. Finally, morning came [Tuesday, March 11] finding us all quiet. On Thursday, the 13th the Rev. Dr. Sunderland of Washington, and the Rev. Dr. Heacock of Buffalo visited us, the latter remaining all night with his brother, Captain R. [Reuben] E. Heacock [Company E].[1] Thursday night we received orders to be ready to move at a moment's notice, and Saturday morning, the 15th, we marched to Fairfax Court House then toward Alexandria. [We] camped in the vicinity of that city at 4 o'clock P.M. It had rained hard all day long and at night. We were a sorry lot, but a big camp fire, around which the field and staff pitched their tents served to cheer and dry us. It also afforded us an opportunity to cook a hot supper and I enjoyed broiling fresh beef on a forked stick. The meat tasted sweeter than if it had been served from Delmonico's grill.

The next day, Sunday the 16th, I received information that my wife was in Alexandria, whereupon, I immediately obtained a pass and visited her at the City Hotel. The ladies had remained in Washington for a few days to learn what our destination would be, and, upon learning that we were ordered back to the vicinity of Alexandria, they took the boat over from Washington Saturday evening. The party consisted of Mrs. [Henry D.] Tillinghast, Mrs. [Daniel D.] Bidwell, Mrs. [William C.] Alberger, and Mrs. [William W.] Potter, and their husbands visited them around noon of Sunday at the city hotel. We remained there until Monday morning [March 16], when I bade my wife good-bye until [Wednesday] December 31st 1862, when I went north for a few days upon my promotion to surgeon of the 57th Regiment New York Volunteers.

Our command remained near Alexandria for a week, awaiting transportation to Fort Monroe. [Major General George B.] McClellan had, by this time, determined to adopt the peninsula route to Richmond. On Sunday P.M., March 23rd, we embarked at Alexandria on the "Arrowsmith," a Long-Island Sound steamer [which had been] chartered for the purpose. We anchored for the night off Mount Vernon. It was even then not safe to sail down the [Potomac] River at night on account of the possibility of encountering Rebel batteries. [We] set sail [the] next morning [March 24] for Fort Monroe, where we arrived the same evening, but [we] did not debark till Tuesday morning [March 25].

Before leaving Old Point, I paid a visit to Fort Monroe, where I saw the then celebrated "Union" and "Floyd" guns. These were the two heaviest guns we had ever cast, and were attracting much attention in ordnance circles just then. The Fort impressed me with its ponderous magnificence, enclosing as it did and does between 30 and 40 acres of ground, and mounting the heaviest ordnance we were capable of producing. At Fort Monroe I had a glimpse of the "Monitor," which had then so lately fought the most celebrated naval battle of the age within sight of our present camp, where the spars of the "Cumberland" were yet standing obliquely out of the water, monuments to the death of wooden vessels of war.

Col. [Daniel D.] Bidwell was left at Washington sick when we sailed, and the command of the regiment devolved upon Lieutenant Colonel [William C.] Alberger. Dr. [James A.] Hall was also left behind to look after the sick and the property of the brigade, [and] to report in person as soon as that duty was performed. This left me in medical charge of the regiment. The first surgery I had was the extraction of a ball from the wrist of one of the men on [Tuesday] March 25th, [which had been] fired by some soldier in a neighboring regiment.

General [John] Davidson and staff came with the 49th [New York] on the "Arrowsmith." He was our brigade commander now, having in January succeeded General [J. M.] Brannan, who had been ordered to the South Carolina coast. [Brannan] took the 47th New York with him. The 77th [New York], Colonel [James B.] McKean (commanding), was assigned to us in place of the 47th, making our brigade consist of the 33rd, the 49th, and 77th New York, and the 7th Maine Volunteers.[2] I took supper Monday evening and breakfast Tuesday morning at the Hygeia Hotel with Mr. [Harry] Harbeck, and during the forenoon we took up our march toward Newport News, where we encamped for the night. We halted for dinner at Hampton, which had been burnt the summer previously by General [John Bankhead] Magruder [C. S. A.]. Hampton had been a pretty village, built almost entirely of brick, and had a population of about 2,500 inhabitants before the conflagration. It was frequented as a summer resort before the war, by wealthy Southerners, and was a place of much aristocratic fame.

The officers were now without tents, excepting the D'abri or shelter tent. I used a hospital tent for my quarters, which the major [George W. Johnson] and [the] quartermaster [Henry D. Tillinghast] occupied with me.

[Thursday] March 27th. [William F.] Smith's Division made a 5 mile reconnaissance in the direction of Yorktown, driving some cavalry videttes away in the vicinity of Young's Mills. We remained out all night, bivouacking on lines lately occupied by the enemy, and returned to Newport News [the] next morning. [We] camped on the banks of the James [River] about a mile above Yorktown. Our camp was named "W. F. Smith," in honor of our division commander, who was familiarly known as "Baldy," a soubriquet [which] he acquired when [he] was a cadet at West Point. During the few days we were here we frequently obtained fresh oysters from the [Chesapeake] Bay, and by [Sunday] March 30th, I noticed [that the] peach trees [were] in blossom. I picked up a porcupine-fish skeleton on the beach at Newport News on the 31st that I sent [home] and [I] still have [it] in my possession.

We now began to see the desolation of war. All [of the] houses were in ruins and scarcely a living thing "native and to the manner born" remained. The inhabitants, excepting the slaves, fled with [the] retiring foe, leaving not even a stray chicken for the dreadful "Yankees." (Newport News was not a town, as might be supposed, but simply a military post where 5,000 men were quartered in barracks, under the command of General [Joseph] Mansfield [U. S. A.].) On [Monday] March 31st the rebel gunboat "Teaser" steamed down the James [River] and commenced throwing shells at our camp. After discharging three shots, she turned around and went back to Richmond, having done no damage.

[Tuesday] April 1. (From this time I shall write generally in the present tense, as it is the most convenient.)[3] Today we made another reconnaissance in the same direction as before. We deployed a battery and fired a few shots at some cavalry. [We] returned to camp about 3 o'clock P.M. without accident or casualty. The field and staff being still without tents, I borrowed a hospital tent of Dr. [Sylvanus S.] Mulford, surgeon of the 33rd [New York], and we are all occupying it as one family.[4] Colonel [William C.] Alberger is not well but keeps about camp. Major [George W.] Johnson is in command. The comforts of Camp Griffin are often referred to these days, in contrast to the beggary of our present life.

Friday. April 4. At six o'clock A.M. the army took up its advance upon Yorktown, our division leading on the line. We marched 10 miles the first day, reaching and bivouacking in the vicinity of Young's Mills. Here we found barracks for three regiments, which were so lately deserted by the enemy that fires are still smoldering in the chimneys. We started again this morning, [Saturday] April 5th, at daylight, our brigade leading the march of the 4th Corps. We found the enemy before noon, who resisted our advance in the rain, and we spent the P.M. in skirmishing losing, in the 49th [New York], one killed [Private Milton Lewis, Company K] and one wounded [Private Christian Hehr, Company B].[5] By 4 o'clock [P.M.] we had reached the position that the enemy sustained along the Warwick River, the strength of which proved sufficient to bring us to a halt. We established our pickets within 300 or 400 yards of the enemy's works and lay on our arms during the night. We were in a piece of woods in which it was difficult to manoeuvre artillery. We lay [here] during Sunday and Monday, [April] 6th and 7th. Shells from the enemy's batteries frequently fell amongst us, and on Sunday the 49th [New York] had 5 men wounded.[6] I picked up a spent canister shot, that expended its momentum at my feet.

It was now evident [that we were] determined to siege the enemy's position as, on Monday evening [April 7], we were withdrawn to a safer and more comfortable position, after having been about 60 hours under fire. This withdrawal was accomplished with difficulty, the utmost secrecy being maintained, lest the enemy should become aware of our purpose. I remember an incident that will illustrate the caution observed. In falling back two of my hospital attendants were carrying some camp-kettles on a pole. The rattling of the kettles attracted the attention of General [John] Davidson, who was sitting on his horse all alone in the woods [near] where we were passing. He flew into a great rage, scolding me soundly for permitting the men to make such a noise. It was nearly dark and raining at the time, and I reached our appointed place in anything but good humor.

Routine camp life now went on for several days, during which time we heard of [Ulysses S.] Grant's victory at Shiloh. [Second] Lieutenant [Charles H.] Hickmott [Company F] preferred charges against me about this time for alleged neglect of duty, in refusing to attend one of his men [Joseph Weiler] in the night, who shot himself purposely, as I believed, to escape duty, causing only a slight flesh wound of no special importance.[7] The weather was rainy and unpleasant up to [Friday] the 11th, when the sun once more appeared. Meanwhile, the roads had become almost impassable, rendering it extremely difficult to get up our stores, which were brought from Newport News—18 miles distant—in wagons, 24 hours being required to accomplish the distance.

Fatigue parties in large numbers were sent out to corduroy the roads and a highway was finally constructed to Ship Point on the James [River]—7 miles distant—where a depot of supplies was established. On the 11th I took two loads of sick [men] back to Young's Mills, where a hospital had been established in the rebel barracks there, and Dr. [William P.] Russell, of the 5th Vermont, [was] placed in charge.[8] Our position was now before Lee's Mill opposite the enemy's right, which was protected by water, [and] dammed at intervals to deepen the stream. On [Wednesday] April 16th a reconnaissance was made at Dam No. 1 between Lee's and Wynn's Mills, where General [William F.] Smith tried to force a passage and attack the works or [to] develop their strength. He did the latter. [Brigadier General W. T. H.] Brooks's brigade of Vermont troops was assigned to the duty [with] our brigade in support. It proved unsuccessful as far as getting a foot-hold in the works, but some important information was obtained. The 3rd Vermont lost 75 men, of whom 22 were killed. I saw General [George B.] McClellan on the field in conference with General Smith about 4 o'clock P.M. We returned to camp about 6 o'clock P.M. without [a] casualty.

Colonel [Daniel D.] Bidwell returned to the regiment on [Friday] the 18th, looking thin and pale, having lost about 50 lbs. of flesh during his illness. On [Saturday] the 19th the 49th [New York] took its turn in support of the batteries for the night and I went along to look after any sick or wounded who might require medical services. [First] Lieutenant William McLean of the 5th U.S. Cavalry, formerly of Lancaster [New York], accompanied me and we busied ourselves trying to keep dry—for it was a rainy night—[by] whiling away the time as best we could in story-telling and smoking.[9] That night was a most dark, inclement one and the rain fell in torrents at intervals. The pickets became alarmed several times during the night and blazed away at

each other [with] the batteries occasionally belching forth their deep
bass intonation, to vary the musical sounds. The flashes of the guns,
athwart the deep darkness of the night, simulated lightning and the
bullets flew over our heads at times in great numbers, sounding like
hail-stones against the great forest trees. It was a most uncomfortable
night, yet we got back to camp next morning without casualty. I was,
however, nearly sick for 2 or 3 days afterwards. I very soon recovered
my wonted vigor. Since entering the service, I had not yet been off
duty a day by reason of illness, this being the nearest thereto that I
had yet come.

McLean's squadron was assigned to duty with General Smith and,
as there was very little opportunity to use cavalry in our present position, he became a frequent visitor in our camp [because] many of the
officers of the 49th [were] his acquaintances. He was a genial companion, a good campaigner, and a valuable officer. Lieutenant, afterwards
General, [George Armstrong] Custer often came with him and spent
an hour or two with me. They were fast friends and both [were] brave
even to audacity.

On [Wednesday] April 23, 1862 [former] Governor [William]
Sprague, of R.I., paid General [John] Davidson a visit, accompanied by
General McClellan's staff and a troop of cavalry.[10] He wore a military
cap, blouse, and sword-belt, and attracted considerable attention by
reason of his prominence as a "war governor," who had equipped and
sent out a regiment at his own expense when the government experienced its first trial. After partaking of General Davidson's hospitality
for nearly an hour, the party proceeded on its tour of inspection. About
this time several of the subaltern officers resigned. There was considerable disaffection in the regiment but it disappeared very soon after
the siege was raised.

On [Thursday] the 24th an order was received designating the
camp as "Winfield Scott"—the name [was] to apply throughout the
army during the siege. While we were here my court-martial trial, on
the charges preferred by Lieutenant [Charles] Hickmott, was called at
brigade headquarters one day. I went up, with Quartermaster [Henry
D.] Tillinghast as counsel, to defend the case. For some reason or another the complainant failed to appear and the judge-advocate dismissed the case.

Large siege guns were now being brought up and placed in position, and operations were pushing with vigor. Dr. [James A.] Hall returned on [Monday] the 28th, much to my gratification and relief, for,
since we left Camp Griffin, I had been in medical charge of the regiment and felt the burden of my responsibility to be rather heavy. I
received visits during these days from Dr. Frank H. Hamilton, Dr. Jo-

seph Robinson, of Hornellsville, and [First] Lieutenant Charles O. Shepard [Company B], of the 82nd N.Y.[11] The paymaster appeared on the last of the month and paid us for January and February. In addition, I discounted my rolls for March and April and thus obtained four months pay, the first I had received since the November and December payment. This enabled me to discharge all my indebtedness and send $250.00 to my wife.

[Thursday] May 1st. We are comfortable for the first time since leaving Camp Griffin, as Dr. [James A.] Hall brought two tents with him from Washington, which we have appropriated to our own comfort. [We are] using one in part for the official headquarters of the surgeons. He brought 4 other tents also, which have been distributed amongst the field and staff officers, so we are all very well provided with quarters. I took my trousers off to-night on going to bed, the first time I have done so in six weeks. We are but half a mile from the rebel lines. No fires are allowed after dark and not a drum has been sounded for a month. If our precise position were known to the enemy, we should probably be shelled out or, to say the least, be kept in a constant tension of dread of such possibilities. From 3 to 5 men are shot daily within a thousand yards of our camp but the 49th has been fortunate thus far in not losing a man since our losses of the first day we came up here. Firing is constantly heard on all sides, chiefly at working parties of ours or theirs.

Saturday night, May 3rd. The batteries all along the lines are firing every 2 or 3 minutes, mostly from [the] siege mortars and [the] 100 pound Parrotts. Everything points to a general bombardment soon, but the firing tonight appears to be simply practice for range. Seven mortars are within a short distance of our camp two of which were placed in position today. We turn out in line of battle from one to three times a day and nearly every morning at daylight there is an alarm of some kind, which brings the whole division to arms. Lieutenant [William] McLean staid all night with us again last night, a thing which he is the habit of doing frequently, and we enjoy his visits very much. He generally brings some important news whenever he comes, which is always acceptable.

WILLIAMSBURG

When we awoke Sunday morning, May 4th, we found the enemy had evacuated his whole line of works during the previous night, and [was] apt to be in full retreat upon Richmond. We were put in immediate pursuit and passed through their fortifications which were very formidable. In their deserted camps were found quantities of rations and camp equipage, including flour in barrels, beans, camp kettles, [and] a few tents. Baggage wagons in large numbers were also secured, and many stragglers were made prisoners. We passed General [John Bankhead] Magruder's headquarters about 10 o'clock A.M., and overtook the skirmishers of their rear guard at 2 o'clock P.M. Our division had the advance, and the 49th [New York] was the second or third regiment in column. About noon I was sent back to our last camp with some orders, and [upon] returning, [I] caught up with the troops about 3 o'clock P.M. By dark we had driven the skirmishers well into Williamsburg, [with] the 6th [U.S.] Cavalry suffering a loss of probably 50 killed and wounded.[12] I dressed one of the wounded by the wayside in the twilight. We rested on our arms that night in line of battle in a wheat field. Colonel [William C.] Alberger and I sought the shelter of a little clump of trees nearby and spread our blankets together for the night. We were awakened about 4 o'clock A.M. by rain falling in our faces and, at daylight, the troops were up and in line, though it rained as hard as ever it could pour.

[Brigadier General Joseph] Hooker, whose division had come up in the night, was placed on our left. [He] pushed his skirmishers forward into the woods beyond at daylight [May 5] and soon found the enemy strongly entrenched behind a slashing of heavy timber. The fighting began at once and [was] kept up all day. At 10 o'clock A.M. [Brigadier General Winfield Scott] Hancock's brigade with two regiments of ours [33rd New York, 7th Maine], by a detour to the right, was swung around on the left flank of the enemy [thereby] capturing two deserted redoubts which commanded the position in front of Hooker. As soon as this was discovered Magruder ordered six regiments to charge Hancock's line, which they did in right gallant style. Hancock reserved his fire until they were well upon him, then delivered it fairly in their faces, driving them back in great confusion with heavy loss. (It seems that Hancock had asked to have the remainder of the division sent to his support, but [Brigadier General Edwin] Sumner, who was in command, refused to comply.) Meanwhile, word was sent to General McClellan of the situation early in the afternoon. (He had remained at Yorktown to superintend the shipment of [General William B.] Franklin's division by water to West Point.) At 4 o'clock P.M. I saw him ride upon the field, accompanied by the Prince De Joinville, the Count De Paris, the Duc De Charters and others of his staff, the whole party literally covered with mud. [General William F.] Smith was promptly at his side and obtained consent to join Hancock. We were off at once, but by the time we got there the affair was over, and darkness was upon us as well. I saw the body of Lieutenant Colonel [John C.] Badham, of the 5th N.C., lying in one of the redoubts, his forehead pierced by a bullet.[13] He was a young man, handsome, and of splendid physique. He was heard to say, just at the climax of the charge, "Now we've got the damned Yankees, give them Bull Run and Ball's Bluff." I stood around a fire all night, for it rained hard, and tried to dry my clothing and keep warm. [I] made no attempt to lie down and sleep. The men slept in the rain and mud as best they could.

When morning came [May 6] we found the works abandoned and the enemy in full retreat. The field was covered with the enemy's dead, and we had over 100 of his wounded in our front to care for. I went over the field Tuesday morning, the 6th, and helped gather up the wounded which were carried to a large barn nearby. The same afternoon I assisted in making the operations. Here, we amputated 10 legs and several arms, the most serious cases having been left on our hands by the hastily retreating foe. I visited Williamsburg on [Wednesday] the 7th, where I saw between 400 and 500 more of their wounded distributed to the various churches and William and Mary College. Twelve surgeons were sent into our lines by [General James] Longstreet, including his medical director Dr. [J. S. D.] Cullen, to look after these wounded. I had an opportunity to talk with some of the prisoners, which was the first time that experience had come to me. [I] also obtained some of their currency which I sent home. They say very little, though enough for me to infer that the men—the private soldiers—don't fare as great heart in the war as their officers.

McClellan paid our command a visit and complimented Hancock and his troops on their soldierly conduct and success. In going over the field again on [Thursday] the 8th, I saw dead rebels lying all through the woods behind logs and stumps. Graves were thick and numerous. This was my first experience in going over a battlefield immediately after the action and it impressed me greatly. Our own dead were very well buried, but the enemy's were more hastily and imperfectly done. The wounded of Smith's division, together with those of the enemy which fell into our hands, were placed on board the steamer "Commodore" and sent to Washington. The wounded in Williamsburg—400 or 500—were left there in care of the rebel surgeons, who were sent into our lines for that purpose. Some of these doctors were quite intelligent looking men, but most of them were shabbily dressed and were only to be distinguished from civilians by the letters "M.S."—signifying medical staff—on their hats. Williamsburg itself is a sleepy old village of probably 2,000 inhabitants in time of peace. Many of them, however, had now retired with the rebel army, so it was quite deserted except by the army of temporary occupation. A state lunatic asylum is located here which, together with William and Mary College, affords it some distinction. Lieutenant [William] McLean paid us another visit on the 8th and was in his usual good spirits.

THE MARCH UP THE PENINSULA

Friday, May 9th. We started at 6 o'clock A.M. and marched 19 miles over the road upon which the rebels retreated, camping for the night near Burnt Ordinary, a small country P.O. We passed broken wagons stuck in the mud (some of them partly burnt), caissons, and other war material which was dropped in the haste of retreat. Our cavalry brought back squads of prisoners captured from the rear guard. At Burnt Ordinary I "captured" large quarto volume of Quain's Anatomical Plates from the house of a doctor which the cavalry had gone through. (I found the book in the yard and still have [it] in my possession as a part of my library.)

Saturday, May 10th. We marched 15 miles starting before 5 o'clock in the morning and at night [we] were said to be but 32 miles from Richmond. Smith's division had the advance, our brigade moving in front. We camped for the night on a field where the cavalry had an engagement the day before and our pioneers buried 80 dead—16 of our own men and 64 of the enemy. The men are constantly capturing stray horses and Dr. [James A.] Hall and I have taken one in partnership to carry our extra blankets, forage, and rations.

On Sunday, the 11th it was rumored that Adjutant [William] Bullymore, who left us on [Sunday] the 3rd, while we were before Yorktown, had died at Fort Monroe. This rumor was, unhappily, confirmed by a letter from quartermaster [Henry D.] Tillinghast the same evening. This was a sad blow to us all, for Bullymore was a promising young officer, whose friends were legion.

We are now near New Kent C.H. On the night of the 11th I went to West Point, 12 miles distant, with a load of sick for shipment to Yorktown. I was out all night, returning to camp just as reveille was sounding. [Harry] Harbeck, our genial sutler, resigned about this time and I sent my porcupine fish by him, when he went home. William Woodruff was appointed sutler in Harbeck's place, and though a good business man, he was not as popular as his predecessor. On [Wednesday] the 14th I was attacked with neuralgia in the face, and was off duty until [Friday] the 16th from that cause. We were then at the White House, where we remained until [Monday] the 19th. The Custiss estate, where we were encamped, was formerly owned by General R. E. Lee. It was here that George Washington courted and married his wife, and it is one of the finest plantations I have yet seen. While we were here the 5th and 6th Provisional Corps were formed, commanded respectively by [Fitz John] Porter and [William] Franklin. Smith's becomes the 2nd Division of the 6th Corps with [Henry] Slocums's division being the 1st.

On the 19th we marched 9 miles farther toward Richmond, [we] being now but 16 miles in direct line from that city. We passed through some beautiful country today, untouched hitherto by the devastation of war,—fields of grain nearly ripe, fine residences, and elegant plantations. Tonight for supper we had duck, eggs, and strawberries, all the products of the country. We moved 5 miles on [Tuesday] the 20th. [We] still live on the country principally—I speak of our own mess— sweet potatoes [new] eggs and chickens being the chief articles of our cuisine. We engaged another, and I hope a better, cook today—one who formerly cooked for General Smith and who understands his business thoroughly.

Thus far into the bowels of the land have we marched without serious impediment and are under orders to March again at 3 o'clock A.M. tomorrow, our brigade to take the lead. Our mails are very irregular now. It is three days since we had the last one. We are pretty hungry for news from home. A march of 8 miles on [Wednesday] the 21st brought us to Cold Harbor. It is simply a crossroads, with a country inn and a smithy. General [George] Stoneman sent up a balloon about 2 miles in advance of us this morning, to reconnoitre the enemy's position. Major [George W.] Johnson [49th New York] is not well these days, but I hope he is not seriously threatened. He is a brave man and a sterling officer. It would be a pity to lose his valuable services. I am in good health and spirits myself. The regiment is reputed [to be] one of the healthiest in the division, and the strongest in the brigade. Dr. S. [Sylvanus] S. Mulford of the 33rd [New York] visits me often. He is in good health and spirits also. He is a good campaigner and an excellent companion.

CHAPTER THREE —1862

THE SEVEN DAYS

MECHANICSVILLE

WE REMAINED AT Cold Harbor until Friday, May 23rd when the 3rd brigade made a reconnaissance toward Mechanicsville, supporting General Stoneman's cavalry. Late in the afternoon, after we marched about 5 miles, a battery opened upon us. Our artillery soon silenced it after exchanging a few shots. We crossed a creek and slept on our arms that night without anything to eat. [The] next morning, the 24th, we stood to arms at daybreak, soon advanced and drove the enemy out of Mechanicsville in a drenching rain. The brigade lost 3 men killed and 5 or 6 wounded—mostly from the 33rd [New York] and 77th [New York] regiments. Our regiment did not lose a man, though it was under fire for an hour or more. Mechanicsville is a hamlet 5 miles north of Richmond, consisting of half a dozen houses, most of which suffered more or less from our artillery fire. We took possession of a beautiful grove in the rear of the principal residence and there remained over [until] Sunday [May 25th]. Our supplies reached us at night and we made ourselves quite comfortable again, though we were without tents. During the day, we picketed one side of the Chickahominy, and the enemy the other. The river runs in a valley, the hills rising on either side. At intervals during the day we saw carriages containing ladies, on the opposite hills, who had come out from Richmond to get a sight of the hated Yankee troops. I am in possession of a saddle captured from a "secesh" cavalryman at Mechanicsville, which comes in play for our extra horse. On Monday, May 26th, bright

26

and early, we were relieved by another brigade, and returned to a position near Gaines' Mill, 4 miles east of Mechanicsville. So the first Mechanicsville affair was at an end. (I visited the place in the autumn of 1886 and sat down upon a log in the same grove in which we passed Sunday, May 25th, 1862. The *Century Magazine* for June, 1885, on page 313 gives a good illustration of our conquest on the place. The artillery referred to in the title of the picture, is the artillery which the 3rd brigade of Smith's division was supporting, as I have described.)

It rained hard on the afternoon and night of the 26th, and on the 27th. The entire regiment was sent out on fatigue duty, chopping trees for timber to build a road across the low ground on either side of the river, apparently preparatory to [a] crossing. The pontoons went down to the river bank on the night of the 26th, and a bridge will doubtless be laid very soon. I picked up a snake skin near my tent this morning, which I propose to send home as a relic and as indicating the two-fold character of the danger we are in. Heavy firing was heard all the afternoon of [Tuesday] the 27th in the direction of Mechanicsville, but we are unadvised as to its cause.

Dr. [James A.] Hall's health is quite poor, and has been so for some time, which adds to my duties and responsibilities very much. Major [George W.] Johnson is, however, in better health than he was a few days ago. I trust [he] will soon be as strong as ever. Dr. S. [Sanford] B. Hunt [9th New York Cavalry] wrote a letter from Fort Monroe, which was published in the Buffalo papers, in which he speaks of having seen [Henry D.] Tillinghast at Old Point.[1] The papers have just been received, and we have been much interested in reading the doctor's newsy account of his visit with "Till." I see Dr. [Frank Hastings] Hamilton quite often these days, as he is medical director on Franklin's staff, and so comes around both socially and officially. On [Wednesday] the 28th we had news of Porter's fight at Hanover Court House, which accounts for the firing we heard yesterday. Dr. Herrick sent a pail of lemons for the sick today, which was a comfort as the boys are fagged. [Thursday] May 29th. I visited General Smith's headquarters today, where I saw a lot of prisoners captured by Porter on the 27th. Major [Edward P.] Chapin, of the 44th New York was wounded in that fight.[2] (He subsequently became colonel of the 116th, and was killed at Port Hudson [Louisiana] in 1863. Chapin Place, out near the park, is named in honor of him.) [Saturday] May 31. We have not moved since we came to this camp [near Gaines' Mill] last Monday morning [May 19], which is the longest time we have spent in any one place since we left Yorktown. Today we hear firing over the Chickahominy on the left on the army, which sounds like a heavy engagement. At night the shells burst over the tree-tops, so we can see them quite plainly. [Orville S.] "Tom" Dewey arrived in camp today, having been commissioned [as the] 2nd Lieutenant in Co. A under Captain [Thomas] Cluney.³ He is a valuable acquisition to the line officer list and will, no doubt, distinguish himself. I saw Professor [Thaddeus] Lowe, the balloonist, and had quite a long conversation with him. His balloon is stationed near us. He tells me that he saw the rebel troops the day before moving toward the field of Fair Oaks and so apprised the commanding general. Lieutenant [James B.] Washington of [General Joseph] Johnston's staff, was captured by our pickets a day or two since, and some important battle-plans were found upon his person. I went down to Dr. Gaines' today to see the rebel wounded whom Porter captured at Hanover C.H.⁴ They are a sorry lot. Two rebel surgeons were caring for them as best they could. All day I was occupied with my monthly report, which must always be sent in promptly, lest there be complaints from headquarters. A severe thunder storm prevailed all last night. One artilleryman is reported killed by lightning at Mechanicsville.

Sunday, June 1st. The battle which began yesterday on our left was renewed this morning and lasted until noon. It is known on our side as the battle of Fair Oaks—the enemy call it Seven Pines. Surely, the oak and pine were contending. We have just received the news of the evacuation of Corinth [Mississippi], and all were very much surprised. The inquiry on every hand is "where have the devils gone?." This Sunday afternoon I went down below Dr. Gaines' where there is an open field looking across the river, toward the scene of yesterday's battle, and on which [Romeyn] Ayres' and [Charles] Griffin's batteries are posted in battery. Both Ayres and Griffin were lying on the ground, directing the artillery practice and chatting about the war, and particularly of the rebel commanders. "Smith G.W." was the familiar name they gave General Gustavus W. Smith, who had succeeded to the command at Fair Oaks, upon the wounding of General Joseph E. Johnston.

Tuesday, June 3rd. We are under orders to be ready to move at a moment's notice—not an unusual order nowadays. The whole regiment was startled today by the receipt of the sad intelligence of the death of Quartermaster H. D. Tillinghast at Buffalo, whither he had gone with adjutant [William] Bullymore's remains. ([He] sickened and, on [Thursday] May 29th, died there.) The loss of these two officers from the staff, so suddenly and so near together, shocked us in the extreme, and was a damaging blow to the regiment as well. Nothing could have surprised us more than this sad news, for it is but a month today since he left us well, excepting some trouble with his teeth which he went to Fort Monroe to have looked after. Mr. T. had the respect of both officers and men. [He] was not a popular and efficient officer but socially he was the best of companions, and he bore the name of 'gentleman' stamped upon his every act.

The rebel General [Johnston] Pettigrew, who was wounded on Saturday [May 31st], has been brought to this side of the river, and is at Dr. Gaines' house where I am contemplating a call upon him. I sent home today a copy of the "Illustrated News," containing pictures of the hospital barns at Williamsburg. I procured the admission of the artist inside the barns while we were operating and was administering chloroform in one of the sketches which he made of the operations.

BEFORE RICHMOND

We left our camp near New Bridge on Gaines' farm at 3 o'clock Thursday morning, June 5th and marched back to the R.R. at Dispatch Station, a distance of 8 miles. Crossing the [Chickahominy] river on the R.R. bridge, we moved west 7 miles toward Richmond, which brought us to Golding's farm, situated about 7 miles from the rebel capital, where we halted. The rains have made the roads and fields muddy and sodden and we bivouacked that night in a clover field where the horses would sink over [their] hoofs in a moment. This is the place we are to stay in for a month.

[Friday] June 6th. The whole regiment is on fatigue duty corduroying roads and building bridges to enable the artillery and baggage trains to cross over from Dr. Gaines', [which is] not more than 2 or 3 miles [away], but [it] cost us a detour march of 16 miles to reach [this place]. On [Sunday] the 8th our baggage train arrived, so we are living again. We are camped within rifle shot of the enemy's pickets, [and are] protected from their view by simply a skirt of woods. Our brigade has a front line and is engaged in throwing up entrenchments. Dr. [James A.] Hall is [feeling] some better but [he is] not on duty. There is considerable feeling of discontent in the regiment, and some of the officers talk about resigning. I wrote my wife today, in reply to a letter from her beseeching me to come home, that I could not think of resigning in the face of the enemy, especially as such an act would subject me to disgrace forever after. [Second Lieutenant] Tom Dewey [Company A] comes in to see me every day, and his face is real sunshine in the camp.

Monday, June 9th. It is cool and comfortable, and the regiment is busy strengthening its rifle pit front. A small redoubt has been built just at our left, and guns are being mounted in it today. It looks very much as though our Yorktown work was to be repeated here. The 20th New York, Colonel [Ernst] Von Vegesack (formerly Max Weber's regiment), joined our brigade today 1040 strong and [it] is a fine looking body of men.[5] They have been at Fort Monroe so long that they look as prim as Regulars—in marked contrast to the other troops.[6]

[Tuesday] June 10. A cold, disagreeable rain set in about midnight, and the weather today seems more like October than June. The enemy complimented us with a few shells and solid shot just at dusk last evening, while Dr. [James A.] Hall, Dr. [Sylvanus S.] Mulford and I were standing in front of my tent. [One shot] struck the ground about 30 yards in our rear; another passed over the fort on our right, and struck near General [William F.] Smith's headquarters, and several shells burst in the air 20 or 30 yards to our left. Today they began the same sort of entertainment again, but the shells all burst farther to our left and fell a little short of the line. Wheeler's battery [Company E, 1st New York Light] is stationed just at the left of our regiment but has not yet replied. Captain [Charles C.] Wheeler intimated to me to-day, however, that he should do so the next time they opened fire.[7]

General [Juan] Prim, lately in command of the Spanish forces in Mexico, paid our camp a visit last Sunday, the 8th, accompanied by General Smith, [the general's] staff, and [a] cavalry escort.[8] He was also attended by several officers of his own suite, wearing the Spanish uniform, which is much more showy than our soiled and tattered dress, presenting thereby a strong contrast. Major [George W.] Johnson is improving in health, and bids fair to return to duty soon. Dr. [James A.] Hall is also some better, but I am very suspicious [that] he will be obliged to give up for a time, and possibly go north before he fully recovers.

[Wednesday] June 11. This evening the "rebs" paid us the further compliment of half a dozen shells, but without damage. One burst near the color line and another in a piece of woods nearby on our left. General [George B.] McClellan and staff paid us a visit today. He and General Smith visited the pickets and reconnoitered the lines together. Captain W. [William] F. Wheeler of "ours" [Company D], not the artillery officer just mentioned, is not well, but I hope his illness will not prove serious. Today we hear that Memphis has fallen, and that the entire Mississippi is in our possession.

[Thursday] June 12. About noon the rebels sent us 4 or 5 shells and again at 5 o'clock P.M., they did the same and yet again at sundown. As Colonel [Daniel D.] Bidwell, Lieutenant [Orville S.] Dewey [Company A], and I were sitting in front of my quarters [when] a shell passed directly over our heads, killing one of the Cameron Dragoons near Hancock's brigade; another of the dragoons was killed on picket today. An alarm on the picket line at one o'clock last night turned out the regiment but it proved a stampede and we went to bed in an hour, after taking a good view of the eclipse of the moon.

[Friday] June 13. The regiment is in line of battle every morning at 3 o'clock and stands under arms until half an hour after daylight, so we don't propose to be surprised by our treacherous foe. This morning we were shelled for 2 or 3 hours, but again without damage. They must have fired 100 rounds at us, but the projectiles either fell short or went over our heads. The don't seem to get our precise range, though they come pretty close to it sometimes. General McClellan visited our lines again today and, as usual, was greeted with great enthusiasm. General [John] Davidson expects an attack tonight, but he frequently gets such an idea into his head, so we don't scare much under that pleasant little bit of camp news.[9]

[Saturday] June 14. It was so extremely hot today that I stripped myself down to my underwear and lay sweltering in my tent at that. Dr. [James A.] Hall is not as well [today] and has been established, just adjacent to General McClellan's headquarters. Captain [Jeremiah C.] Drake [Company G] is also there, and I visited them both today.[10] I can hear the bands in the enemy's camps playing quite distinctly tonight, which generally means mischief, but Lieutenant Colonel [William C.] Alberger and 275 men from the 49th [New York] are on picket tonight, so we shall be quiet I think, for he keeps the line straight when he is field officer.

[Sunday] June 15. The heat continues so intense that I sent to the woods for young trees, and planted them around my tent to protect it from the sun's rays. This P.M. a thunder shower refreshed and cooled us somewhat; but the pickets were driven in somewhere on our left just as the storm subsided. Captain [William F.] Wheeler [Company D] is quite sick, though not dangerously so, I think. He has worked hard of late, having no lieutenant to assist him, and the fatigue has been too great for his endurance. I sent him to the Trent house today, where Dr. [James A.] Hall is, where he will be more comfortable, and where his recovery will be facilitated by removal from the noise and excitement of camp. Major [George W.] Johnson is better, but Colonel [Daniel D.] Bidwell is not well, though he keeps on duty. [Lieutenant Orville] Dewey [Company A] is well, and as genial as ever; so is [Lieutenant Colonel William C.] Alberger.

[Monday] June 16. The weather has turned cooler. These changes produce considerable sickness among the troops, yet our regiment suffers less in this respect than some of the others in the division. Today the long expected flag, presented by the ladies of Buffalo, arrived and was committed to the custody of the regiment with ceremony.[11] The command formed in a Hollow Square and, in the presence of General Davidson and [his] staff, Colonel Bidwell presented the color to the regiment with [the] appropriate remarks, followed by the rousing cheers of the soldiers [and a Tiger].[12] Lieutenant [William] McLean [5th U.S. Cavalry] was wounded and taken prisoner 2 or 3 days ago somewhere in the vicinity of Liberty Hall, or Old Church, where he was doing outpost duty on the extreme right of the army.[13] It appears that the bold rider, [J. E. B.] Stuart, made the circuit of the Army of the Potomac with 1500 of his troopers, striking McLean's squadron at the point named, and rode over it pell-mell, killing Mac's beautiful white mare, and wounding him in the head. We have heard today of McLean's safe arrival in Richmond.[14]

[Tuesday] June 17. This is a quiet day and I took advantage of the lull to visit Dr. [James A.] Hall and Captain [William F.] Wheeler [Company D] at the Trent House, finding them both better. [The] Captain was sitting on the veranda enjoying the refreshing breeze of a mild June afternoon, and I hitched my horse and joined him. We talked over "old times" for an hour, and he seemed better from my visit. It is rumored that the rebels intend to attack us tomorrow, in commemoration of the Battle of Waterloo. We shall see. Mr. [Stephen Morris] De Fort, of Co. D, has been established as my valet-de-chambre, and he keeps my quarters in such fine order as to excite the envy of all my visitors, who are not a few.[15]

[Wednesday] June 18. The enemy attacked General [Edwin V.] Sumner's line [Second Corps] on our left, just at night, killing 6 and wounding 14 men.[16] They sent forward two regiments and deployed their skirmishers on our pickets, but were soon driven off and the lines held as before. We are under orders to move at a moment's notice, and have so been since noon.

[Thursday] June 19. All is quiet along the lines, but I think, from movements and preparations which I observe all around, that something is going to be done soon. The North is impatient [for a quick victory] as I observe from the papers, but this [army] is a great machine to manage and, with a wily enemy opposed [to its presence], movements must be conducted with caution.

[Friday] June 20. By official orders from general headquarters our camp has been designated "Camp Lincoln," in compliment to our illustrious president—a fitting recognition of his greatness. Captain [William F.] Wheeler is improving; Colonel [William C.] Alberger is quite sick; Dr. [James A.] Hall is about the same; Major [George W.] Johnson is on duty again.

[Saturday] June 21. I visited McClellan's headquarters where I found a sutler who had plenty of good things; I bought a box of figs, and tonight Colonel [Daniel D.] Bidwell and Major [George W.] Johnson have enjoyed them with me, in my tent. We are still entertained daily— sometimes 2 or 3 times a day—with the shelling by the enemy, generally, however, without damage to our regiment. 9 o'clock P.M. Colonel Bidwell has just received an order to send out a company to strengthen the pickets, and Co. A goes in compliance therewith.

[Sunday] June 22. This is the most quiet day we have had for sometime—not a shot fired within hearing of our camp. Captain [William F.] Wheeler is better and returned to duty today; [William C.] Alberger still quite sick. Lieutenant C. [Charles] H. Bidwell has resigned—his papers came to-day. He gave me a fine canteen, with an outside pocket for knife, fork, and spoon, and two tin cases for pepper and salt.

[Monday] June 23. Lieutenant Bidwell started for Buffalo today, and I sent a box of cigars home by him, which were made by one of our men [James Kris, Company F], from tobacco that grew on Dr. Gaines' plantation.

[Tuesday] June 24. A great thunder shower prevailed all last night, and another came today. I never experienced anything like such severe storms of that character as we have here. The lightning was so continuous that it was quite light the most of the night, and the electricity came so near the earth as to nearly convulse my extremities, several times. The rebels are building a fort in our front, which we have just discovered. Four prisoners, probably deserters, were brought through our camp today, on their way to headquarters.

[Wednesday] June 25. Today has been one of considerable excitement; we have been under orders to be ready to move all day. The men [are] keeping their belts on, and extra rations and ammunition have been issued. The line on the left was advanced somewhat today, and the artillery on the right, across the river has kept up a continuous fire all day from 3 batteries of 30 pounder Parrotts, apparently at the fort which the enemy is building in our front. Dr. [James A.] Hall is better; Colonel [Daniel D.] Bidwell and Major [George W.] Johnson are in good spirits, while [William C.] Alberger is still sick though a little better today.

[Thursday] June 26. This has been a day of great excitement. About 2 o'clock P.M. we heard guns in the direction of Mechanicsville, about 4 miles away, on our extreme right; within an hour the firing so increased as to lead to the conclusion that an important battle was going on; and within another hour we heard that "Stonewall" Jackson had appeared on our right flank with 30,000 men, and that [Fitz John] Porter, [George A.] McCall, and [George] Stoneman were giving him battle. Long, and anxiously, did we listen to the distant roar of the battle; the cannonading was furious, and at nightfall we began to see the shells bursting over the treetops. About 8 o'clock P.M. a dispatch from General McClellan was read to the troops, stating that we had driven the enemy from the field. The men fell into line, began to cheer, and regiment after regiment took it up along the whole line toward our left, until it seemed as though pandemonium had broken loose. At 9 o'clock another dispatch stated the enemy to be fleeing toward Richmond [with] our cavalry and horse-artillery in pursuit. Again the cheering began, and the bands commenced playing, keeping it up until near midnight, the first music we have been allowed since we left the White House.[17] Our loss is supposed to be considerable, as all the ambulances belonging to our command have been ordered to the scene for duty.

[Friday] June 27. [Winfield Scott] Hancock's brigade and 2 regiments of our own, including the 49th, were ordered out this morning to the picket line, all under the command of Hancock.[18] I, of course, went along. We were partially concealed in a piece of woods, but [we] could see the enemy at work on the fort I have before alluded to. We had not been out long before the 6th Maine regiment, who are experienced wood-choppers, began cutting down the timber that protected our camp from the view of the enemy. Meanwhile, a battery of 17 guns—6 three-inch guns, 6 light 12's, and 5 thirty-pounder Parrotts— was put in battery behind the timber. After it fell [we and they] were in full view. We remained out until this had been accomplished, and then went back to camp, reaching there about noon. The men stacked arms and began at once to cook their dinner. Our own dinner was served as usual under the colonel's fly, and while Colonel [Daniel D.] Bidwell, Major [George W.] Johnson, Captain [William F.] Wheeler and myself were eating, the enemy opened upon us with a heavy fire. The shells flew over our heads thick and fast, a piece of one striking my colored servant's tent just in rear of my own. He was lying down fast asleep at the time, and it awakened him with such [a] fright that he ran away across the field and never came back. (I never saw him afterwards, but learned that he made his way to Harrison's Landing with the army, where he took the first boat for the North. He called upon Dr. McCray, in Buffalo, [while] on his way to Detroit where he lived. He had met the doctor [during] the winter previous, when he visited me at Camp Griffin.) The regiment immediately fell into line, and soon we were ordered to the left in support of the battery which had just been erected, occupying some breastworks vacated by [John] Sedgwick's division, [when it was] sent elsewhere. Here we remained all the afternoon, and from this point we could plainly see the Battle of Gaines' Mill, which was then going on under General [Fitz John] Porter.

By nightfall it was plain to be seen that Porter had lost ground, but we did not then realize the full significance of his battle. We went back to our own camp again just at night, and while the men were having supper, an order came for our brigade to go to Porter's assistance. While the regiment was marching out by the flank to obey the order, the enemy opened upon us with artillery; shells began to fly all around us, one bursting in the flank of the regiment, killing and wounding several men. I dismounted and took the wounded forward into the rifle pits for shelter, when the order for us to move was countermanded. One of the men killed was the man who made the cigars, that I sent home by Lieutenant [Charles H.] Bidwell.[19] We remained in line under arms all Friday night, under the greatest tension of nerve and muscle, hourly expecting the enemy to attack.

[Saturday] June 28. The night passed without event, and this morning I rode back to the Trent House hospital, to see about my wounded who had been sent there the night before. Here I found everything had been ordered away toward Savage Station, Dr. [James A.] Hall having gone with the rest. I returned to camp. While I was away on this mission the rebels attacked our line with the 7th & 8th Georgia regiments, and were driven off handsomely, leaving Colonel [Lucius M.] Lamar, of the 8th Georgia in our hands, severely wounded.[20] Captain Theodore B. Hamilton (Company G) of the 33rd [New York] was taken prisoner by the rebels in this affair.[21] [He is the eldest son of Dr. Frank Hastings Hamilton.] This ended the fighting for the day so far as we were concerned, and at night we lay in the woods on our left supporting Mott's battery [3rd New York]. Colonel [Daniel D.] Bidwell, Captain [Thaddeus P.] Mott, Major [George W.] Johnson and myself slept on the ground, in a tent which we found deserted.[22] Our own camp was left standing, but during the night the tents were cut into ribbons, to render them useless to the enemy.

[Sunday] June 29. Our orders were to remain until daylight, then to retire guarding Mott's battery, which we did, and reached the Trent House about 8 o'clock A.M. where we found the division drawn up in line. We then moved down along the Chickahominy [River], guarding the fords and bridges during the forenoon, and [we were] brought up on the field of Savage Station about 2 o'clock P.M. Here we found [Edwin] Sumner's 2nd Corps drawn up expecting the enemy. Our division took position over on his left near the Williamsburg Road, and rested for an hour or more. Soon after 4 o'clock, as the enemy did not appear, we moved down the Williamsburg Road about a mile, and rested again. At 5 o'clock the enemy arrived and attacked Sumner at the station, whereupon we were recalled to assist him. Brooks' Vermont brigade engaged the enemy at the opening through which the Williamsburg passes out into the field, and lost quite heavily. Some other portions of the division also suffered, but not as severely as Brooks. These wounded were collected at a house and shop about a mile down the road from the field of action, where a temporary hospital had been established.

A PRISONER

About 8 o'clock in the evening of the 29th, Sunday, while I was busily engaged in the care of the wounded, Dr. Brown, Franklin's medical director, came to tell me that the army was in full retreat, that these wounded men were to be left behind, and that, by General Franklin's order, he would detail me to one of the medical officers to remain with them. Dr. [William P.] Russell of the 5th Vermont, and Dr. [William J.] Sawin of one of the Vermont regiments [2nd Vermont], were also to stay.[23] We kept at our work most of the night, but finally, at near 3 o'clock A.M. [Monday, June 30, 1862], We laid down for a little rest, from sheer exhaustion. Meanwhile the army was passing in steady tramp until mid-night, when the rear guard went by, leaving only a battery behind, by mistake.

Surgeon William J. Sawin, 2nd Vermont
(USAMHI)

Though so very tired, I could not sleep from the excitement of the situation, and at dawn I arose and began work. I soon heard the enemy's skirmish [line] advancing slowly through the woods, and presently it came to a halt on a line with the house where we were. I was examining a man's face at the time, who had some of his teeth knocked out, and had placed him in the doorway to get more light when, looking around, I saw some mounted men peering in at me. They proved to be some of General [Thomas J.] Jackson's officers, whose column was moving on this road, so I told them, briefly, by what authority I was there, and what my business was. One of them, comprehending the situation at once, remarked that he would report the matter to General Jackson. [He] turned upon his horse to go and do so, when Jackson himself rode up. I briefly told my story to him, stating that I [had] no rations, and needed a guard to prevent the troops from over-running the place, and particularly to preserve the water supply. He directed that a sergeant and 12 men be detailed as guards, committed other questions arising from our presence there to his medical director, and ordered the column to advance.

Sometime during the morning, about 10 o'clock I should think, the head of D. H. [Daniel Harvey] Hill's division halted near the hospital, and from General Hill a pass was obtained which authorized me to visit the field of battle, in quest of any wounded who might have been overlooked. About 2 o'clock P.M., armed with the pass and accompanied by one of the guards, I proceeded to the field for the purpose mentioned. In going I was obliged to pass the Confederate column, which was still marching along the Williamsburg Road, en route for White Oak Swamp. They were a cheery lot, flushed with their recent victories which they vainly supposed decisive, and greeted me with many playful expressions, such as "On to Richmond," [and] "You are on the right road." Their uniforms were tattered, but their muskets were bright, and their cannon, though mostly drawn with rope traces and marked "U.S." were quite capable of doing effectual service.

On the field I met a well-dressed, intelligent Confederate ambulance sergeant, who greeted me pleasantly upon my explaining my mission, and who stated that he was there for a like purpose. He had found a few wounded, and they were removed to Savage Station on the opposite side of the field, where our army, on retiring, had left about 2,000 wounded, chiefly from the Ellerson's and Gaines' Mill battles. I counted about 70 Union dead lying in the open space through which the Williamsburg Road emerged into the Savage Station field, whose uniforms were mostly new, and whose pockets were inside out, indicating that they had been rifled. These dead belonged, for the most part, to Brooks' Vermont brigade. After an hour or so spent in this way upon the field, I returned to my hospital and resumed work. All the weary day long, the Confederate column marched down the road leading past our place, and at night some of their trains camped in the woods near us. During the afternoon we heard the firing at White Oak Swamp, where a battle was in progress.

July 1. On Tuesday morning we were moved up to Savage Station with our wounded, and merged into that hospital. Dr. John Swinray, of Magruder's staff, had been designated as military commandant by the Confederate authorities.[24] I remained at Savage Station two weeks, and assisted in the care of the wounded. The first day, Tuesday, we distinctly heard the guns at Malvern Hill, and soon learned of the terrible punishment that the Army of the Potomac there gave to Lee and his host.

I had charge of about 200 wounded at this hospital and made a number of capital operations, besides innumerable minor ones, and assisted at about 100 operations made by others. The weather was hot and, as a consequence, many of the wounded did badly, from septic causes. The enemy took possession of a considerable part of the rations and stores which were left for us, appropriating them to their own use regardless of our necessities. While at Savage's [no sarcasm intended] a sergeant of the regular army transferred a colored boy, a servant of his captain, to my custody, who passed as my servant thereafter.

IN RICHMOND

On Sunday, July 13th, we were loaded upon platform cars and moved into Richmond. Arriving there late in the evening, and finding no ambulances in waiting, we remained at the station all night. In the morning [July 14] we were distributed to the various tobacco ware-houses then used as hospitals. I was assigned quarters in Libby Prison, with the other medical officers. In the afternoon Lieutenant Turner, the commandant of the prison, ordered a search of my person, claiming that he did so to ascertain if I had any counterfeit Confederate money in my possession. I was not the unhappy possessor of that valuable circulation medium, but did have some gold, having been paid partly in that coin a few days before. He cast longing eyes at it, but did not dare to take it. It must be remembered that I was a medical officer left with wounded [men] under proper orders, and not a pris-oner of war in the ordinary acceptation of the term. I was soon as-signed to the care of wounded in warehouse No. 4, about four blocks east of "Libby," on Cary Street. The weather was very hot and [the] stifling air of the building, saturated with the odor of [the] State To-bacco Company and without any conveniences whatever, was some-thing almost unendurable. It is a wonder that even so many survived as did. I went to Libby for my meals, and also slept there on the bare floor. I met Dr. Joseph W. Robinson on my arrival at Libby, who had been captured at White Oak Swamp. We joined the officers mess, pur-chasing our food with the gold and U.S. currency which we had, and which the Rebels were very glad to get in exchange for their merchan-dise of any kind.

July 17. Thursday. I obtained a pass from Turner and visited the officers' prison on 18th Street, where Lieutenant [William] McLean and Captain [Theodore B.] Hamilton were confined, and whose joint guest I became for the night. They were both very glad to see me, and did all in their power to entertain me pleasantly. McLean was cheer-ful, making the most of everything, and taking his imprisonment as kindly as possible, but Hamilton was the reverse, feeling downcast in the extreme. However, we had a pleasant visit, and the next morning at 9 o'clock [July 18] I returned to Libby. On my arrival there I found that about 500 wounded [men] were being exchanged, and that a part of them had already been loaded into ambulances, which were drawn up in front of the building. I applied to Dr. Cullen, under whose direc-tion the exchange was being made, for permission to go with them. He readily granted my request, and I boarded a convenient ambulance, taking a seat with the driver. The little colored boy, who became sepa-rated from me on my arrival at Libby, now came running up with tears in his eyes, begging to go along too. I told him to get aboard, the driver having consented, and we were driven to Aiken's Landing on the James River, about 10 miles below Richmond.

On our arrival at the landing we found the hospital steamer "Loui-siana" at the wharf awaiting us, and the afternoon was occupied in transferring the wounded to the boat. Lieutenant Colonel [Jacob Bowman] Sweitzer [62nd Pennsylvania] of General [George B.] McClellan's staff, was the truce officer in charge, and this was the first transaction under the cartel, [which had] just then [been] agreed upon between the hostile powers.[25] I succeeded in getting the colored boy past the guard and safely on board, through the kindness of the ambulance sergeant who was in charge at the wharf, and who was the same whom I had met on the field of Savage Station on June 30th. Dr. Robinson was with me, and we were rejoiced to get under the protection of the Stars and Stripes once more.

HARRISON'S LANDING

We steamed out into the river after we were loaded up and cast anchor for the night, as our flag would not protect us from the shore batteries of the enemy after dark. We got up steam at daylight [July 19], and in a few hours "hove to" off Harrison's Landing. Soon after we came to anchor General McClellan boarded the "Louisiana" by steam launch, and proceeded to the cabin where two regular army officers, Major H. B. Clitz and Captain [William Parham] Chambliss [5th U.S. Cavalry], were lying upon cots.[26] McClellan spent nearly an hour in low conversation with them, evidently for the purpose of ascertaining all he could of affairs in Richmond. (General J. E. B. Stuart came almost daily to see these officers in Libby, sitting between their cots which were contiguous, and spending a short time in conversation with them. These two officers were wounded and captured at Gaines' Mill, June 27.) Finally, the medical officers and nurses were put ashore and sent to their respective regiments, while the "Louisiana" proceeded north to distribute the wounded to the various hospitals.

I reached the camp of the 49th [New York] about 2 o'clock P.M., Saturday, July 19th, and everybody greeted me with kind words, anxiously inquiring after any of their friends in Richmond, and as to my treatment by the enemy. I hardly had time to get some dinner before General [John] Davidson sent for me, and I spent an hour or more with him in telling him my experience, and in describing what I saw in Rebeldom. General Davidson was very gracious and seemed much pleased with the interview. He mentioned me in his report, besides giving me a letter to Governor [Edwin D.] Morgan recommending me for promotion.

[Sunday] July 20. I visited Dr. [Frank Hastings] Hamilton at General [Erasmus] Keyes' headquarters, where he was serving as medical director, and gave him the first news he has received of Theodore [Hamilton]. We spent an hour or more in agreeable conversation, and he thanked me very kindly for coming to see him with such good news. On my return from Richmond I found the regiment quite sickly—

more so than it had been at any time before. Colonel [Daniel D.] Bidwell had gone home on sick leave which came back approved on July 20th. The paymaster arrived on the 19th to pay the brigade, and we were paid on the 22nd, up to July 1st. I sent home $150.00 by Dr. [James A.] Hall on the 23rd.

I left [William] McLean in good spirits in Richmond. [He was] taking his imprisonment quite philosophically. He was wounded by three sabre-cuts, two upon his head laying open his scalp quite extensively, and another in one arm. They all healed kindly, after which he was put on duty in the office of the commandant of the prison. About 200 officers were confined in the building with him, among whom were Generals [George A.] McCall and [John F.] Reynolds. Our camp at Harrison's was pleasantly situated on a knoll, about 2 miles from the landing at Berkley where we had a regimental hospital once more, the first since we came on the peninsula. A cow—tell it not in gath—was obtained for the use of the hospital, and thus we were afforded nice milk twice a day, which, together with fresh vegetables, made us seem like living again.

[Tuesday] July 29. I heard from home today—the first letter in 4 weeks. Dr. [James A.] Hall has promised to use his influence to secure a promotion for me while he is away, and it is rumored that Colonel Folsom is expected to command a regiment to be raised in Wyoming County, which, if true, may afford a chance of success.

[Wednesday] July 30. The weather is very hot, and has so continued for several days, with no prospect of abatement at present. On the night of the 31st the Rebels opened [fire with] their batteries from the south side of the river, attempting to disable our shipping at Westover, the lower landing. The gunboats soon replied, and after an hour or so silenced the enemy. The scene of the bursting of those immense shells in the middle of the night was grand, but no great damage was done to us.

[Sunday] August 3. We had rain which left the air cooler, and the health of the army began to improve. Our regiment shows a smaller sick list by one half than it did two weeks ago. This morning, I reported 16 sick in [the] hospital, and 27 in quarters, mostly cases of diarrhoea which is quite obstinate, in character.

The attitude of the North, in relation to the demand for more troops, surprises us here in the army. There is very little use in teasing, hiring, or buying soldiers to defend our country. Men must be had, and if they won't come voluntarily, they must be made to come. This army, and [General John] Pope's, must be reinforced largely and speedily. Drafting must inevitably be resorted to sooner or later, and it might as well be done now as ever. It will never do to handle the rebellion with kid gloves, as there is very little Union sentiment remaining in the South, and we need [to] have no fear of injuring this supposed class by an aggressive warfare of the most unrelenting kind. These are some of the views entertained in the army at this time—views which are freely expressed on all hands.

[Wednesday] August 6. The weather is hot again, and our division is under orders to be ready to move at a moment's notice. The health of the regiment is very good at present, and the sick list is daily diminishing. An assistant surgeon has been temporarily assigned to help me while Dr. [James A.] Hall is away, which affords me some relief from the pressure of the routine duties. Captain [Erasmus W.] Haines [Company F] and Lieutenant [William S.] Bull went home on sick leave today, and Quarter Master [James A.] Boyde went to Fort Monroe on business for the regiment.[27]

[Saturday] August 9. I have been suffering considerably with pain in my front teeth, so much so, that my face is swollen quite badly. I have applied for leave to go to Baltimore and have them cared for by a dentist.

[Monday] August 11. My face is better, and my application for leave came back disapproved, which didn't surprise me much. Everything is packed up in camp ready to move, and we are sitting around upon the boxes waiting for the orders to start. The name of my assistant is Dr. Meekley, of Pennsylvania. General [John] Davidson has been assigned to another command, and will not return to us. He goes to St. Louis, I believe. Captain [Reuben E.] Heacock [Company E] has gone home on recruiting service.

[Tuesday] August 12. It is very hot and we are still waiting to move, expecting the order momentarily. Preparations are going on all around us, which indicate a movement of the whole army.

[Wednesday] August 13. We are still hourly expecting [a move and] living out of doors, as our tents and camp equipage are all packed and the wagons have moved off. This suspense is more trying than the labors of an active campaign. Captain [Theodore B.] Hamilton [Company G] of the 33rd New York returned from Richmond today, and reports that [Captain William] McLean, who was released with him, was off for Fort Monroe and probably the North. The weather is cooler, but I feel very much depressed in spirits—don't know why.

[Thursday] August 14. We are not off yet—waiting, waiting, waiting. [Captain William] McLean, much to our surprise, came to our camp yesterday, and is now staying with his brother-in-law, [Orville S.] Tom Dewey [Company A]. General [William F.] Smith has just returned from 20 days' leave spent in the North, and comes back a Major General, which we all think he deserves as much as any man. He has taken his division through some severe campaigning, and always skillfully, with little loss and no disaster. He is cool under fire, and altogether an ideal division commander.

Chapter Four —1862

THE MARYLAND CAMPAIGN AND FREDERICKSBURG

ALEXANDRIA - POPE

[THURSDAY] AUGUST 21. After six days of hard marching we are at Hampton [Roads] preparatory to embarkation, though we are unadvised as to our destination. The march down the Peninsula, especially that part of it between the camp we left at Harrison's [Landing] and the Chickahominy [River], was so hot and dusty that we all looked like millers just out of duty in a flouring mill. The flies perplexed us greatly the first day. We were obliged to carry tree branches to brush them off our horses as well as ourselves. We passed over the old battlefield of Williamsburg, and through the heavy works at Yorktown—places of familiar and historic interest.

We embarked at Fort Monroe, Friday, August 22, on the steamer "C. [Cornelius] Vanderbilt" and reached Alexandria Saturday evening [August 23]. [We] remained on board all night and disembarked this morning [Sunday, August 24]. The regiment was sent to camp about 2 miles out of Alexandria on the Fairfax Road, and I obtained a pass and took the boat for Washington. O. H. O. Dorrance of Attica, a military telegraph operator, went with me and we staid all night at the National Hotel. I had known Dorrance in my youth, he was a good companion, and we had a pleasant visit discussing the times of our boyhood days.

[Monday] August 25. I returned to camp this morning and find that our horses have not yet arrived from the Peninsula. It looks as though we would be sent out to assist [General John] Pope who, I fear, is getting into some difficulty. On the boat coming from Fort Monroe to Alexandria I lost my baggage, a satchel containing my clothing and some valuable papers, including my rebel passes. I busied myself Tuesday, the 26th, in replenishing my scanty wardrobe at Alexandria, buying however only such articles as I stood in immediate need of. Dr. [James A.] Hall and Colonel [William C.] Alberger returned from sick leave the 26th, both looking well, and Major [George W.] Johnson forwarded his application for leave. We are located by the roadside between Forts Ellsworth and Lyon, and it is so dusty that we suffer considerably from it. As we are without horses we are obliged to stay in camp or go about on foot.

Friday, August 29. Franklin's Corps, consisting of Smith's and Slocum's divisions, was ordered to go to the scene of Pope's operations supposed to be somewhere near Manassas, and whose guns we had been hearing for a day or two. We were obliged to start without our horses, which was a serious inconvenience. Dr. [James A.] Hall and I kept up with the troops the first day, as the march was not a long one. We slept together that night under an apple tree in an orchard near our bivouac, without covering save a borrowed blanket. Saturday morning [August 30] we moved on early, but Dr. [James A.] Hall and I were obliged to lag behind for a time. However, we soon found an ambulance going to the front, the driver of which was persuaded to give us a ride, thus enabling us to overtake the regiment [on] Saturday evening between Centerville and the Second Bull Run battlefield. The closing scenes of which engagement were just then being enacted.

August 31. Sunday morning found us all back at Centerville, [John] Pope and the Army of the Potomac as well, in the midst of a drenching rain, without any place to even sit down upon excepting the mud. We remained there until Monday night [September 1], when we fell back to Fairfax Court House. [On] Monday P.M. a severe thunder storm set in, and I could find no shelter save the canvas covers of the artillery, and this was not safe on account of the danger from lightning. That night after we reached Fairfax I broke open a store, and lay down upon the counter at 3 o'clock A.M., sleeping until daylight. Tuesday, September 2nd we remained near Fairfax, marching and countermarching all day, and at night returned to our former position near Fort Lyon, from which we [had] set out five days before to join Pope. Our horses met us Wednesday morning [September 3] just as we were approaching Alexandria again, so we had no use of them during this fatiguing but fruitless affair. To add to my discomfort I had on a pair of new boots when I left Alexandria, and was tortured by them more or less during the whole trip.

THE MARYLAND CAMPAIGN - ANTIETAM

[Thursday] September 4. Today [General George B.] McClellan is assigned to the defense of Washington, which brings us once more under his command. How long it will last or what [happens] next I cannot say, but God be praised for delivering us from Pope. Dr. [John] Jenkins reported to us as 2nd assistant surgeon on the 5th.[1] He had formerly been in the employ of Dr. [Milton E.] Potter, of Cowlesville, and brought news of the people in that region.

September 6. Saturday P.M. we crossed the Potomac over Long Bridge, marched through Washington and Georgetown out the Tennallytown Road, and bivouacked for the night near the latter village. This was the beginning of the Maryland Campaign, for news had now been circulated that the Rebels had crossed into Maryland above Harper's Ferry. It was late in the evening when we passed through Washington, but the people were up to greet us, and we were received with demonstrations of enthusiastic applause at almost every corner, especially at Willard's Hotel where a large crowd had collected. The people evidently regarded the Army of the Potomac as their savior, and were grateful that it stood—a mighty barrier—between them and the rebel horde. As we passed General McClellan's residence we gave nine rousing cheers, which were taken up by each regiment as it passed. At a number of places during our passage through the city, I observed ladies supplying the soldiers with water, always so needful upon the march, and particularly in hot weather.

September 7. We lay in bivouac above Tennallytown until late Sunday P.M., and then we set out toward Rockville, Maryland. Soon after starting we came to a stream, a small creek which I think was Rock Creek, where stood a carriage near the ford, in which sat President Lincoln, Mr. [William] Seward, the Secretary of State, and Mr. [Edwin] Stanton, the Secretary of War. The soldiers cheered them lustily, and they all acknowledged the attention with bared heads and waving hats. We marched on by moonlight until 11 o'clock P.M., when we again went into bivouac.

September 8. Monday was hot and dusty, and, though we did not start very early, we kept it up until late at night to make up. This was a good plan, for it enabled us to avoid the great heat of mid-day, and we continued to do so through the week after this fashion. On the 11th, we bivouacked at Barnesville, and by Saturday, the 13th, we had reached Jefferson where we again bivouacked for the night.

[Sunday] September 14. Sunday morning the sun rose bright, betokening a hot day, and after a hasty breakfast we started on the road to Crampton's Gap in the South Mountain, that was visible in the distance. We soon began to hear firing and see the smoke of battle at Turner's Gap, a few miles to our right, but the Sixth Corps was destined to engage in a battle of its own at Crampton's later in the day. About noon we rested in a piece of woods, and cooked coffee. Henry Slocum's division being in advance, pushed on up to the gap, [and] we of Smith's soon followed. Just at night we reached the foot of the mountain, when we were welcomed by a few shots from a battery belonging to Howell Cobb's brigade stationed at its summit. The guns could not be depressed enough to get our range. Most of the projectiles passed over us without damage. It was quite dark by the time we were fairly ascending the mountain, and, hearing the groans of [the] wounded men in the woods off the road, Dr. [James A.] Hall and I dismounted and went to their relief. We found a number of Rebels scattered through the woods, most of whom were mortally wounded in the abdomen or chest. After ministering to them the best we could, we sought the regiment, which had passed on over the mountain, and was in bivouac on its western slope. We reached it late at night, tired and worn by the fatigues of the day, and slept soundly on the ground.

September 15. Monday morning the Sixth Corps was ordered to go to the succor of Harper's Ferry, but had not gone far before an order came calling us back, that post having already surrendered. We remained in camp near Rohrersville during the balance of Monday, and all day and night of Tuesday. Tuesday, the 16th was the anniversary of our departure from Buffalo. What memories clustered around the day. What a year of camping, marching, and fighting we had seen— and the end was not yet. Dr. [James A.] Hall and I visited the South Mountain battlefield at Turner's Gap, on this Tuesday P.M. It was a beautiful day, and the scenery was something indescribably grand. Before us, looking east, was the Frederick Valley [Middletown Valley], with the city nestling in its midst a few miles away. Behind us lay the Washington Valley, equally picturesque, but where even firing was going on between some of the contending forces, maneuvering for position near the Sharpsburg field. Some of the enemy's yet unburied dead lay at our feet as we were sweeping the horizon with our glasses, and altogether it was a sadly beautiful picture of peace and war. We reached our regiment in the early evening with appetites sharpened for supper by the keen air. We soon partook of [supper] and then lay down to sleep and rest, preparatory to the coming of the morrow with all [of] its dreadful carnage.

September 17. Wednesday morning we awoke early and prepared to march in a misty rain. I shaved myself while my tent was being struck, which is the last time my upper lip has felt the touch of a razor. We were off betimes, and soon passed through Rohrersville en route to the Antietam Field, which we reached about noon. The Sixth Corps was thrown in on the right to relieve [Edwin] Sumner, and the third brigade of Smith's division (commanded by Colonel [William]

Irwin, 49th Pennsylvania Volunteers) made a charge on the enemy at the Dunker Church on the Hagerstown Road. [This is illustrated in the *Century*, June 1886, p. 298.] Surgeon W. J. H. [William James Hamilton] White, medical director Sixth Corps, was killed by a sharpshooter while sitting on his horse very near General [William B.] Franklin.[2] [He was] the first casualty in the corps in this fight. The 49th New York lost 2 killed, and 21 wounded. Lieutenant Colonel [William C.] Alberger, [who was] struck in the face by a fragment of a shell, was among them. He was taken to the Second Corps hospital. The Sixth Corps did not establish separate hospitals for itself, and I spent part of the day with him there on the 18th. During this day there was no fighting to speak of, and everybody who could do so rested as much as possible.

September 19. The enemy retreated during the night of the 18th, and on Friday morning we found he had escaped to the other side of the [Potomac] river, where he stood at bay. I visited the famous "Sunken Road" where I saw the dead lying in swaths, and in the Cornfield they were also thickly strewn. The number of dead bodies that I saw must have aggregated nearly 500. I counted 11 dead near a caisson that fell into our hands. During the next few days we moved about considerably, but never very far at one time. On Sunday, the 21st, we marched to the vicinity of Williamsport, where our baggage came, so that night I enjoyed the luxury of a tent once more. On the 22nd, I rode 12 miles to General McClellan's headquarters to obtain Colonel [William] Alberger's leave, and I brought it back with me duly approved. He went home rejoicing that his wound was no worse. On [Tuesday] September 23rd we moved about 4 miles down the Potomac, and camped at Dam No. 4, to guard it, which is about half way between Williamsport and Sharpsburg.

These were bright days for us, for we felt the influence of the victory gained at Antietam. The weather was pleasant, though the nights were cool. The old troops are very much worn in vigor, besides being poorly clad, and are particularly suffering for shoes. The country we are in is the finest we have seen in the South, resembling New York more in its thrift and enterprise. Under its genial sun the health and stamina of the army is improving. On [Saturday] September 27th, being still at Dam No. 4, we were reminded that is just a year since we first crossed the Potomac into Virginia.

[Sunday] September 29th, we are still at Dam No. 4, which is a longer time than we have been in any one place since we left Harrison's Landing. I am very short of money, having had no pay since July, and no prospect of getting any at [the] present, as the government coffers are reported as nearly empty. Rumors are afloat that we [will] go to Hagerstown soon, which I hope are true for that is said to be a delightful region. Our mails are very irregular, sometimes a week apart, for which there seems no good reason. We are certainly in a more accessible region than Virginia, but we do not fare as well in regard to our mail facilities, as we did there.

[Tuesday] October 1, today I attended the funeral of one of our men, the first that has died in camp since we left Camp Griffin. Others have died, but at the different hospitals where they have been sent. We were surprised by the receipt of a mail today, with [a] letter from home [written on] September 19th. Rain fell today for the first time in many weeks, which was refreshing in every sense of the word.

[Thursday] October 3, we were reviewed by the President and General McClellan, which is the first review we have had since we were at Harrison's Landing. The Sixth Corps did itself credit as usual, and the affair passed off pleasantly. We have a new brigade commander in place of General [John] Davidson who, it will be remembered, left us at Harrison's Landing. Brigadier General Francis L. Vinton, nephew of the Reverend Dr. Vinton of New York, is our new general.[3] He, [who] has just been promoted from colonel of the 43rd N.Y. Volunteers, is a young looking man, but may do well.

[Wednesday] October 8. We received 54 recruits from Buffalo today, which is a substantial and much needed addition to our wasted ranks. General McClellan's headquarters were moved to Harper's Ferry today, which is thought by some to indicate a forward movement soon. Major [George W.] Johnson has been in command of the regiment since Colonel [William C.] Alberger's wounding. He is a cool, brave officer, but [is] not generally popular. I like him very much myself, for I know him well—probably better than any other officer, for he has no intimates. Tom Dewey was wounded in the heel at Antietam, but is on duty and is well.

[Friday] October 10. We have just been surprised again with a mail, the first in 10 days, which is a welcome change. Letters and papers from home are our great consolation, and when we are deprived of them [for] so long it seems as if life were a blank. Mr. [William] Woodruff, the sutler, has just arrived in camp, the first time he has been with us since [we left] Alexandria. We still remain quiet, having occupied this camp at Dam No. 4 [for] about 17 days. We are midway between Sharpsburg and Williamsport, and 9 miles from Hagerstown, in the very garden of Maryland. Generals [William B.] Franklin, [William F.] Smith, and [William T. H.] Brooks have their wives with them at Hagerstown, which is a very pretty place according to report.

[Saturday] October 11. About 1 o'clock this morning Major [George W.] Johnson came to my tent, saying we were ordered to move immediately. It was raining at the time, and there was much mystery in the suddenness of the movement in the middle of the night, when we had not seen a Rebel for nearly three weeks. However, we started at 4 o'clock

A.M., and at 9 A.M. [we] passed through Hagerstown. We then learned that [J. E. B.] Stuart had made a raid around our rear, burnt stores at Chambersburg, and that we were being sent out to aid in intercepting him. He was too nimble and fleet footed for infantry. Eluding our cavalry, he passed over the Potomac at Point of Rocks without interruption, after making the complete circuit of the Army of the Potomac for the second time in four months. Our services, therefore, being of no further use, we went into camp in a beautiful woods one mile and a half from the town, and on the 13th, Dr. [James A.] Hall and I visited the city for the first time. The nights were beginning to grow cool, and we therefore availed ourselves of this opportunity to purchase a small cast iron stove, which we brought home with us and set it up in our tent that night, having the first inside fire of the season. The popularity of the scheme was attested to by our numerous visitors, not only this evening, but on various other occasions during the next few weeks.

The 3rd brigade has a brass band again, which is the only one in the division at present. The bands were all mustered out on the 1st of August and we have had no music since [then] until now, excepting such as the fife and drum furnished. Tom Dewey has not been well for a day or two, but seems better this evening, and sits by my fire enjoying its benefits and comforts.

[Saturday] October 15. Dr. [John A.] Jenkins has been quite ill for the past week, and I imagine he is not over charmed with military life. A little sickness is apt to remove all illusions as to the delights of camp, especially in an active campaign. Dr. [Sylvanus S.] Mulford has just returned from an absence of 30 days, having obtained his leave through the influence of judge advocate Levi C. Turner, of the War Department. He calls two or three times a day, and is feeling quite happy.

[Saturday] October 18. The weather is beautiful—like Indian summer—and today Dr. Mulford and I went into Hagerstown, where we saw the ladies promenading the streets, the shops busy, and all looked like civil life again. We also saw Mrs. General Franklin and Mrs. General Smith at the Sixth Corps headquarters, where everything was gaily festive. General [Henry] Slocum has been assigned to the command of General [Nathaniel] Banks' corps, and General [Darius] Couch has been ordered to Hancock, Md. today. Colonel [Daniel D.] Bidwell has returned to camp, having reported yesterday, and is looking quite thin for him. Today I was assigned to the medical charge of the 77th N. Y. Volunteers, as it was without a medical officer, the surgeon and assist-surgeon both being away on sick leave. Tom Dewey has been ordered home on recruiting service, to relieve Captain [Reuben B.] Heacock, who has been absent sometime on that duty.

[Wednesday] October 22. We moved in the night to Clear Spring, several miles toward Hancock, where we remained a week, guarding one of the dams or fords. While at Clear Spring about 20 officers boarded at the hotel there, which we enjoyed very much, as it was a pleasant change. We were all without money, but the landlord kindly trusted us until we should get our pay, the quartermaster becoming responsible. I had charge of the 77th New York [during] the week we were there. On [Wednesday] the 29th we broke camp at 3 o'clock P.M. and moved to Williamsport, where we arrived at 11 o'clock at night, and [we] remained [there] during the 30th. Colonel [Daniel D.] Bidwell is with the 49th New York but [is] not on duty yet, as he is not feeling strong enough to assume command.

[Friday] October 31. We moved from Williamsport to Boonsborough today, about 12 miles, where we arrived at noon, and then had our bimonthly inspection and muster for pay. Mrs. General Pratt accompanied her husband on the march today, and tonight they are at the U.S. Hotel in Boonsborough. Our brigade band is serenading them this evening, the weather being warm and the night delightful. Gen'l Pratt was formerly colonel of the 31st N.Y., the reg't that Dr. Hamilton went out with as surgeon. (General Pratt is now judge of one of the courts in Brooklyn, where he resides.) We are ordered to move at 6 o'clock A.M. tomorrow, but whither bound we do not know—some say to Harper's Ferry, others to Frederick—but the morrow will tell.

[Sunday] November 2. We made a rapid and long march yesterday from Boonsborough to Petersville, passing through Turner's Gap where Reno and Burnside had their battle on [Sunday] September 14, and then through Burkittsville, at the foot of Crampton's Gap, where Franklin's Sixth Corps was engaged the same day; but all evidences of the carnage had disappeared, save only the bullet marks on the trees and fences. We are two miles and a half from the Potomac, and 6 miles below Harper's Ferry. A hospital was established for the Sixth Corps at Hagerstown, and we left 700 sick there. We expect to cross into Virginia tomorrow, and then farewell to the delightful scenes of southwestern Maryland—my Maryland—where we have had so much of joy and sadness commingled. We have now been campaigning for 8 months, which has worn us down in body and discouraged us in mind to a considerable degree, and I think we all dread going back into Virginia, where the old ground is evidently to be fought over again.

ON THE "SACRED SOIL" AGAIN

We have heard distant firing in Virginia at intervals all day, which appears to be in the vicinity of Snicker's Gap, and have been under orders to move since morning, but night finds us still here. We have, however, received final orders to march at 6 A.M. to-morrow. Tom Dewey did not go on recruiting service as expected, but sent his resignation a few days ago. I believe he expects to enter the artillery service. I am sorry to have him leave the 49th, for he is one of our best officers. Adjutant [George H.] Selkirk departs for Buffalo in the morning, on recruiting service in Dewey's stead.

[Monday] Nov. 3. We crossed the Potomac on a pontoon bridge at Berlin this morning, and have marched about 17 miles to-day, reaching Purcellville where we have encamped for the night. I was chilled through on the march, as the weather was very cold; our stove comes in place most delightfully to-night. To-morrow will be election day in New-York, and I regret that I cannot be present at the polls to cast my vote against [Horatio] Seymour, who is the Democratic candidate against General [James] Wadsworth. On [Tuesday] November 4th, we reached Union, Virginia. (What's in a name?) [We] went into camp at 3 o'clock P.M. for the night, but we remained there until 1 P.M. of the 5th. [Then] we moved 6 miles farther and encamped in the woods after dark. We were without tents and a colder night we had not seen.

[Thursday] November 6. We marched 12 miles which brought us to White Plains, on the Manassas Gap Railroad. I lost my gloves and so [I] had cold hands today. General Seth Williams [Adjutant General, Army of the Potomac] told Dr. [Sylvanus S.] Mulford yesterday, so the latter informs me, that the Sixth Corps would be given the reserve position, and would always be near McClellan's headquarters. Dr. Mulford also says he intends to resign from the 33rd New York, and enter the volunteer staff corps. I shall be sorry to have him leave our brigade, but so it ever is. Our friends are constantly looking to advancement. The changes in the personnel of the army, through promotion, casualties, and other causes, is something remarkable. One scarcely knows his friends from campaign to campaign. [1st Sgt.] Mart Clark [Company G] of the 21st New York came on [Friday] the 7th, and spent the night in our camp.[4] It is cold and snowed all day, but our stove makes it comfortable for ourselves, as well as others who call. We were thronged in our quarters today, and Colonel [Daniel] Bidwell spent the entire day with us.

On Sunday, the 9th, we moved from White Plains to New Baltimore, a distance of 8 miles, over a mountainous country and in a searching wind. General McClellan has been removed from command, and General [Ambrose] Burnside [has been] appointed [to the command of the Army].

EXIT McCLELLAN - ENTER BURNSIDE

[Tuesday] November 11. Today, General McClellan took leave of the Army, and the Sixth Corps was paraded to bid him farewell. He bade his adieus to the music of drums, cannon, and cheers. He looked sad as he rode along the lines, and many were moved to tears as he passed. Altogether, it was sad and affecting. The news of [Horatio]

Seymour's election too, coming at this time, is especially dispiriting. We are still [Thursday, November 13] at New Baltimore, and I presume our quietude is to enable the new commander to seize the reins with a firm hold. We have heard firing beyond Warrenton today, but know nothing of its import.

[Saturday] November 15. [It is] still quiet at New Baltimore, and the weather is delightful. It is rumored that [William B.] Franklin is to have command of a grand division, to consist of 2 or 3 corps, in which case [William F.] Smith will have the Sixth Corps, and [Albion P.] Howe the 2nd Division. Captain [William F.] Wheeler [Company D] is reported at Warrenton, and if so he will soon be here. He has been absent since we were at Fort Monroe, and his long absence has furnished occasion for unfavorable comment in certain quarters.

THE FREDERICKSBURG CAMPAIGN

[Monday] November 17. We left New Baltimore early yesterday morning, and encamped last night about 2 miles east of Catlett's Station. This morning we started again at 6:30 o'clock, and marched about 15 miles, which brings us to a point about 15 miles north by northwest of Fredericksburg. On [Tuesday] the 18th, we moved to Stafford Court House and camped in a dry woods near an old brick church. Our base of supplies is at Aquia Creek, seven miles distant. Captain [William F.] Wheeler has returned to the regiment, and on [Saturday] the 22nd had a trial for absence without leave before a military commission. I was, of course, summoned as a witness. The weather is bad and we are "stuck in the mud."

[Monday] November 24. The grand division organizations have been perfected and [William B.] Franklin has the Left Grand Division, [William F.] Smith the Sixth Corps, and [Albion P.] Howe the 2nd Division. The Left Grand Division comprises the 1st and 6th Corps, the 1st [Corps] being commanded by [John F.] Reynolds. The 21st New York is in the 1st Corps, and I paid that regiment a visit yesterday in company with Dr. [Sylvanus S.] Mulford and Captain [William F.] Wheeler, where I saw Mart Clark but spent most of my time with Captain "Al" [Alger M.] Wheeler, who is about the only officer left there of my particular acquaintance.[5] Captain W. F. Wheeler has been dismissed [from] the service for absence without leave. He was one of our best officers, and his dismissal is one of those unfortunate combinations of circumstances that often happen in the service. I hope the order will be revoked, as it is, in my opinion, a most unjust and cruel judgement. I believe that there was some neglect [to] present the case properly before the commission, and that, further, a re-hearing should be demanded by Captain Wheeler on that ground.

[Tuesday] November 25. [Second] Lieutenant [William T.] Bliss [Company F] returned from leave, and brought me a package from home containing gloves, stockings, etc.[6] Tomorrow will be Thanksgiving Day, and we are making some extra preparations for dinner on that account, though nothing very elaborate can be served, as we are not in a region of abundance. However, we shall have a roast turkey and some potatoes, both sweet and Irish, so I fancy we'll get along without starving. The weather is unfavorable for military operations, the frequent rains having made the roads almost impassable.

On Friday the 28th, I went to Aquia Creek Landing to draw medical supplies for the brigade, and saw Tom Dewey off for home, his resignation having been accepted at last. He was one of our best subaltern officers and Colonel [Daniel] Bidwell told me he would recommend him for captain of Company D, if he would remain. I hear that Captain [William] McLean [Company H, 5th U. S. Cavalry] is on recruiting service in Elmira. Lieutenant Charles O. Shepard of the 82nd New York Volunteers has also resigned, and he went north on the same boat with Tom Dewey. I bade them both goodbye at the wharf, wishing them much joy upon their release from the dangerous and irksome duties of field service.

[Sunday] November 30. This being the last day of the month I am busy with the monthly reports, which I have always to make up. Dr. [James A.] Hall is now surgeon-in-chief of the brigade. Dr. [Sylvanus S.] Mulford, who was holding the place by virtue of seniority, has resigned and gone north. Dr. Oliver Adams, brother to Dr. N. H. Adams came down to the army with Lieutenant [William T.] Bliss the other day and I understand he has been appointed assistant surgeon in one of the New York regiment's, the 78th New York, I think. The weather is better than at the last record, but the roads are still horrible [and] impassable for heavy trains and artillery. Colonel [Daniel] Bidwell's health is quite poor, and I fear [he] will break down completely if we have an active campaign.

[Thursday] December 4. The weather is bright and we are under orders to move at 11 o'clock A.M. today (rumor says to Belle Plain below Aquia Creek Landing).

[Saturday] December 6. We left our camp near Stafford Court House [the] day before yesterday as expected and our baggage train did not arrive until late into the night. We were without tents. Yesterday, we moved 4 miles again, but the artillery and trains did not get up until noon of [Sunday] the 7th. I was out of doors all night of the 5th, without cover of any kind, excepting my overcoat. It was the most severe night I had experienced in the service. I revolved before a camp fire all night long, but it was so cold [that] I could not sleep a wink. The ground is covered with snow and the ambulances are stuck in the mud for miles along the road. My horses have had no grain for two days and I have lived during that time on hard bread, with short allowance at that. Four men died in the ambulances yesterday while we were on the march. Just before our last move I was detailed to the medical charge of the division ambulance train, which adds to my duties and responsibilities very much. It is the duty of the medical officer in charge of the train to examine all passes given to the sick and to pick them up if he approves of their authority to "fall out," and to minister to their wants or necessities during such [a] march.

[Monday] December 8. We are at Belle Plain, or near there, but [we remained] quiet. In fact we cannot move on account of the mud. This is the most trying campaign we have experienced, yet I am in good health and gaining in flesh all the time. [Wednesday] December 10. [We are] still at the same place, though we have been under orders to march at a moment's notice since yesterday. With three days cooked rations and 60 rounds of ammunition, it looks like a fight. [First] Lieutenant [George W.] Gilman [Company E] has gone home on leave.[7] He is a faithful, deserving officer and I am glad [that] he has been allowed this indulgence.

[Saturday] December 13. I had been appointed recorder of the 2nd Division hospital, 6th Corps. We had moved down to the Rappahannock River [during the] night before last, and crossed the river yesterday morning early on two pontoon bridges, about two miles below the town of Fredericksburg. Our hospital is located at Mansfield, Bernard's Mansion, on the south bank of the river near the bridge head. We had a battle today in which the 49th New York lost 10 or 12 men, mostly wounded.[8] [First] Lieutenant [William T.] Bliss was slightly wounded in the head—the only officer struck. [Edwin V.] Sumner's Right Grand Division suffered a heavy loss, we hear, having made repeated assaults upon the enemy's strong position in front of the town. It is expected the battle will be renewed in the morning. I send my letters by the correspondents of the N.Y. Times and Tribune, who come to the hospital to get the lists of killed and wounded, and accord me that privilege in return for courtesies shown them. This is a great advantage, as we have no mail facilities during a battle.

[Sunday] December 14. The battle was not renewed today as expected, General [Ambrose] Burnside having countermanded the order which he first gave to do so. General George D. Bayard, of the cavalry, was struck by a solid shot while in conversation with General [William B.] Franklin, and I had him brought in immediately. He was on the lawn in front of the hospital when it happened, and I was standing on the steps at the time. The shot rolled along and expended its force against the foundation walls of the building. The injury is a mortal one, and it is doubtful if he lasts out the day.

[Tuesday] December 16. We remained quiet during the 14th & 15th, except [for] the usual skirmish firing and an occasional gun, and last night [we] recrossed the Rappahannock in safety. We are now on the north bank about 1 & 1/4 miles from the river, having been busy all night in removing and caring for the wounded. We seem to have been fortunate in extracting ourselves from a bad box. The Battle of Fredericksburg will always stand in history as a monument to the folly and incompetency of the second commander of the Army of the Potomac.

[Thursday] December 18. I was ordered to take the wounded of the 2nd Division to Washington. They were collected at Falmouth and put aboard of the cars, whence they were transported by rail to Aquia Creek, where we arrived [at] about 8 o'clock in the evening. Two transports at anchor off the landing were brought to the wharf, and the transfer of the wounded to the boats was accomplished by three o'clock A.M., whereupon we steamed for Washington, arriving there by 7 o'clock. The wounded were fed by the Sanitary Commission's agents while they were transferring to the ambulances, but it was three o'clock P.M. before they were all off for their various hospitals. Up to this time I had not eaten anything since leaving Falmouth the night before, so I was nearly famished. I made haste for a good hotel where I soon obtained the needed food and rest. The troops had not been paid since June, and I was quite out of money, so I availed myself of this opportunity to visit the pay department, where I drew four months' pay on [Saturday] the 20th, sending $300 home by the first express.

FAREWELL TO THE 49TH NEW YORK

I remained in Washington until [Tuesday] the 23rd, for rest and recuperation, when I started back for the army. Arriving at Falmouth late in the evening, I rode to [William B.] Franklin's and [William F.] Smith's headquarters in one of General Smith's headquarters wagons which I found at the station. Here I obtained supper about 9 o'clock P.M. and [I] remained over night as the guest of Dr. Basil Norris, the Medical Director of the Left Grand Division. [The] next morning, [Wednesday] the 24th, I made my way on foot to the camp of the 49th New York, about a mile and a half distant, and on my arrival there I found a letter from Dr. Vanderpoel, Surgeon General of the State of New York promoting me to be surgeon of the 57th Regiment New York Volunteers.

Thus it came about that, after 15 months' service as assistant surgeon, I found myself suddenly invested with the full rank of surgeon, and not yet quite 24 years old. This seemed to present the opportunity for me to obtain a leave of absence, which, as I had not been thus indulged since entering the service, I thought myself entitled to

[it]. Armed with my letter of promotion, I took myself back to Grand Division Headquarters, and presented the case to Dr. Norris, knowing full well he would do all in his power to aid me. The orders at this time in force on the subject of leaves of absence for officers were very strict, but Dr. Norris took the letter in to General Franklin and stated the case to him. Franklin, though a disciplinarian, was a kind officer, but was powerless to act, no matter how deserving the case, in the face of positive orders. This was the report Dr. Norris brought back to me. I then suggested to Dr. Norris that I could resign as assistant surgeon to accept promotion. He asked Franklin how that would do. The general readily assented to such a plan, stating he would approve such a paper, and that I might take the responsibility of going home upon that authority, though suggesting that the visit be a short one.

These negotiations consumed the day [of] the 24th, and as the next day was Christmas nothing was done. On the 26th I sent up my resignation as indicated, which came back duly approved on the 27th, and the necessary order was issued. In the meantime, on Christmas Day, I visited the 136th New York which was lying near Falmouth, seven miles away, where I met many old acquaintances—[Sergeant] Gad Parker, [Corporal] John McCray, [Corporal] John Boyd [all from Company H], Dr. Edwin Amsden, and others.[9] Dr. Amsden was anxious to be promoted to surgeon, as he had been in service sometime. I am persuaded that he did not altogether enjoy himself with his superior, who was Dr. B. [Bleecker] L. Hovey, now of Rochester.[10] I engaged to speak a word for him to surgeon general Vanderpoel, in case I got away as expected. Another object of this visit to Falmouth was to ascertain something of the 57th [New York], which I understood was encamped near there. I saw the regiment in its camp, and learned that it belonged to the 1st Division, 2nd Corps. I did not pay it a call lest, if I did, my plans for going home would be spoiled.

Sunday was the 28th, and I spent the day in packing up, bidding good-bye to the officers and men. In preparing to leave Monday morning, December 29th, bright and early, I bade adieu to the 49th [New York], after 15 months continuous service with it, and sped my way to Falmouth Station to take the train to Aquia Creek. When the time finally came to depart I was loath to go, for I had many friends who were tried and true, whereas, in my new field, I was a total stranger, not having a solitary acquaintance in the regiment. However, go I must, no matter how regretfully, and go I did, with many [of] a kind expression from both officers and men of the old 49th. From Aquia the boat carried me up the Potomac to Washington, where I arrived near 3 o'clock P.M. I was anxious to reach the pay department before the office should close, so took a carriage at the Sixth Street wharf and drove rapidly to the office, where I had my resignation paper properly endorsed for pay by E. H. Brooke, the chief clerk. He referred me to Major Rochester [now paymaster-general] for payment, but by the time I reached his office it was too late. He was just closing up for the day and asked me to call the next morning, when he would pay me my balance for November and December 1862. I was impatient, and took the evening train for N. Y. without waiting for pay. I reached New York on the morning of [Tuesday] December 30th [and] spent the day there in obtaining a new uniform to correspond with my increased rank, Major of Cavalry, and proceeded to Albany the same evening, where I arrived at 10 o'clock P.M. I took rooms at the Delevan House, and [the] next morning [I] proceeded to the capitol to interview the surgeon general, Dr. S. Oakley Vanderpoel.

I found Dr. Vanderpoel in his office at 10 o'clock A.M., and had a very pleasant visit with him for half an hour. This was the last day of the year, and also his last day in office, as governor elect [Horatio] Seymour would take office the next day, and, of course, appoint a Democrat to succeed Vanderpoel. I took occasion to thank him for his kindness to me in various ways, and particularly in looking after my interests in the way of promotion before he left office. He replied, that it was his policy, as far as possible, to promote all the old assistant surgeons before retirement, and that my record was such as to merit what I had received. I then told him how I had succeeded in getting away from the army for a visit home, whereupon, he smilingly said that I had better make the visit as brief as possible, so as to give his successor no cause for complaint. I said I would return at the end of 20 days, which was the usual length of leaves of absence to officers. Finally, I asked him to promote Dr. [Edwin] Amsden before retiring, but he said that would be impossible as it might look like forestalling the action of the new surgeon general if he [Vanderpoel] made appointments or promotions on the last day of office. The interview terminated. (I enjoyed Dr. Vanderpoel's personal friendship in after years, meeting him often at the State Medical Society, and we rode together from Albany to New York only a few days before his death, which occurred March 13, 1886.) I took the afternoon train for the west arriving at Lancaster about midnight, where I persuaded the conductor to let me off, as the train did not make a regular stop there. It was nearly one o'clock A.M. when I reached the house and awoke my wife who, up to this time was unaware either of my promotion or of my coming. My son Frank was then nearly three years old, and even at that late hour was aroused by my arrival, when we all had a happy meeting.

Chapter Five — 1863

CHANCELLORSVILLE AND GETTYSBURG

THE "FIFTY-SEVENTH"

DURING MY VISIT home my wife and I went to Michigan to visit my mother at Okemos. While there I was invited to a supper given by Zachariah Chandler to the legislature and other guests, to the number of 600, at the Benton House in Lansing, upon the occasion of his re-election to the U. S. Senate. At the termination of my leave, or the time I had allotted to be absent, viz., [Monday] January 19, 1863, I started back for the army. I lost my baggage on my homeward trip somewhere between Albany and N. Y., so I returned by the same route spending a day in Albany in search for it. I finally found it at the Chambers Street Depot in N. Y., which was then the terminus of the N. Y. Central R. R., and arrived in Washington on the morning of [Wednesday] the 21st. I reported immediately to the surgeon general, who found no fault because I had been away. He ordered me to report to Captain De Russy at the War Department for muster, and this officer requested me to call the next morning when the papers would be ready. I did as requested, and on Thursday, January 22nd, [I] was mustered out as assistant surgeon to date January 21, and mustered in as surgeon to date January 22, 1863. My next step was to visit the paymaster general's office for payment as assistant surgeon, for November and December to January 21, 1863. I was there informed that my case could not be reached in turn until Monday the 26th, which would compel me to remain in Washington till Tuesday [January 27].

I met A. C. Winter, of Lansing Michigan, paymaster U. S. Navy, at the National Hotel [on] Sunday evening the 25th, in company with

57

Mr. Leach, late member of Congress from the Lansing District, and whom I had met a few days before at Chandler's big supper. During my stay in Washington I met Dr. [James A.] Hall, who had been ordered up from the army [no leaves were granted at this time] to see his son Theodore, who was sick in [the] hospital. He found, however, on his arrival that the poor boy had died, and now the problem was to get permission to take the body home. Theodore had enlisted in the 154th New York Volunteers without his father's knowledge or consent, and of course the family were very much heart broken.[1] (No leaves of absence were granted to officers at this period, which was just at the termination of Burnside's career when everything was in a state of confusion, and no one could predict what would take place next.) I proposed to Dr. [James A.] Hall that we interview Senator James R. Doolittle of Wisconsin, whom I had known before the war when he lived in Wyoming County, and see what he could do in the premises. We met the senator in the hall of the National Hotel, and followed him to his room where I introduced the doctor, and stated our errand as briefly as possible. Without a word in reply, the senator sat down and wrote a letter to the Secretary of War, stating the case in detail and closing with these words: "Now, my dear Secretary, even the sternest rules of war must permit a father to bury his dead son." I remember them as well as though it were yesterday.

Armed with this letter we proceeded to the War Department, where it immediately brought us an audience with the Secretary, who, without hesitation, ordered a 10 days leave of absence for the doctor, and also pay for November and December. Dr. [James A.] Hall was so relieved that he thanked me over and [over] again, [with] the tears rolling down his cheeks in great drops as he bade me good-bye.

I left Washington, Wednesday morning, January 28th, for the Army of the Potomac, reaching Belle Plain Landing at 6 o'clock P.M. in the midst of a most disagreeable snow storm. It was impossible for me to proceed that night to the camp of the 49th New York, whither I was bound, so I found quarters for the night at the landing through the courtesy of an officer of the Q. M. Department. The next day, the 29th, I sent up for my horse, but by the time I reached camp it was nearly dark. My baggage was not brought up until near dark of the 30th, which occasioned another day's delay. The Army of the Potomac is literally, completely, and totally stuck in the mud. It requires a whole day for teams to go to Belle Plain and return to White Oak Church with 8 bags of grain, a distance of 4 miles and back, and yesterday they did not bring up any excepting on horse back.

A change of commanders has again taken place. [Joseph] Hooker relieves Burnside of command of the army. [William B.] Franklin goes away altogether, and [William F.] Smith is also given another com-

Major William Ellis
(NYSAG, USAMHI)

Colonel Samuel K. Zook
57th New York
(Frederick, Story of a Regiment)

mand. Colonel [Daniel] Bidwell [49th New York] is very kind to me, and Major [William] Ellis is as gay and happy as ever.[2] I enjoyed the two days spent with the 49th, at this time very much indeed, and began to dread the separation which must now be final.

I started for the 57th New York Regiment [on] Saturday morning, January 31st, and reached there about noon. Calling at division headquarters on the way, I saw Major John Hancock, A. A. General, and others of the staff whom I had known in the Sixth Corps before General [Winfield S.] Hancock was assigned to the Second [Corps]. General Hancock was away on leave, and Colonel Samuel K. Zook, of the 57th, was in command of the division.[3] I learned from him the location of the camp of the 57th, and about noon I reported to Lieutenant Colonel [Alfred B.] Chapman for duty, he being in command of the regiment.[4] The officers are a very fine body of young men, and all received me very cordially, though [they] are frank to express their disappointment in the failure of Dr. H. [Henry] C. Dean, the assistant surgeon, to receive the promotion.[5] Dr. Dean is very kind to me, and altogether I cannot be otherwise than pleased with my reception. The regiment is small, having only about 170 men present for duty, and today, [Monday] February 2, they are, for the most part, busily engaged in constructing log huts, so that in a few days they will be very comfortably situated. There are very few on the sick list as the camp is pleasantly located on a sandy knoll, so we are not troubled with the mud as much as many other portions of the army are.

Major Alfred (Alford) B.
Chapman
57th New York
(Frederick, _Story of a Regiment_)

Captain James G.
Derrickson
Company D, 66th New York
(Faville, _Diary of a Young Officer_)

[Thursday] February 5. The entire field and staff occupy a hospital tent as [a] sitting room and mess-room, behind which and communicating with it is a wall tent, that I occupy as my sleeping apartment. I like the officers very much indeed, and hope my first impressions will continue. Lieutenant Colonel [Alfred B.] Chapman is a young looking man with [a] smooth face, dark hair and eyes, about 27 years old, and [he is] a splendid disciplinarian. It is snowing today quite hard, and such a storm in the north would soon make sleighing [possible], but here it only means more mud.

[Sunday] February 8. This is my second Sunday with the 57th New York. Last Sunday Dr. [Henry C.] Dean took me over to corps headquarters, and introduced me to the medical director, Dr. Taylor, who is a brother of Bayard Taylor [correspondent for the New York _Tribune_]. Dr. Nelson Neely, our 2nd assistant surgeon, is a character, tall, phlegmatic, slow, but bright and dry with his wit. [6]

[Saturday] February 7. Yesterday we moved our camp about 400 yards, and are very pleasantly situated. I have a nice old fashioned fireplace in my quarters, that is now giving forth large dividends of both light and heat. I have a hospital tent for my front room, and a wall tent for my sleeping apartment, which is no longer used in common with the other officers as a mess room. My large apartment is, however, a convenient rendezvous for the officers at evening, and they congregate there for social and friendly intercourse. Indeed, it is quite like a club room in the evening. Lieutenant Colonel [John S.] Hammell, Dr. [Charles S.] Wood, Dr. [Albert] Van Der Veer, Captain [James G.]

Derrickson [Company D], and other officers of the 66th [New York], as well as some from other regiments, frequently join us in our evening's entertainments, and we make up quite a merry party.[7]

[Thursday] February 12. The times are very dull in camp these days, as the roads are so bad that riding is not agreeable, so we are committed to the dull routine of eating, reading, and sleeping in the daytime. In the evening we have quite jolly times. Some of the officers are very good singers, among whom may be mentioned Captain [Augustus M.] Wright [Company F], [First] Lieutenant [Orlando F.] Middleton [Company D], and Colonel [John S.] Hammell of the 66th, who is always willing to lend his voice to aid in the entertainment of our visitors.[8] Captain Rasdurichen, a Russian officer on General [Joseph] Hooker's staff, is a frequent visitor, and he occasionally passes the night with me, as I have an extra bed for guests.

[Monday] February 16. I have been suffering with the toothache for a day or two. Today, however, the pain is gone, but my face is very much swollen. (It is a reminder of the time I had at Harrison's Landing last summer.) The officers are very kind to me, and treat me as though I was an acquaintance of many years, instead of a comparative stranger. Many officers are now obtaining leaves of absence for ten days, under an order permitting a certain number from each regiment to be away at a time. This is Monday, and on Friday last [February 13] I visited the 49th New York, where I spent a part of the day very pleasantly. Colonel [Daniel] Bidwell had gone home for ten days, and Dr. [James A.] Hall had not returned from the sad mission which called him home. When General [William F.] Smith was ordered away from the 6th Corps, the officers of his old division, the 2nd, paid him a visit en masse to bid him good bye and god speed. He is very much liked by them all, and a movement is on foot to present him with a set of silver plates to cost $1,000.

On Saturday last [February 14] I visited Stafford Court House, where I saw the 136th and 154th regiments. I there met Gad Parker, Daniel Post, and Levi Vincent, also Colonel [James] Wood who commands the 136th New York.[9] At the 154th New York, I called upon Dr. [Henry] Van Aernam and Dr. Dwight [W. Day] three days past, and I have been improving the opportunity.[10]

[Thursday] February 19. We have just passed through one of the most severe storms that I have experienced in Virginia. It snowed Monday night [February 16] and all day Tuesday [February 17], and by Tuesday night we had over a foot of snow. It then set in and rained, the rain continuing all night Tuesday and through the day Wednesday and Wednesday night [February 18], ceasing about 10 o'clock this [Thursday] morning, and now the mud is ankle deep or over. Dr.

[James A.] Hall came to see me Monday the 16th, and is feeling very much depressed from the loss of his son.

[Sunday] February 22. This being Washington's birthday, salutes are being fired at several points within the lines—at General [Joseph] Hooker's headquarters, Stafford Court House, Aquia Creek, and Belle Plain. It snowed all night last night [February 21] and a good part of today, with high wind this P. M., and the [snow] is now drifting badly. It was so cold this morning that I did not get up until noon, as I could not get my fire started, and I found about 6 inches of snow in my tent when I awoke.

[Friday] February 27. The roads are very bad and it is very dull in camp as a consequence. We cannot pay visits nor receive them until we get some drying weather. Under the order granting leaves to a certain number of officers at a time, I may be able to go home next month for ten days. We shall see.

[Sunday] March 1. I visited the 49th New York yesterday and saw, among others, Colonel [William C.] Alberger who was paying a visit to the old regiment. He is in the Veteran Reserve Corps now on account of his wound, which renders him unfit for field service. We were put through our regular bimonthly inspection and muster for pay yesterday, which fell on Sunday this time.

[Tuesday] March 3. Today was appointed for a review by General Hooker, but it was postponed on account of the weather. I saw, and had a pleasant visit with, Colonel [Daniel D.] Bidwell at the 49th New York the other day. He appears to be in much better health, and has resumed his usual urbanity of manner.

[Thursday] March 5. General Hooker reviewed the 2nd Corps to-day. The troops looked well, though their ranks are thin. After the review we entertained a number of visiting officers in our (my) quarters.

[Tuesday] March 10. The weather is disagreeable again, and a damp snow is falling. My horse is looking fine, as I have a good groom in the person of Patrick Corbley, one of the 57th New York's soldiers and an old stable man from New York City.[11]

[Friday] March 13. Captain Rasdurichen, of General Hooker's staff, has been staying with me for two days. He is an agreeable companion and a friend of several officers of the regiment. Yesterday, the 12th, [Thursday] a wedding took place in the 3rd Corps, which attracted great attention from the novelty of the affair. Captain D. [Daniel] Hart, [Company C] of the 7th New Jersey Volunteers, was married to Miss Lammond, of Washington, and it was made an occasion of great festivity in his regiment.[12] A large platform was erected covered in on three sides with evergreen trees and boughs, upon which the ceremony took place, in the presence of General [Joseph] Hooker and [his] staff, two other major generals, 10 brigadiers, and a large concourse of officers, soldiers, ladies, and civilians. Mollie Lewis, of Washington, whom I [had] met several times at Mrs. Ridgeley's, was one of the bridesmaids. The band played "Hail to the Chief" on the arrival of General Hooker, and amidst displays of bunting, salvos of artillery, and bursts of music the two were made one. Leave of absence for 20 days was granted the groom, and the party goes to Washington by special boat after the festivities are over.

[Monday] March 16. Tomorrow will be St. Patrick's Day, and great preparations are being made for its celebration by the Irish Brigade which belongs to this division, and whose camp adjoins ours. General [Thomas] Meagher [pronounced "Marr"] is first and foremost in the affair, and we are expecting many visitors from other portions of the army at our camp during the day.

[Wednesday] March 18. Yesterday the celebration came off as expected and, it being a beautiful day, everything conspired to make it as jolly as possible. Horse races, the soaped pole, [the] greased pig, and sack racing were among the features of the day. After these were concluded all were invited to General Meagher's headquarters to luncheon and a race. The bridal party of last week was in attendance, and I had the honor of an introduction to the bride by Mollie Lewis. Today, the party goes to Washington, and then north. Major [William] Ellis [49th New York] and Lieutenant Colonel Theodore [B] Hamilton, of the Sixth Corps, and other officers of that corps, besides many who were friends of the 57th New York officers, were entertained in my quarters after the races, and the fun was kept up until a late hour of the evening.

[Friday] March 20. It is cold and snowy today, and it is difficult to keep a comfortable fire on account of the changeable nature of the wind. There has been a cavalry fight somewhere on our right, as we heard distant firing at intervals during yesterday.

[Monday] March 23. It was a year today since we sailed from Alexandria for the Peninsula. What changes have been wrought in that time! Who can tell what another year will bring forth?. Today it is warm, with threatening rain, and the snow is all gone. Dr. H. B. Miller, of Alexander, New York, paid me a visit yesterday, which I enjoyed very much. He is spending a few days in the army, and is quartering with the 136th New York at Stafford Court House. On the 13th [of this month] I made application for leave of absence, but it was returned on the 14th disapproved. Today, as it was intimated that it would go through, I renewed it.

[Thursday] March 26. My application for leave came back today approved, authorizing me to be absent for ten days from the 27th. So

I started on Friday morning, March 27th, and reached Lancaster on Saturday night, the 28th, [by] persuading the conductor to let me off though the train did not make a regular stop there. At the expiration of my leave, not being able to return, I forwarded a surgeon's certificate of disability to cover twenty days more. On [Monday] April 20th I started back, reaching Washington on the morning of [Tuesday] the 21st. I went immediately to the Pay Department to obtain my pay to [Sunday] March 1st, but Major Potter, who pays our brigade had gone down to the front for that purpose. On reaching the camp, [Wednesday] April 22nd, I found I could not draw [my] pay until a military commission had settled the question as to the cause of my absence [to decide] whether it was a good and sufficient one or not. This is in accordance with recent orders from the War Department in reference to officers absent on surgeon's certificates of disability. When I reached Brooks' Station, the nearest one to our camp, on my return I walked over a distance of two miles. It was a very hot day and I was very much overcome on reaching my quarters. The regiment was in the same location and nothing of importance had transpired during my absence, so I had lost nothing by my month's visit home. Now everything looked like an immediate move, orders of a preparatory nature being constantly received. This is Wednesday [April 22nd] and I should not be surprised if we had a battle before the week ends. This is the impression that I reached from [a] conversation with Colonel [Alfred] Chapman and other officers, whose judgement is reliable.

[Friday] April 24. We are still in a state of disquiet. Orders upon orders [are] being received, but the final one to start has not been issued yet. While I was home we heard of the death of Captain [William] McLean, 5th U.S. Cavalry, which occurred suddenly in Washington, and rumor had it that he died in a debauch.[13] (This seems to have been the report made by Surgeon Basil Norris, U.S. Army, who was called, but did not see the captain during life. This report prevented his widow from obtaining [his] pension, and after the war I obtained a correction of the record upon representing to Dr. Norris the soldierly qualities of McLean, and his sabre wounds in the head, received during Stuart's raid around the Army of the Potomac, June 13th 1862. I procured a letter from General [George A.] Custer substantiating my statements, whereupon Dr. [Basil] Norris revoked his former report, and the pension was duly granted. This was during 1866 & 1867.) To return from this digression, I found the regiment in good health on my return and all were glad to see me back, finding no fault because I had prolonged my stay.

Sunday, April 26. [We are] still on the Que Vive, expecting to move at any moment. The weather is warm, and everything is in readiness for the start.

CHANCELLORSVILLE

[Monday] April 27. 3 P.M. We are under orders to move at half an hour's notice, and all expect to be off before morning. We have now been in this camp over three months, and in the vicinity of Falmouth much longer. It is desirable that a change should be made, even if we go but a short distance. The 5th Corps is moving on our right today, and we received a call from Dr. [Henry C.] Dean, who has been promoted to be surgeon of the 140th New York in that corps. He is full of animation as usual, but only stayed with us a few minutes while his regiment was passing.

On the morning of the 28th, Tuesday, we marched at sunrise, and bivouacked for the night near Banks' Ford. On the afternoon of the 29th, we went forward to U.S. Ford, and bivouacked again in the rain and mud. A bridge was laid on the morning of [Thursday] the 30th, and we crossed the Rappahannock [River] the same afternoon, bivouacking near Chancellorsville late that night. We lay there during the greater part of the forenoon of [Friday] May 1st, and then moved out beyond Chancellorsville about a mile on the road to Fredericksburg. The 1st Division was acting in connection with the 5th Corps at this time, and we reached the full view of the enemy's position, fully expecting to fight him. About 2 o'clock P.M. we received an order directing us to withdraw and fall back on Chancellorsville. We did this reluctantly and slowly, finally forming near the Chancellor House in support of artillery.

While I was sitting on my horse awaiting events, I had an opportunity to survey the position. The field was full of troops, artillery, ammunition wagons, and ambulances. A few shells from the enemy, which we were expecting every moment, would have created a panic, I am sure. While thus waiting, the head of the 3rd Corps, with General [Daniel] Sickles and [his] staff at its head, came up the U.S. Ford Road, and deployed on the right of Chancellorsville. Finally, we were given our position well out to the front center [of the field], and on one of the roads leading to Fredericksburg.

The first division hospital was located in the woods about half a mile in rear of the Chancellor House, but we were not allowed to bring up our wagons, as nothing on wheels was permitted on this side of the river excepting artillery, ambulances, and ammunition wagons. So we had the men gather leaves, spread blankets upon them, and thus prepared beds for the wounded. Early Saturday morning [May 2] I amputated a finger for a man who was wounded the night before, and soon the wounded began to arrive at our hospital. During the day Colonel Nelson A. Miles, 61st New York, was brought in wounded, under the conduct of Ambulance Sergeant [George S.] Joyce [Company F], of the same regiment. It was thought at first that his wound was mortal, as he was suffering from collapse from a bullet wound on the abdomen.[14] He rallied however, and the missile was cut out of his back near the spine, it having passed around between the muscular layers. He recovered promptly, and came back in time for Gettysburg. Saturday evening, just at dark, the 11th Corps gave way on our right, and their stragglers came through the woods where our hospital was located in such numbers as to nearly overrun us, and really endanger our wounded. The stampede was soon checked, however, though the woods were filled with stragglers most of the night. Sometime during the evening I saw Dr. [Henry] Van Aernam, of the 154th N.Y., who told me his regiment was near by. Near 11 o'clock P.M I laid down on a blanket with A. B. Talcott, the head correspondent with the 2nd Corps, and while we were talking the artillery had a severe duel, [with] the shells bursting above the tree tops and the explosions lighting up the heavens most brilliantly. This died away after midnight to an occasional gun, after which I obtained some sleep.

May 3. [On] this Sunday morning we were up with the dawn. The fighting soon began and then the wounded poured in so we were busy, too much so to think about the ever shifting lines of battle, and to realize that a new line was being laid out which came very near our position. So the fighting went on during Sunday, to be renewed Monday morning [May 4], with disjointed and fitful intervals of quietude, only to be again broken by the sound of musketry and cannon, now in fearful proximity to our hospital. One of our wounded men had been rewounded while lying on the ground, and one of the ambulance corps was killed while directing the unloading of an ambulance at the hospital station. But all things must have an ending, and so with battles. On the afternoon of Monday, May 4th, an ambulance train was loaded with wounded for shipment to Potomac Creek Hospital, which was located about half way between Falmouth and Aquia Creek landing, and I was ordered at U. S. Ford, and moved along the north bank of the Rappahannock until near Banks' Ford. [I] then diverged to the left and struck across the country to Potomac Creek. It was near dark when we passed along the region of Banks' Ford, and we could plainly see the bursting of the shells where [General John] Sedgwick was having a struggle to cover the crossing of his 6th corps. Finally, late at night I reached the hospital and delivered the wounded. [I was] glad to get where I could have a night's sleep again without fear of being awakened by the sound of guns and the noise of contending armies.

The next day, Tuesday, May 6th, I was ordered on duty at the hospital, where I remained nearly three weeks, when I was relieved at my own request, as the wounded were all cared for as far as immediate operations were concerned. The surgical staff here is not adequate to do all the work, hence the surgeon in charge was anxious to retain me. Our loss in the late battle has been heavy, and large numbers of the wounded have fallen into the hands of the enemy. I came near being hit myself several times, so near, indeed, that men on each side of me were killed and wounded. I am nearly worn out with fatigue and hunger, but shall soon recuperate here.

[Saturday] May 9. I have been busy daily since my arrival here. [I] have made a number of operations, and shall amputate an arm the first thing tomorrow morning. Some estimate our loss at the battle of Chancellorsville at 20,000 men, killed and wounded. At all events, we were ingloriously defeated—beaten in detail because our commander was not equal to the emergency.

[Wednesday] May 13. [We are] still at Potomac Creek Hospital and as busy as ever. We are now receiving the wounded that fell into the enemy's hands. They were delivered under flag of truce, and are glad enough to get with us. One man, whose wounds I dressed, gave me a Richmond paper of May 11th, containing an account of the death of Stonewall Jackson, which I sent to my wife and it is still preserved with my papers.

[Friday] May 15. [I am] still busy with the wounded, and have 3 or 4 operations to make tomorrow morning. Until today the weather has been very hot, but a cooler wave has struck us which makes the wounded men more comfortable. As soon as the wounded are sent away I shall return to my regiment.

[Monday] May 18. The weather is very hot, and it is very fatiguing to work over the wounded at such a time. Just at evening I rode over to the 6th Corps hospital, where I saw Dr. [John A.] Jenkins, of the 49th New York [who was] on duty. He says his regiment lost very few men in the late battle. The 57th New York lost 2 killed, and 29 wounded, besides a few missing. I visited the 136th regiment on Saturday, the 16th, where I saw Gad Parker and others who were all right.

[Wednesday] May 20. The weather is still hot and I am suffering with the toothache, which adds very materially to my discomforts. The wounded are doing well for the most part, and I shall probably get away very soon. Dr. [Marvin C.] Rowland, of the 61st New York, is associated with me here, and is a very competent medical officer.[15]

Sunday May 24. I am once more in camp with my regiment, and [I] am very glad to get back again. I was relieved from duty at the hospital yesterday, and started for the 57th New York at once. All the operations had been made and I could not derive any benefit from a longer stay there, so I applied to be relieved. The weather is so hot [that] I am not anxious to work any harder than is absolutely necessary, and here with the regiment I have very little to do, as we have but two men on the sick list.

[Tuesday] May 26. The 57th New York is in nearly the same place where it wintered, having returned to the old camp after the battle. It seemed like getting home again to the boys. I expect to go to Aquia Creek Landing today to make arrangements for ice for the hospitals of the brigade, similar to the plan of last year at Harrison's Landing.

[Thursday] May 28. [It was] very hot. Our division has just been reviewed by General [Winfield Scott] Hancock, who now commands the 2nd Corps. Rumor has it that General [Darius] Couch, after Chancellorsville, refused to serve longer under General [Joseph] Hooker, and was relieved at his own request. The 21st New York regiment has been mustered out of service on [the] expiration of [its] term, and is now home in Buffalo where it has been received with honor. It was a good regiment, and deserves recognition at the hands of the citizens of Buffalo for the service it has so honorably performed.

[Saturday] May 30. Everything is extremely dull in and about the army these days, though [the] day before yesterday, the 28th, we had orders to be ready to fall in at a moment's notice but it created no excitement as everybody regarded it as a bit of a scare. It is rumored that Lee contemplates an attack upon our right [flank], but I hardly think it probable that he will. The whole army is very anxious for him to do so, for we think we could whip him handsomely if he would only attack us once. We have always been the attacking party, and that works to our disadvantage.

I made a large number of operations after Chancellorsville, and they all did well with one exception. This case—a man belonging to the 88th New York, Irish Brigade—I amputated midway between the ankle and [the] knee joints. Eight days afterward his nurse, in removing the dressings one morning, tore out all the ligatures causing [an] alarming hemorrhage. This we arrested as soon as possible, but as he had two other wounds, the discharge from them together with the loss of blood proved too exhausting, and he died at the end of ten days.

The leaves of absence for ten days that have been granted for the past few months have now been suspended. Officers can only get away at present on [a] surgeon's certificate of disability, or for five days in cases of great urgency. A great many officers are, as a consequence, obtaining sick leaves just now.

Monday, June 1. Yesterday, Major [John H.] Bell [57th New York] and I dined with Dr. [James D.] Hewett, surgeon of the 119th New York.[16] The Doctor is a friend of Major Bell's, and we went by special invitation at 6 o'clock P.M. at which hour, with several other guests, we sat down to the table. The menu consisted of oyster soup, claret punch, spring lamb and mint sauce, potatoes, green peas, asparagus, apple pie, ice cream, fruit, and coffee. The company did not break up until near midnight, and Major Bell and I stayed all night at Dr. Hewett's.

On our way home this morning we called at General Hooker's head-quarters on some friends.

[Thursday] June 4. Yesterday I paid a visit to the 49th New York, and had a nice old fashioned visit with Dr. [James A.] Hall and others. General [Albion P.] Howe gave a ball there last night but I did not remain. Mrs. Colonel Lewis is visiting her husband in the Vermont brigade. The Lewis' are from Buffalo.

[Friday] June 5. The rebels are reported as having left their forti-fications above Fredericksburg, and [are] moving we know not whither. Heavy firing has been heard below the town this P.M., but it was chiefly to protect the bridge building. Two pontoons are across at Franklin's old crossing, and the 6th Corps has thrown over a division, I presume to feel the enemy and see if he is still there in force. We are under orders to be ready to move at a moment's notice with three days ra-tions and 60 rounds of ammunition, which looks as though something was up. Bands are playing in all directions tonight (11:30 o'clock)—an ominous sign of a move.

[Monday] June 8. We are still in the same old camp, but are con-stantly receiving orders indicative of a movement, and today all our sick were sent away—a pretty sure indication of activity. Yesterday, I visited the left of the army to see what the 6th Corps was about, and found the "Old Division", the 2nd, across the Rappahannock, [with] the 49th New York on the extreme left of the line near the Bernard House, where our hospital was at the first battle of Fredericksburg in last December. The house itself is a partial ruin from fire though, be-ing of stone, the walls yet stand intact. I spent about an hour there, and had a pleasant visit with Major [William] Ellis [49th New York]. Recrossing the river at 5 o'clock P.M., I called at the division hospital where I found Dr. [James A.] Hall in charge. His wife had arrived about an hour before, and he was very happy. I met Mrs. Colonel [John R.] Lewis [5th Vermont] across the river, whither she had gone to pay her husband a visit. She was in good spirits and quite brave, having had an opportunity to see the division in line of battle.

[Thursday] June 11. We have not moved yet, but are expecting orders at any minute. I visited the 6th Corps again yesterday, where I saw Dr. Hall and [his] wife, Colonel [Daniel D.] Bidwell, Major [Will-iam] Ellis, and others. The 49th has been relieved from duty on the other side of the river and is now encamped on the heights on this side. A great number of ladies are visiting the 6th Corps now. [The] day before yesterday the paymaster made his appearance, and I drew pay for the balance of January and for February, March, and April, and sending $300 home. No military commission was ever convened in my case, so I drew pay upon the ordinary vouchers, filing my mus-ter-in roll as surgeon as well.

The Gettysburg Campaign

[Saturday] June 13. 7:30 P.M. I am strongly of the opinion that we shall march before tomorrow at this time, but we are, of course, in ignorance of our destination. Just now the quartermaster informed me that he has orders to take the corps supply train to Stafford Court House tonight, with the expectation that we follow early tomorrow morning.

[Wednesday] June 17. Near Fairfax Station on the Orange & Alexandria Rail Road. We marched on Sunday the 14th, and reached this place last night, coming via Dumfries. The First Division has had some slight skirmishing with the enemy, but no general engagement as yet. We are now about 16 miles from Alexandria. The North must be in a state of excitement now, for the rebels are reported to have invaded Pennsylvania. I am glad they are there for it will undoubtedly have a tendency to shorten the war.

[Thursday] June 18. We have moved two miles to Sangster's Station since yesterday, and are now about 18 miles from Alexandria. The day has been very hot, but now, 4 o'clock P.M., there are signs of rain. Major [John H.] Bell leaves tonight for Washington to enter the Veteran Reserve Corps, and has been ordered to report for duty to Major Diven at Elmira.

[Friday] June 19. It rained hard all night, and fortunately we did not move. The 49th [New York] is only about a mile from us, and Colonel Bidwell gave me his photograph when I was there [the] day before yesterday. Dr. Hall's wife has gone home, but Mrs. Lewis is still with her husband.

[Monday] June 22. Near Gainesville. We camped at Centerville Friday night, and Saturday moved up here where we have been since. We are six miles from Thoroughfare Gap. Yesterday, [General Alfred] Pleasonton's cavalry and a part of the 5th Corps had a battle with [J. E. B.] Stuart [on] the other side of the Bull Run Mountains, near White Plains where we lay last fall when McClellan was removed. The rumor is that Stuart was beaten. Last night General [Julius] Stahel, with several thousand cavalry, passed along the road toward Warrenton. We are on the Warrenton Turnpike about 12 miles from Warrenton, in the most beautiful part of Virginia that I have yet seen. Our camp is located in a delightful meadow, and a cool breeze is rendering the air quite balmy. It looks, however, as though we should move today.

[Sunday] June 28. Near Frederick, Maryland. We left Gainesville [on] Thursday [at] noon [on] the 25th, crossed the Potomac at Edward's Ferry on the 26th, and reached Frederick at noon today. I don't know the distance from Gainesville [to] here, but we have marched day and night since leaving there with only short intervals of rest. General [Winfield S.] Hancock passed the column about 7 o'clock this morning, and I rode with him a short distance, having a pleasant visit with himself and [his] staff. It is said here this evening that General [Joseph] Hooker has been relieved from the command of the army, and that General [George G.] Meade, of the 5th Corps, has been appointed in his stead. We shall probably march early in the morning.

[Monday] June 29. Last night at 9 o'clock the 57th [New York], with a section of artillery, was ordered to guard a bridge over the Monocacy River about 2 miles north of Frederick, and we remained out upon this duty all night. It seems there was a suspicion that the enemy might undertake to burn the bridge, but if any such idea ever pervaded his mind he made no attempt to carry it out while we were there. This morning we were ordered to join the Corps which was on the march toward Westminster, but owing to some delay in the transmission of the order we did not start until near 9 o'clock A.M. and consequently did not overtake the command until after midnight. I don't know just what time we did make junction with the remainder of our division, for sometime during the night, being tired and hungry, I reined into a lot, and sat down on a cock of hay with Captain Rose, our Commissary of Subsistence. Discovering a cow in the field nearby [in the] moonlight, we got one of the soldiers to milk her and after refreshing ourselves with hardtack and milk, we soon fell asleep. When I awoke it was daylight [on Tuesday June 30]. My horse had straggled off a little way, and was grazing in a clover field. I was alone, Captain Rose had gone, and I could see no troops anywhere. I mounted my horse and rode on. I soon came across the regiment, and then stopped at a farmhouse where I got breakfast, and fed my horse some grain purchased of a farmer. At this house I wrote a letter home at 6 o'clock A.M. which I mailed at Union Bridge, Maryland, a small village nearby which was, however, called Uniontown in our orders. We remained [there] all day and, we were there mustered for pay in the afternoon.

[Wednesday] July 1. This morning we were served with orders to be ready to move at a moment's notice, and stood to arms waiting the final order to march until afternoon. Meanwhile, we could see the bursting of the shells above the treetops beyond Gettysburg, Pennsylvania which proved the beginning of the great battle. While here General [Winfield S.] Hancock was directed to turn the command of the 2nd Corps over to General [John] Gibbon and proceed posthaste to Taneytown to report to the commander-in-chief. The troops finally received orders to proceed thither also, where we arrived about dark. Here we learned that, owing to the death of General [John F.] Reynolds of the 1st Corps General [Winfield S.] Hancock had been sent to Gettysburg to assume command of all the troops then present on the field. We little understood the full import of this important assignment at the time, but it proved a duty of vast moment for Hancock, as well as a fortunate selection for the Army of the Potomac. It appears that Hancock soon brought order out of the chaos which the death of Reynolds had precipitated, and [he] decided it [was] a proper position for the Army of the Potomac to take up as a defensive line. He so advised [George G.] Meade, who at once ordered up the whole army. After resting for an hour at Taneytown, we proceeded on our way to Gettysburg, following after our restive and famous commander as fast as our legs could carry us. We halted for a rest between 11 P.M. and 12 o'clock A.M., and I sat down upon a haycock in a field along the roadside, to rest and graze my horse. General [Samuel] Zook soon joined me, sitting on the hay beside me, and we entered into [a] conversation about the importance of the work before us. The moon would occasionally break through the flying clouds. The general had bought a horse in Maryland that day, for which he paid $250. It was a handsome animal, and he said it was a good purchase if he lived through the impending battle, but if he should be killed, not so. In that event, he desired the horse [to be] sold. I inferred that he felt apprehensive for his own welfare, and that he might not survive. I cheered him with a few encouraging words, reminding him of his previous good fortune in battle. (In less than a day he had received his mortal hurt.)

We soon started on our weary way, and a little after daylight [Thursday, July 2] in a misty rain, [we] marched upon the field of Gettysburg, taking position on the left center of [the] line. Just after our regiment had assumed its appointed position, I received an order to report to the division hospital as assistant to Dr. Charles S. Wood [66th New York], one of the chief operating surgeons of the division. The place selected for the hospital was in an oak opening east of the Taneytown Road, between it and the Baltimore Pike. After breakfast, I laid down and slept for several hours, as all was quiet.

I awoke about noon, and soon we had dinner. Still there was no fighting. Finally, taking advantage of the dullness and quietude, I mounted my horse and rode over to General Meade's headquarters at the cottage on the Taneytown Road. I hitched to the palings of the fence and went inside the yard, where I met several officers of my acquaintance, visiting with them for perhaps half an hour. I expressed a desire to take a look at the field, and was advised to proceed to Cemetery Hill, 3/4 of a mile north, where I could get the best view. I did so, and soon became absorbed in the wonderful scene before my eyes, which I surveyed with the aid of a field glass. Looking directly west into the enemy's lines I saw, in a gap in the woods, troops moving toward our left in considerable numbers. I could readily distinguish the regiments as they passed and felt sure at the time that the movement was of serious import. Sweeping my glass still farther to the left, I soon saw a line of battle advancing toward the front, which proved to be the 3rd Corps moving to take possession of the Emmitsburg Pike. It had been cloudy all day until now, but the sun just then burst through the clouds and glinted across the long line of bayonets. The colors, unfurling and waving in the bright sunlight, presented a most entrancing sight to the observer. In a moment the beauty of the parade was changed [into the] mad clamor of actual warfare. The enemy's batteries opened as soon as the line had advanced sufficiently far to give them enfilading range. The first smoke brought forth the exclamation from a voice near me, "There, General, go the enemy's batteries," and on looking around to my left and rear, I saw Generals [Abner] Doubleday and [Oliver O.] Howard in conversation together, and it was Doubleday who had spoken.

I soon became satisfied myself that they were the enemy's batteries we saw, for the shells commenced coming toward Cemetery Ridge and [Cemetery] Hill so I turned my horse into the road and started on my way back to the hospital. I halted again at Meade's headquarters, on the way back, and went into the yard for a moment. Soon everybody there began to take to horse, [George G.] Meade for the front, [Alfred] Pleasonton for his cavalry on the left, and other officers for their various posts of duty. The fact is the fire fairly drove them out. I followed Pleasonton who was going in the direction of the hospital, and on the way the shells burst over and around us in frightful rapidity and proximity. No one was hurt as far as I could observe. Arriving at the place where I had left the hospital, not a person was to be found, and no traces of it could be discovered. I began searching for it, and soon found its new location near a stream, protected by a ridge from [the] great danger of [the] shells. We were somewhat nearer the lines than before. It seems that, during my absence, the hospital was literally shelled out of its first position, and this new place was sought out of necessity.

The advancing line which I had just seen proved to be General [Daniel] Sickles's 3rd Corps moving to take up position on the Emmitsburg Road. The enemy, too, had been maneuvering for an attack upon our left all the afternoon. These two mighty forces came together with an impact, which made the wood resound with the crash. Sickles soon became nearly overpowered, and Hancock went to his rescue with a part of the 2nd Corps. The first division caught the heaviest of the blow. Many killed and wounded were the result. The wounded were now being brought to the hospital in great numbers. While busily engaged in their care, I received word that General [Samuel] Zook had been grievously wounded and was being moved to a farm house on the Baltimore Pike. I immediately repaired to the place and discovered at once that he was fatally shot, a shell having torn open his left shoulder and chest, exposing the heartbeats to observation. I remained with the general until about 11 o'clock P.M., and left word with [First] Lieutenant [Josiah] Faville [Company H, 57th New York], of Zook's staff, that I would come again in the morning should he survive the night, which now looked very improbable.[17] Soon after leaving the house I met a detail of 40 soldiers bearing General [Daniel] Sickles, to Westminster, 25 miles away. [His] thigh had been amputated on the field that evening. This expedient no doubt saved his life, as to have been driven thither in an ambulance would probably have proven fatal.

After working till the small hours of the morning of the 3rd, I laid down and obtained a little sleep, but was up and at it again by daylight. After assisting at many operations, as well as making a number myself to spell the chief operator, I once more repaired to General Zook's side, finding him still alive, but rapidly sinking. He lingered, however, until near two o'clock P.M., passing away without a murmur of complaint and in the full possession of all his mental activity.

The famous cannonade, the prelude to Pickett's heroic charge, was in full blast at this hour, and Zook breathed out his life amidst the uproar and mad clamor of two hundred guns—the grandest combat of field artillery the world ever beheld. As soon as the general breathed his last I made haste for the front, where I knew my services were needed. I arrived at the hospital not a moment too soon. After the sound of the cannon died away there was a short interval of comparative silence. Then came the infantry battle. The 2nd Corps received the weight of the shock, and our hospital was soon overflowing with wounded men, in the care of whom we were busy all night. I took a short nap near morning, but began work again soon after daylight [on] the 4th.

A heavy rain poured in upon us during the night. Continuing during the 4th, [it] nearly flooded us out. During the 4th, in the midst of a heavy shower, I amputated the thigh of a rebel captain whose name I have forgotten. He belonged to a North Carolina regiment [and] was full of hope and courage. I have no doubt [that] he recovered. So the work went on for the next three days until, on the 7th, [when] we were relieved by surgeons from Washington and the North.

Chapter Six —1863

Gettysburg to Mine Run

The Retreat and Pursuit of Lee

THE ARMY WAS moving to intercept Lee, if possible, and we [had to] go with the troops, where our services were likely to be needed at any time. General Meade did not permit our hospital wagons to come up until the battle was over, so we were not able to shelter our wounded very well, but in all other respects they were well cared for.

[Thursday] July 9. Yesterday it rained nearly all day, and quite hard for a considerable part thereof. Nevertheless, we made a march of 25 miles, reaching Frederick about 4 o'clock P.M. Captain James D. Brady, of the staff, and I visited the city in the evening, but all was confusion in the town and we returned to camp, tired and disgusted with our attempt at recreation. Today we are destined for Crampton's Pass, where the 6th Corps had a battle on the 14th of September last.

I stopped at a farm house near noon owned by a man named Roderick, and wrote a letter home. The family was very kind [to] me, inviting me to visit them after the war, which I partly promised to do.

[Sunday] July 12. We are again positioned before the enemy near Jones's Cross Roads, having come through a pass in the South Mountain, and are now about five miles from Williamsport near the road leading from Sharpsburg to Hagerstown. Our skirmishers are "at work" about half a mile to our front, the nature of the fire indicating that they are meeting quite stubborn resistance.

[On Monday] July 13th, we were busy all day perfecting our breastworks and otherwise preparing for active work with the enemy, and at

75

night received orders looking to an attack upon his position at dawn [the] next morning, but when we awoke on the 14th we found the enemy gone.

[Tuesday] July 14. We followed on the heels of the retreating foe as fast as foot, hoof, and wheel would carry us, the 57th [New York] being deployed as skirmishers. Before night the First Division had captured nearly 2,000 stragglers from their rear guard. The recent rains made the roads and fields one vast sea of mud. When we bivouacked at night we were a sight to behold. Every officer and man was covered with mud from his heels to his head, and the animals were as though they had been plastered.

[Thursday] July 16. In the field near Harpers Ferry. We bivouacked on the Virginia side of the Potomac near Williamsport Tuesday night, the 15th, and moved down the river to this point yesterday. We returned to the Maryland side of the river, and passed through Sharpsburg on our way hither, where we saw evidences of the battle of last September in the yet unrepaired damage to the church and some of the houses. We are in that delightful spot known as "Pleasant Valley," and need rest from the fatigues of the hard fighting, and the long and rapid marching of the past month. I don't think we will be allowed to remain here very long.

[Friday] July 17. It looks as though we would push into Virginia again tomorrow, although we have been quiet today. We left Pleasant Valley Saturday morning, July 18th, and marched every day until the 24th, save one, which brought us to Manassas Gap. On the 24th we rested for a few hours in the gap, the enemy being not far away. Ammunition was issued to the troops at 2 o'clock P.M. Dr. [Robert] Corry, my 2nd assistant surgeon, left today for Washington on sick leave, and I forwarded a letter by him to be sent home.[1]

Monday, July 27. Near Warrenton Junction. We have made long and tedious marches for the past 10 days, the heat being very oppressive, but we are fortunately resting today. On the night of [Saturday] the 25th, we camped at White Plains, where the 6th Corps stopped for three days last fall. Yesterday, we marched 20 miles in the broiling sun, passed Warrenton about 5 o'clock P.M. and reached this camp at 10 o'clock at night. (Warrenton is the prettiest southern village I have seen. [It] is delightfully located, and possesses some fine buildings.) A great many of our men are barefooted, and some are half naked but we may get supplies here. Our horses have been several days without forage, subsisting entirely upon grass. As for myself blackberries, of which there is an abundant supply, have been my chief article of diet for a week. We have had no mail since crossing the Potomac, but [First] Lieutenant [Stephen R.] Snyder, quartermaster of the 57th New York, goes to Washington tomorrow to procure clothing for the division.[2] I can send a letter by him to keep them at home advised of the fact that I am still alive and well.

[Tuesday] July 28. We have received two mails since yesterday with home dates to [Wednesday] the 22nd. My wife writes as though she was anxious for me to leave the service but the recent successes that have attended our arms, both [in the] East and [in the] West, have inspired me with new courage. I have always thought the Army of the Potomac would strike the final blow at the rebellion, and I have a strong desire to be "in at the death." So I shall stick [it out]. Thus far I have been present at every battle this army has fought since its organization under McClellan, and I take some pride in maintaining such a good record. (No doubt many find fault because Lee's army was not destroyed before we recrossed the Potomac, but when the entire facts are known General Meade will be fully justified in the course he pursued. It is useless for me to endeavour to vindicate the Army of the Potomac, or its commanders. History will do us full justice, I have no doubt.)

[Thursday] July 30. Still near Warrenton Junction. Yesterday, in company with Colonel [Alfred B.] Chapman, I paid a visit to the 11th Corps which is near us, where I saw Gad Parker, John McCray and others. Parker tells me that John Boyd, who belongs to his company, was severely wounded at Gettysburg. We also called upon Lieutenant Colonel Stewart L. Woodford, of the 127th New York, who is a friend of Colonel Chapman.[3] The weather is cooler as we have had rain. We are quiet but I think we shall move again within a day or two.

[Saturday] August 1. We are again within 6 or 7 miles of the Rappahannock at a place called Morrisville, having moved from near Warrenton Junction [the] day before yesterday. We are opposite Kelly's Ford where we may cross, but [we] are now simply guarding the passage. The weather is extremely hot, but I am in good health and spirits. Captain James C. Bronson [Company C] left for New York today to fetch on the drafted men for our command.[4] How I envy his prospects for numerous juleps and ices.

[Monday] August 3. Morrisville was formerly a village of two houses, but one having been totally destroyed by fire, the "town" is only half its original size. I took a

Captain James C. Bronson
Company C, 57th New York
(Faville, *Diary of a Young Officer*)

ride in company with Quartermaster [Stephen R.] Snyder to Elkton yesterday, four miles distant toward Warrenton Junction [by] going through a region infested by guerrillas. We returned in safety at 7:30 P.M., not having seen one of that much dreaded "chivalrous gentry." [Second] Lieutenant E. [Elisha] L. Palmer [Company A], of the 57th [New York], in charge of a picket detail, disappeared on the same road we travelled [the] night before last, about half way between here and Elkton, and is supposed to have been captured by the guerrillas.[5] Sickness is increasing owing to the heat. Today I report 6 men on the sick list, more than at any time since we left Falmouth.

Major [John H.] Bell, [of the] 66th New York, had an adventure with the guerrillas near Warrenton, when we were approaching that place a few days ago, an account of which appears in the New York Herald. (It will be found in my scrapbook.) My brigade was in the rear of the wagon train that day guarding it, and the 57th [New York] was the rear regiment. I was in conversation with Major Bell near the broken down ambulance spoken of not five minutes previous to the appearance of the guerrillas, and came very near being mixed up in the affair myself. Our tents are now pitched in the edge of a beautiful wood, and we are delightfully situated in every way, but no telling how long we shall remain so.

[Thursday] August 6. [The] day before yesterday we changed our camp, moving about a mile and a half, for the purpose of getting better ground and having water more convenient. Our regimental headquarters are now delightfully located on a beautiful knoll, upon the green summit of which stands a large cherry tree and our tents are pitched around the tree facing inward, which affords us shade all day long. I hope and believe we shall not have any fighting for a month which, if my prediction falls true, will give us a much needed rest [in] this hot weather.

APPOINTMENT TO THE CHARGE OF THE HOSPITAL

[Saturday] August 8. Today, while we were sitting around our cherry tree enjoying our postprandial [after dinner] dish of conversation, an orderly rode up and placed in Colonel Chapman's hands an order, which, upon opening [it] proved to be an appointment for me, placing me in charge of the field hospital of the First Division [and] relieving in that duty Surgeon George L. Potter of the 145th Pennsylvania Volunteers.[6] I went to headquarters immediately to learn the particulars of the change, and to arrange for the transfer of the property, which will take place tomorrow when I assume charge. My tent leaked badly last night, the water saturating my bed in places. I shall have the tent condemned and get another. We are now living on green corn, cucumbers, fresh bread, canned tomatoes [and] peaches, so we need not complain.

[Monday] August 10. I am very busy now putting the hospital in order, and systematizing the work. The place I hold is one of hard work and responsibility, but I do not complain. Many an older man than I might feel proud to get the position and I shall endeavour to discharge the duties pertaining to it in such a manner as to merit, and I hope [to] receive, the commendations of my superior officers.

[Wednesday] August 12. I regret to hear that Frank Folsom is drafted, but he will, no doubt, get relieved from serving on account of his health. I have 30 men daily on fatigue duty building cots, ditching, building arbors across the front of the hospital, and otherwise making it comfortable.

[Friday] August 14. Today has been cooler, with a shower just at night. I harnessed my horse and hitched him before a top buggy that was captured by the provost marshal and drove him out four miles and back today. It was considered quite an event, many looking on with interest and enjoying the unusual scene. The papers report the 6th Corps at Warrenton, as having a great time giving balls and parties, which the women of that village attend. It is reported in the Buffalo papers received tonight, that Lyman Bass and Oscar Folsom have both been drafted. They will, of course, both escape service by some device or other. It is also rumored that General [Winfield Scott] Hancock will be appointed to the command of the Army of the Potomac as soon as he is able to take the field again. I hope this may prove true, but I question very much whether the government will make another change in commanders soon, unless there should arise strong reasons therefor.

[Sunday] August 16. Colonel [Alfred B.] Chapman has received a letter from Lieutenant [Elisha L.] Palmer, who was captured on picket two or three weeks ago. He is now in Libby prison, Richmond. We have [heard] rumors of a speedy move but I have received no orders in regard to the hospital yet. I hear, though, [that] the troops are under orders to be ready to move at a moments notice.

[Tuesday] August 18. A cool, comfortable day comparatively. I have bought General [Samuel K.] Zook's saddle cloth which, with a new russet bridle obtained in Washington, sets off my black horse well, and makes him look quite handsome. I get my pay every month now, which is one of the advantages of being detached from the regiment on this kind of service.

[Thursday] August 20. I went down to Bealton Station today, and sent my July pay home by express. While there I fell in with an artist in tintypes and had some pictures of my horse taken. On the way back to camp [First] Lieutenant [George] Mitchell [Company G] of the ambulance corps, who was with me, found a pocketbook containing $75.00

or $80.00 in greenbacks.[7] He sought, but never found, an owner for it. Calling at one of the houses in our neighborhood a few days ago, one of the women of the household gave me a sample of cloth which she wove, and like which was the dress that she was wearing at the time. It is called "dixie gingham," and I sent the sample home.

[Friday] August 21. Yesterday I witnessed the execution of a deserter [unidentified] in the 2nd Division—the first time the death sentence has been invoked in the 2nd Corps. It was a melancholy spectacle, but a just way to deal with such dangerous men. We are having quiet times now. The hospital is running smoothly. The entire command is in very good health. We are beginning to receive some of the fruits of the draft now going on in the North, which will reinforce our thinned and weakened ranks. A motley group of these raw soldiers arrives almost daily, a goodly number of which seek the hospital upon the first excuse. Some of them [come in] needfully, as they [have] become ill from the change of climate, as well as a radical revolution in their mode of living. The old soldiers are inclined to look with a jealous eye upon these drafted men and substitutes, but I think most of them will make good soldiers after they get tempered to the work.

Monday, August 24. I wrote home today on a sheet of note paper taken from a rebel soldier's knapsack at Falling Waters, [West Virginia] where we crossed the Potomac July 14th, when we were pursuing Lee after Gettysburg. I have carried it ever since, but did not think to use it until today. It is of a dirty brown color, coarsely ruled, and not very good in quality, yet it answers [its] purpose just as well, I presume, as though it were made in Belfast. Yesterday was the hottest day of the season, and a julep and an iced lemonade were refreshing. These are luxuries which we can now boast, as I get 150 pounds of ice a day. The consequence is [that] I have plenty of company—visitors who call for a drink of ice water.

[Friday] August 28. We are having beautiful moonlit nights now, and every evening a cavalcade of 8 or 10 officers visits my quarters, when we all go out for a ride, generally taking the Bealton Road. After riding about four miles we all return to my tent, where an hour or two is spent in conversation, smoking, [and] cobblers. Two more deserters were shot in the 2nd Division today.[8] The entire division was drawn up in line and the doomed men marched to the place of execution behind their coffins, which were drawn in a wagon. The guard detailed for the shooting made bungling work, which added to the horrifying nature of the spectacle.

[Monday] August 31. The month closes with quietude, and we are still at Morrisville. I think, however, that we shall not remain here much longer. Things military seem to be pointing to a movement of some kind.

[Tuesday] September 1. I hear from home of a visit to my wife by Mrs. [Daniel D.] Bidwell, which was a pleasant reminder of the winter of 1861-2 at Camp Griffin. The 2nd Corps has gone on a reconnaissance to Falmouth, leaving one regiment to guard the camp and the sick, so I am in supreme authority today. Quartermaster [Stephen R.] Snyder is quite sick in the hospital.

[Friday] September 4. The Corps returned today without having met with any special adventures. It seems the purpose of the movement was to aid in the destruction of some gunboats [which] the enemy had placed in the Rappahannock. I never heard whether the boats were even seen by any man of the command. Dr. Mary Walker rode up to the hospital just at dusk last evening and I gave her quarters for the night.[9] She appears to be one of those women cranks, who imagine they have a mission to perform in the army, and so pester the doctors with their care.

[Saturday] September 5. These are quite busy days as I have several very sick men with typhoid fever [and] dysentery. I have lost but one patient since assuming charge on August 9th out of over 150 different patients treated, and [we] now have 65 on hand. I made application last Sunday, the 30th, for leave for 7 days to go home to Mary Bostwick's wedding, but as the corps moved out on the reconnaissance to Falmouth on Monday, and did not return till yesterday, it is doubtful if I get it in season to reach Lancaster by September 9th. The mails come with regularity now which is a great comfort, furnishing letters and papers from home almost daily.

Wednesday, September 9. The supply of ice and lemons is ample, and I am thus enabled to make the men in [the] hospital very comfortable during this very hot weather. This evening the wedding takes place at home, but I am not there as I hoped to be. This is the lot of a soldier—doomed to disappointment—but if life and health are only spared 'tis well.

Friday, September 11. My leave came last night and I started this morning, reaching Alexandria late in the afternoon, owing to the delay of the train. I engaged a livery man to drive me over to Washington in time for the 6 o'clock train north, for which he gets $5.00 if we succeed. On the Long Bridge we met a long train of army wagons which promised, at first, to impede our passage. I happened to have a cavalry sabre with me that I picked up on the field at Bealton after a cavalry fight and which I was taking home. It was supposed that I was a staff officer with important dispatches, as I waved a large envelope and motioned the train to give way to the left. This the officer in charge readily obeyed. The roadway across the bridge was cleared, and we reached the Baltimore & Ohio depot in season for the train.

I arrived home Saturday evening, September 12th, much to the surprise of everybody, not to say their gratification. On Monday [September 14] I had a new plate of teeth made by Dr. Theodore G. Lewis. [I] started back for the army on Wednesday [September 16], and reached Washington to get my pay for August. Friday evening [September 19] I attended Ford's Theater, where I met Dr. and Mrs S. B. Hunt and their son. I sat beside Mrs. Hunt during the play, and had a delightful visit with her. Dr. Hunt has medical charge of Convalescent Camp near Alexandria, and says he would make me his executive officer if my rank was not so high. I could not think of advancing backwards like a crab, even with so tempting an offer as that, for I am well pleased with my present position, and think it is all I deserve at my age. I hear that the 2nd Corps has moved out beyond Culpeper Court House, since my departure.

AT MITCHELL'S STATION

Saturday, September 19. I started for the front this morning, reaching Culpeper about 5 o'clock P.M., where I remained over night. On the following morning, Sunday [September 20], I joined the command near Mitchell's Station, which is the last R. R. Station before the O & A [Orange and Alexandria] Railway crosses the Rapidan. Our camp is near the Rapidan River, and the Rebel camps are in plain sight of my tent on the heights opposite. We are 10 miles from Culpeper Court House, and about 25 miles from our last camp at Morrisville. I am still with the hospital though we have very few sick, most of them having been sent away before the move.

[Tuesday] September 22. We are in plain view of the Rebel batteries on the opposite side of the Rapidan, and from their position they could shell our camps if they saw fit. The cavalry has been fighting on our right, apparently near Madison Court House. We have orders for 8 days rations and to be in readiness to move at a moment's notice, which looks like work soon.

[Friday] September 25. Our sick were sent off today to Culpeper Court House, another indication of a move. One of the enemy's signal stations is plainly visible and I see their flags waving at all hours of the day. I have a Richmond paper of the 23rd, which says [James] Longstreet's and [A. P.] Hill's Corps are out west opposing [William S.] Rosecrans, and claiming a great victory for their side at Chickamauga on the 19th. The 11th and 12th Corps from this army have been sent west to reinforce Rosecrans, which reduces our status to a strict defensive.

[Sunday] September 27. We don't move yet, but the indications are that we shall soon fall back toward Alexandria. The enemy is on the alert, feeling our flanks, and may precipitate a move at any time. At all events there is much mystery in the situation as it appears to me.

[Wednesday] September 30. [We are] still waiting and hourly expecting [something to happen], but no definite orders to move as yet. I have been two years in the service, the 2nd anniversary of my muster-in having occurred the day I left home, two weeks ago. One year yet remains before my term expires, and who knows what it will bring forth? Time alone can answer the question, and it only remains for me to do my duty to the best of my ability, trusting the result to Him who "doeth all things well."

[Friday] October 2. It has rained steadily for the past 12 hours, and altogether it is one of the most disagreeable days I have known for a long time. Yesterday we had a little excitement in the way of a horse race at Mitchell's Station between a horse owned by Captain Rose, commissary of the 3rd Brigade, and one belonging to the staff at corps headquarters. Colonel Smith, Chief Commissary of the corps, and myself were the judges. Rose's horse won by half a neck. The Rebels looked on from the heights opposite, quiet and interested spectators. Today a man was shot in this division for desertion—the first execution in the First Division.[10] I have had my horse mustered in to service at a value of $225, so that I can recover [the money] in case he is killed. We have been troubled for supplies for our mess since we have been here, but tonight we are to dine upon roast pork, mashed potatoes, and onions.

[Sunday] October 4. Today has been a beautiful day in marked contrast to the weather lately, and especially to Friday last.

[Wednesday] October 7. We were relieved on [Monday] the 5th from our uncomfortable and dangerous position at the front by the 6th Corps, and yesterday [we] retired to Culpeper Court House, where we are now encamped. It is raining quite hard again and we have just received orders to send away our sick tomorrow, which looks like activity again. Dr. [Jonathan] Letterman, medical director of the Army of the Potomac, goes north tomorrow to be married.

[Saturday] October 10. We moved our camp a short distance yesterday, and are again ordered to move immediately.

AUBURN AND BRISTOE

October 11. Sunday, 5 o'clock P.M. We have been on the march since 12 o'clock last night, and have just reached Bealton Station on the north side of the Rappahannock. The army has evacuated Culpeper by this time, as the last train on the Orange & Alexandria Railroad has just passed here for Alexandria. What the movement signifies I cannot say, but it looks as if the enemy was upon our right flank, and we would retreat toward Alexandria in the morning.

[Friday] October 16. We have been constantly on the move since Monday [October 12], and [have been] fighting a good part of the time. The Army of the Potomac is back at Centerville, and the 2nd Corps was the rear guard during the movement. It appears that Lee's army got upon our right flank, as was intimated [to be] probable a little way back, and we were obliged to march fast, fight a good deal, and maneuver still more to save ourselves and our trains. We did it and, besides, made the enemy pay dearly for the trouble he put us to. On Monday, the 12th, we recrossed the Rappahannock, moving from Bealton to Brandy Station, but found no great force of the enemy there, as was expected. We came back and bivouacked at Bealton late that night. [On] Tuesday morning [we] moved in the direction of Warrenton. At 9 o'clock P.M. we bivouacked in a cornfield near Auburn, not over 400 yards from the enemy's pickets, building large fires to deceive them as to our numbers. [We started] next morning at daylight [October 14] with the expectation of reaching Catlett's Station in two or three hours. The enemy, however, planted a battery across our path and shelled the First Division while [they were] cooking coffee at Auburn. I had a large load of sick in the ambulances, and they shelled our train pretty severely, driving back the cavalry on our flank. I thought at one time our whole train would be captured, but the First Division charged and drove off the rascals in season to save it. General [Gouverneur K.] Warren now came along to the head of the train and gave orders for it to give way to let a battery pass, which was soon put into action and did good work. I was obliged to unload the sick and take on the wounded, which I brought safely to Centerville after dark. We passed Catlett's Station near noon, where I saw General [George G.] Meade, [his] staff, and escort drawn up in line.

At Bristoe, just at nightfall, we had another encounter with the enemy, who sought to cut off our retreat by getting possession of our road where it intersects the one they were moving on. The Second Division was pushed forward, seizing the railroad cut which served as a breastwork, and gave them a terrible thrashing. We captured five guns, two colors, and over 400 prisoners [before] retiring afterwards to Centerville under cover of the darkness.

I was busy all night operating and dressing the wounded, with one assistant surgeon, [and] relying upon the hospital stewards and nurses for further aid. I amputated an arm for a cavalry captain about 2 o'clock A.M., who thought he could not endure the suffering until morning. Next day, Thursday, the 15th, we were ordered to send the wounded to Fairfax Station for shipment to Washington. One poor fellow, [Private Frank] Rose [Company D] of the 57th [New York], who was suffering so from shock that we thought best not to operate upon him, must now receive attention.[11] Upon Dr. [Alexander N.] Dougherty's advice, I amputated his right thigh and left arm [with] four men holding a rubber blanket over the table to keep the rain off, while the operation was being made.[12] The train had gone on, but I kept one

ambulance back to take him, and after the operation he was put carefully aboard, given half a glass of brandy and sent on to overtake the
others. Just as the ambulance was moving off he asked: "Doctor, you
think I'll get well now, don't you?" and, sure enough, he did recover.
(This case is reported in the "Medical & Surgical History of the War,"
part second, surgical vol. [X], p. 711, and part third, surgical vol. [XI],
p. 253.)

Today, Friday, 16th, I am not well from an attack of colic. It has
rained ever since yesterday when I was operating on Rose. The corps
is in line of battle, and everything looks gloomy enough.

Sunday, October 18. We have been here at Centerville since
Wednesday night, but I fancy we'll not stay much longer. The movements of the past week have given the 2nd Corps new honors, and
General Meade has complimented us in orders. Today has been the
warmest and pleasantest day we have had for a long time.

[Wednesday] October 21. Near Auburn. I was in the saddle 13
hours yesterday. We left Centerville Monday morning [the 19th] early
in a terrific rain storm, and marched to Bristoe Station, where one of
our battles was fought a week ago today. Yesterday we moved up here,
which is about half way between Catlett's Station and Warrenton. The
exact spot where we are now encamped is the scene of our first battle
of this day week, when the Rebels attacked my train early in the morning. [The] night before last it was reported that Hill's and Ewell's Corps
were at Warrenton, and last night it was reported that all the Rebel
forces had recrossed the Rappahannock about two hours before we
arrived here. I am inclined to credit this last report, as we are not
moving today, as we probably would be, were they [on] this side [of]
the river. They have entirely destroyed the railroad from Bristoe Station to Warrenton Junction, and I presume as far as the Rappahannock
too. The day is very warm, but I feel almost sick with a sore throat. I
took cold at Centerville, and am still suffering from its effects. I saw
[George A.] Custer on the march yesterday at the head of his cavalry
brigade, clad in velvet and gold lace, his locks waving in the breez-
ing—a perfect Murat in manner and appearance.

[Saturday] October 24. We moved about 5 miles on the 22nd,
and are now encamped on the Warrenton Railroad midway between
Warrenton and Warrenton Junction. I went up to Warrenton [the] day
before yesterday on a pleasure ride, where I saw the 6th Corps. They
always appear to get a good place somehow, but have less actual fighting than the 2nd Corps. [The] Division hospital has been temporarily
abandoned, but I still retain charge of the ambulances and the ambulance corps.

I have been appointed one of the chief operating surgeons of the
division, which, however, will not interfere with my charge of the

ambulance corps. I presume this appointment was made on account of my conduct at Centerville. The medical director, Dr. Alexander N. Dougherty, spoke in complimentary terms thereof, not only to me personally, but to others who have mentioned it to me since. My appointment is to fill a vacancy occasioned by the resignation of surgeon C. S. Wood, 66th New York, who has been appointed medical director, Department of the Pacific, with headquarters at San Francisco.

[Monday] October 26. Yesterday we changed our camp a short distance to get out of the mud, and now [we] have a fine place in a dry pine grove. The weather today is like a northern autumn. We have just received orders to pack up and get ready to move at a moment's notice.

[Wednesday] October 28. We did not move [the] day before yesterday as expected, and are still here in the pine grove. Today we are having a fireplace built in our tent, so we expect to be comfortable tonight with an indoor fire. My cold is not well, but [I] am better.

[Friday] October 30. We captured a camera at Morrisville last summer, and a few days ago obtained chemicals from Washington, and are now in full blast taking tintypes, which affords entertainment as well as useful employment. Our fireplace is a success; the chimney does not smoke—a wonder—and everybody is happy. Dr. Brower Gessner, of the 3rd Division ambulance corps, is chief photographer, and I act as [his] assistant.[13] Captain Livermore, Chief of ambulances for the corps, Lieutenant Pelton, of the 3rd Division train, and two officers of the 2nd Division corps, are with us every day, sitting for their pictures in all sorts of groups and positions. A photograph in my military album shows a group of the ambulance officers, and it was copied from one of the tintypes that we took at this time.

[Saturday] October 31. The weather is very fine, and we are quite comfortable with our fireplace to warm us at evening. The month closes with the uncertainty of a possible movement of the army at any time, but [we are] in [a] comparative quietude for the moment.

[Sunday] November 1. This has been one of the finest days imaginable, just the sort of day to march in, but we do not move yet as expected.

[Tuesday] November 3. It was certainly anticipated that we should move before this, and I hear that a movement is on the tap which is likely to occur very soon. The weather could not be more delightful. Indian summer has set in. The trees are losing their foliage amidst their ever changing hues, and everything looks autumn-like, much as it does north a month earlier. I expect to return to my regiment in a few days if we do not move, as I have nothing to do here.

[Thursday] November 5. The weather continues pleasant, but orders do not come for us to move yet. Yesterday, however, the sick were all sent to Washington—a pretty sure indication that we shall march soon.

Tomorrow night [Friday, November 6] we intend giving a party at this camp, providing, of course, we do not move. Our headquarters tents are trimmed with evergreens, a band of music is engaged, and all preparations are completed for a jolly time. Last night, the 4th, the 2nd Delaware Volunteers gave a party, where a large number of the officers met and had a very enjoyable time.

[Monday] November 9. We broke camp [near] Warrenton [the] day before yesterday early in [the] morning, and marched all day in the worst dust I almost ever saw. Yesterday morning early we crossed the Rappahannock at Kelly's Ford without much opposition. The 6th Corps crossed at Rappahannock Station, taking 1100 prisoners and 4 cannon in a redoubt at the railroad bridge. We are not anticipating the enemy will make much of a stand this side of the Rapidan. Our party came off on Friday night as planned, though it broke up at midnight on account of the orders to move early [the] next morning. We had about 50 guests, good music, a collation [light meal], and milk punch and everybody was happy, or seemed to be, at least.

November 12. This is Thursday, and for two or three days past it has been cold with a little snow. This morning it is warmer and consequently more pleasant. We have been constantly changing position for the past three or four days, but nothing has been accomplished beyond getting the several corps well into line.

November 14. Saturday. There is a feeling afloat that we shall move on next Monday, but it is difficult to say on what it is based.

November 16. Monday. A terrific rain storm passed over us last night, but this morning it is pleasant. Firing has been heard at intervals during the day along our front and that of the right wing, owing to an attack of the rebel cavalry, in which they are reported to have driven ours back upon the 6th Corps. We are ordered to hold ourselves in readiness to move at a moments notice, but I didn't anticipate a general engagement until this army moves forward again, which is likely to be sometime this week. I shall not return to my regiment as I thought probable a few days ago, as there is something to do here as long as we are actively campaigning.

[Tuesday] November 17. We are near Brandy Station, the weather is very fine now, but we shall probably move soon. In regard to the cavalry fight of last Sunday, the 15th, it is said by some that we got the worst of the bargain and lost 500 men. I rather think we were beaten, but cannot learn the particulars.

[Thursday] November 19. We are still here and hourly expecting [to move]. Some English officers were entertained yesterday with a review and drill of the 2nd Corps, and expressed themselves as much pleased with the American soldiery.

[Saturday] November 21. A drizzling rain has kept up since daylight, and as a matter of course the mud is pretty deep tonight.

[Monday] November 23. We are ordered to move tomorrow at daylight.

[Wednesday] November 25. We did not move yesterday as ordered. Our tents were struck, wagons packed, and the head of the ambulance train pulled out for the start—all in the midst of a heavy rain—when the orders came countermanding the movement. Every man cheered lustily. The woods for miles rang with the echoes of applause. The mud is knee deep or thereabouts, which is the explanation of the change of orders. I presume the movement is only temporarily in abeyance. The rain is still pattering on my tent, but as soon as the roads are sufficiently dry we may expect to be off. Tomorrow will be Thanksgiving Day, and our dinner will consist of pork and beans, bread without butter, and no et ceteras.

MINE RUN

On Thanksgiving Day, Thursday, November 26th, we broke camp at daylight and marched to Germanna Ford on the Rapidan, a distance of 7 miles, which we had reached before noon. The enemy made no resistance to our crossing there, but owing to the steep banks on either side of the river it was late at night before the entire corps, including the artillery, had crossed. Some of the [artillery did not] even get over until the next morning. We camped at 9 o'clock at night about 2 miles beyond the Rapidan, on the road leading from Culpeper Court House to Fredericksburg, and about 5 miles from Robertson's Tavern. By 7 o'clock on the morning of the 27th, the corps was well under way [with] the 2nd Division leading, the 3rd Division next, and the 1st Division bringing up the rear.

By 10 o'clock the skirmishers had encountered the enemy, and a rattling fire of musketry was kept up for two hours [with] the Rebels falling back to Robertson's Tavern on the Orange and Fredericksburg Pike. Skirmishing was kept up until nightfall, with occasional discharges of artillery, and the casualties of the corps had reached, probably, fifty men. During the night of, Friday, the 27th, the enemy fell back to Mine Run, where he was strongly fortified.

We followed at early daylight, and the 28th was spent very much as the day previous in skirmishing and feeling the position. On the morning of the 29th the 2nd Corps, with one division of the 6th, all under [the] command of General [Gouverneur K.] Warren, moved by a circuitous route around to the enemy's right flank, with the design of turning his position.

We arrived there about 5 o'clock P.M., too late to accomplish much that night, and the next morning, [the] 30th, it was discovered that their fortifications there were even stronger than those we had left in the center. We spent two days in skirmishing and feeling.

At 9 o'clock P.M., December 1st, [we] turned our backs upon the "rebs" and their fortified position, and commenced retracing our steps toward our old camps. We marched all night in the clear, cold air, suffering intensely, and by daylight, Tuesday, December 2nd, the whole army was safely on the north side of the Rapidan again.

This is a brief sketch of what we actually did. I shall not attempt to say what we might have done. It is sufficient to remark that the army feels entirely satisfied with General Meade's decision not to attack such formidable works as he found, no matter what the people of the North may say about it. We had no communication with Washington for the 8 days we were away.

On Friday, the 4th of December, I was sent to Washington with a R.R. train load of wounded from the 2nd Corps, reaching the city at midnight, and remaining till the 8th.

Wednesday, December 9. I left Washington during the previous morning, but did not reach camp until this forenoon. I arrived at Brandy Station at a late hour last night, and was kindly offered quarters by Dr. J. Bernard Bridenton, the army medical purveyor. I enjoyed the brief visit to the Capital, for it is a relief to get away from the army even for a few days, especially after such a severe campaign as we recently had over the Rapidan. The weather was extremely cold; we could have no fires that were at all comfortable. The army suffered severely. I don't think we will make another aggressive campaign this winter, but we shall probably move to a more favorable spot for winter quarters, where timber and water can be had more plentifully. There is very little of either.

[Friday] December 11. The weather is very cold and we haven't even a comfortable place to write a letter. By tomorrow night we expect to be comfortably domiciled in a log house we are building. The weather reminds me much of the season [in the] North, being about the same temperature. An order was issued last night restoring the 10 days leave of absence to officers. One surgeon can be absent from each brigade at a time and this may give me an opportunity to visit home in January.

[Wednesday] December 16. Rumors were rife yesterday that we should move today, but the day has nearly passed and no orders have yet been received indicative of a movement. Many officers are of the opinion we will stay here during the winter, but I have not yet settled into that belief myself.

[Friday] December 18. It has rained almost uninterruptedly for 36 hours and the roads, as a consequence, are simply horrible. In fact, one cannot step outside of quarters without going ankle deep in the mud. I have not been outside of camp for 5 days, and don't pretend to go anywhere except on urgent business. This would be considered lazy in the North. It is not so here, where one becomes so completely enervated after a campaign [from] deprivation and suffering.

[Sunday] December 20. Today is a clear, cold, bright, winter day, which is an agreeable change after the rain of the past week.

[Wednesday] December 23. Yesterday I visited the 6th Corps and the 49th [New York], where I saw Colonel [Daniel D.] Bidwell, Dr. [James A.] Hall, Major [William] Ellis, and other officers of my acquaintance. Major Ellis went away last night for 10 days, leaving in his usual good spirits. Today is a pleasant, cold day, much like a December day in the North. It is my present purpose to apply for a leave about January 10th, which will fetch me home about the 15th, or 18th.

[Saturday] December 26. Christmas Day passed off yesterday in a very quiet manner with us. We dined on roast turkey and had porter to drink. Dr. B. [Brower] Gessner, medical inspector of the 2nd Corps, was our only guest. He has been recently married and proposes fetching his wife down to the army next week. If I should have a hospital as I now expect, perhaps I will not ask for leave, but [will] have my wife come and visit me instead.

[Monday] December 28. We are still at the same place, but I may leave the ambulance corps in a few days if I take charge of the division hospital again. It has been raining very hard for 24 hours.

[Tuesday] December 29. Division hospitals have been ordered reestablished, and I have been appointed to the charge of the First Division hospital. I have drawn 10 new tents today, and shall commence putting them up tomorrow. In the course of another week everything will be in running order. Several ladies have already arrived in camp and more are expected soon. Dr. [Brower] Gessner goes north tomorrow to fetch his wife and every train is bringing the women into camp. General Meade has issued an order permitting the wives, sisters or mothers of officers to visit the army for 20 days and the order is being complied with most heartily.

Thursday, December 31. [It is] the last night of the year, with the rain falling in torrents making everything cheerless and gloomy. 'Tis my birth day as well. [It is] also the anniversary of my visit home last year and of the visit of my wife to Camp Griffin two years ago. I have written my wife to make all preparations to visit me, and to start on the 12th of January. I [am] to meet her in Washington on the 13th.

CHAPTER SEVEN —1864

THE OVERLAND CAMPAIGN

FRIDAY, JANUARY 1. [It is] a very cold and wintry day, with a raw, searching wind. I worked all day at the hospital, having chosen a site on the plain towards the Fitzhugh homestead, but when General [Winfield S.] Hancock, who is on a visit to the corps, got sight of the tents going up, he interfered, saying it was not a safe place for the hospital. I came back in the midst of a snowstorm and pitched my tent for the night near corps headquarters. The hard work of New Years Day went for naught.

The next day [January 2] was spent in choosing a site for the three hospitals of the corps and I was out with Dr. [Alexander N.] Dougherty upon that business until near night. Finally, a spot was fixed upon in the woods along the corduroy road about half way between corps headquarters and Brandy Station.

Monday, January 4. I took a large fatigue detail into the woods and commenced falling the trees, clearing the ground, and otherwise preparing it for the tents. The work is a laborious one and will occupy us for some days before we shall be ready for the sick.

[Tuesday] January 5. [We are] still very busy at work getting the hospital in order. We have two saw mills within the lines of the First Division on the banks of a small stream that furnishes the power to run them. They have been put in order by Captain Hoyt, chief quartermaster of the division, and he has furnished me with a supply of lumber for hospital use. The tents are being floored with this lumber, and it comes in very conveniently for many other purposes also. This work went on for a week when everything was declared in readiness

91

for the reception of the sick. I had written my wife to start for Washington on [Tuesday] the 12th, and that I would meet her there, having obtained permission for her to visit me for 20 days.

On [Wednesday, January] 13th, I went to Washington on a two days leave to meet her according to promise. She arrived late at night and I found her in the dining room of the Metropolitan Hotel taking supper at 11 o'clock P.M., with Major [William] Ellis, 49th New York, in whose company she had traveled from Buffalo. We remained in Washington during [Thursday] the 14th, and in the evening [we] attended the theater [Ford's,] where we met General [John C.] Caldwell and [his] wife. On the 15th, Friday, we went down to the army and fairly established ourselves for the winter. I obtained a lady's saddle in Washington, and we were in the saddle together almost every day for the next two months. Mrs. Payne, Mrs. Arnold, Mrs. John Hancock, Mrs. Caldwell, Miss Jennie Kerner, and a few other ladies were our most intimate acquaintances in the First Division. Several ladies from the Second Division were our frequent guests.

The 3rd Corps issued invitations for a grand ball to be given at General [Joseph B.] Carr's headquarters on [Monday] the 25th of January, and we received cards thereto on [Monday] the 18th. We attended the ball on Monday, January 25th, going over in an ambulance with Dr. and Mrs. [Brower] Gessner. It was a successful affair in every way, and was attended by the ladies and their husbands, as well as many other officers. The Honorable John Minor Botts, who lived in sight of the ball, attended with his two daughters. The supper, an elegant one, was sent down by [a] special train from Washington.

MORTON'S FORD

On Saturday, February 6th, the 2nd Corps was ordered down to the Rapidan at Morton's Ford and had a skirmish there with the enemy. The 3rd Division, commanded by General Alexander Hays, was thrown across the river, and had a severe skirmish with the force defending the ford. That division lost about 200 men in killed and wounded. I did not go down to the ford myself, as I had no orders, and did not even learn anything of the movement until I heard the firing, the sound of which was quite distinct at the hospital, and then inquired as to its cause. The wounded, chiefly of the 3rd Division, were brought up and distributed to the hospitals of the corps, and cared for by us until their recovery. This was the first instance, so far [as I] know, during the war where the wounded after a fight were treated from first to last in field hospitals.

I made several operations of a capital order and sent the specimens to Washington where they were deposited in the Army Medical

Museum. One man died with lockjaw several days after the fight. He was wounded in the thigh and the ball was impacted just above the outer condyle of the left femur. At the autopsy it was discovered that the femur was fissured longitudinally, extending from the point of the impaction of the ball to the trocanters—an unusual wound. My wife had an opportunity to assist in the care of these wounded soldiers, which she did with a kindly heart and thoroughly useful manner.

THE SECOND CORPS' BALL

On Monday, February 22, Washington's birthday, the Second Corps gave a grand ball at the headquarters of the corps near Stevensburg, or, to be more precise, at the Thom House on Cole's Hill. Adjoining the house a dancing hall was built, which required 12,000 feet of lumber to floor [it]. This was seasoned pine borrowed of General [Rufus] Ingalls, Chief Quartermaster, Army of the Potomac, which was smoothed and fitted by carpenters detailed from the ranks. The sides of the building were constructed of green hemlock which our sawmills furnished, and the roof was of canvas. It was lighted with 600 Adamantine candles, the holders for which were specially made in Washington. The supper was furnished by Gautier, a Washington caterer, for which we paid him $2200.00 and furnished transportation for it to the camp. It was a subscription ball, no fees being taken for anything on that night, and no officer outside of the corps being allowed to subscribe. In other words, every visitor was considered the guest of the managers. Officers in the 2nd Corps who were solicited, subscribed according to rank or position and my subscription was $20.

General [George G.] Meade, General [John] Sedgwick, General [Alfred] Pleasonton, and other high officers were present, besides Vice-President [Hannibal] Hamlin and daughter, Governor [William] Sprague and [his] wife, [Kate Chase Sprague], Senator Wilkinson, of Minnesota, and other distinguished civilians. The distinctive flags of the corps and the camp and garrison flags, were festooned in an artistic way about the room. An orchestra was built up across on end of the hall, upon which were mounted two brass Napoleon guns with the requisite ammunition, and three bands furnished uninterrupted music till morning.

The pickets at the Rapidan were doubled that night, and a brigade was sent down within supporting distance of the picket line, so as to be in readiness in case of a surprise. Happily, there was no attack, and all went off in splendid style. This was, undoubtedly, the largest, strictly military ball ever given in this country, a pleasure to the participants, and a credit to the managers.

[Tuesday] February 23. General [George G.] Meade reviewed the Second Corps and [Hugh Judson] Kilpatrick's division of cavalry in honor of the visitors which the ball had attracted. It was a beautiful day, soft and balmy as spring. The ladies attended in full force and fine array, many of them mounted upon fine horses, and many others in ambulances and spring wagons. Colonel Ulric Dahlgren, of the cavalry, a son of Admiral [John Adolph] Dahlgren, was conspicuous that day as the only one-legged officer present. He was noted for his excellent horsemanship, notwithstanding his physical imperfection. Alas! He was soon to meet his death, even within a few days [March 3], which occurred during Kilpatrick's celebrated raid to the environs of Richmond, which he started out upon the next day after the review.

At the First Division headquarters a fine music hall was constructed early in the season, and here we met almost every night for some sort of an entertainment, lectures, balls, and hops being the chief amusements. Grace Greenwood [Mrs. Lippincott] gave us three or four of her characteristic talks, that bristled with wit, wisdom, and genuine loyalty. The days were spent in riding, visiting, witnessing drills , and artillery practice. The evenings [were spent] in cards or at the entertainments at [the] music hall. The ladies entered into all the ways and sports of camp life with a will and before the season was over were really veterans in all the methods and habits of military life. During the winter about 4,000 women visited the army under the generous permission of the commanding general, and I am sure it did both them and the army much good.

I had my wife's visiting permit extended twice for 20 days each time, so that she was with me 60 days altogether. We had fine quarters, a hospital tent 14 x 16 feet for the front room, and a regulation wall tent 9 x 9 feet for the sleeping apartment. These rooms were both warmed by stoves, carpeted with army blankets and were very comfortable indeed. I obtained a church door down at a cavalry picket on the Rapidan and had it fitted as a front door to my tent, which was the envy of all our visitors, as well as the pride of ourselves.

One day, about the 1st of March, while General [John C.] Caldwell and [his] wife were dining with us, in walked our cousin, Milton G. Potter, then in his senior year at Rochester University, [who was] visiting the army for recreation and information. He had been spending a few days with the cavalry on our right near Culpeper Court House and was quite surprised to find everything so comfortable and home-like in our quarters. He joined us at dinner and remained with us a few days, though it was only his purpose to make a short call when he came. I took him to Division Headquarters the next day and there made him acquainted with all the officers, which his previous meeting with General Caldwell greatly facilitated and relieved [us] of that stiffness incident to first introductions. We also visited the 6th Corps and other points of interest during his visit. He was so well pleased with the manner of the entertainment we provided that he prolonged his stay to nearly a week, finally leaving with sincere expressions of regret. He wrote me afterward how much he enjoyed his visit to the First Division. This letter is preserved among my military papers. So the winter wore away, all too rapidly to be sure, for those of us who were so pleasantly situated.

On [Saturday] the 12th of March, I obtained a leave of absence for 10 days to go home with my wife. On a bright Monday morning, March 14th, we bade adieu to the festive scenes of camp life and turned our faces regretfully northward. From Washington we went to New York where we spent two days, reaching home on [Thursday] the 17th. After a week of rest, part of which was spent in visiting friends, I started back on [Thursday] the 24th, arriving in Elmira [on] Friday morning, the 25th, just 10 minutes too late for the train over the N.C.R.R. for Baltimore, which compelled me to wait 12 hours for the next one south. I did not reach Washington until after midday Saturday [March 26].

Sunday, March 27. I started for the front this morning, reached the hospital this P.M., and found everything in good order, Dr. [Marvin C.] Rowland having been in charge during my absence. I found the army in a sea of mud, [from] the effects of a 10 inch snow fall the previous Tuesday, which had now melted and left the surface of the ground in a liquid state. Dr. Aiken, in charge of the 2nd Division Hospital, is sick. Otherwise everything is as usual about the whole camp. I learn that negatives of the hospitals have been taken by [Alexander] Gardner during my absence, and two pictures have been ordered for me, that are to be delivered very soon.

[Tuesday] March 29. It has been raining hard all day, which will delay a movement of the army for the present. General [Ulysses S.] Grant has arrived at Culpeper Court House, where he has taken up his headquarters. The army has been reorganized, as has been contemplated for sometime. The corps [are] reduced to three: the 2nd, 5th, and 6th—commanded by [Winfield S.] Hancock, [Gouverneur K.] Warren, and [John] Sedgwick, respectively.

The 3rd Division of the 2nd Corps has been broken up and distributed to the 1st and 2nd Divisions. General [Alexander] Hays takes command of a brigade in the 3rd Division ([David B.] Birney's from the 3rd Corps) General Caldwell goes to Washington upon court martial duty. General Francis C. Barlow, formerly colonel of the 61st New York, takes command of the 1st Division. Colonel [James A.] Beaver's regiment, the 148th Pennsylvania goes to the 4th Brigade.[1] General [Alexander S.] Webb goes back to a brigade, and General [John] Gibbon is assigned to the command of the 2nd Division. The 2nd Corps

Colonel James A. Beaver
148th Pennsylvania
(Muffly, Story of Our Regiment)

now has four divisions. Two are made up of its own original three, and two come from the old 3rd Corps.

Dr. [Frederick A.] Dudley, 14th Connecticut, is now in the 2nd Division, and does not like the change at all.[2] Dr. [Brower] Gessner also goes to the 2nd Division. Lieutenant Pelton is promoted to captain, and is appointed chief of ambulances in Livermore's place. These are some of the changes that affect my friends or acquaintances. I visited the 57th [New York] yesterday and found the officers all well excepting Dr. [Nelson] Neeley, who returned from his leave on Saturday, the 26th. Colonel [Alfred] Chapman has offered his resignation, but is doubtful about its acceptance.

Friday, April 1. Everything is going on in the most quiet manner possible. There are but 21 patients in the hospital now, as the most of them were sent away last week, including the wounded of Morton's Ford, and Dr. [Marvin C.] Rowland accompanied them to Washington. Dr. [Justin] Dwinelle [71st Pennsylvania], of the 2nd Division, has not returned from his leave yet.[3] I had a small card party last night composed of doctors, among whom were Aiken, Dudley, and Neeley. The latter remaining as my guest for the night.

The 57th moved its camp yesterday, occupying the hill where General [Joshua T.] Owen's brigade formerly camped. It is expected that General Grant will review the army by corps very soon, though it is not yet definitely known when the 2nd Corps' turn will come. All the ladies have left the camps and everything is settling down to business. It is not probable, however, that the campaign will open before [Sunday] the 1st of May, and nothing, of course, can be learned of even its probable character. A column of troops passed along the corduroy road today for the front, probably recruits and convalescents. It is supposed the Army of the Potomac now numbers upwards of 100,000 men.

[Sunday] April 3. The 3rd Division hospital is broken up and distributed to the 1st and 2nd Divisions, to conform to the consolidation of the troops. Miss [Cornelia] Hancock, a nurse who has been with the 3rd Division hospital all winter, comes to my hospital. Her house was moved today and set up alongside of my quarters. Dr. [Frederick A.] Dudley, in charge of the 3rd Division hospital until now, goes back to his regiment, the 14th Connecticut. The recent rains have made the mud very deep. I have just been summoned to division headquarters for a consultation about medical matters of the division.

April 5. Tuesday. It has stormed almost continually for the past week—rain, snow, and wind—and the rain has not ceased to fall for 24 consecutive hours. On my way to division headquarters Sunday I met Captain [William A.] Arnold near the bridge, and he gave pleasant news from his wife, who arrived home safely.[4] Captain [James] McKnight's battery, late of the 3rd Corps, is to join the 2nd Corps in a day or two. Lieutenant W. [William] S. Bull, formerly of the 49th [New York], is an officer in McKnight's battery, and I shall be glad to have him near me again. General [Francis] Barlow has arrived and assumed command of the division. He appears to be much [like] a man as Hancock—nervous, impatient, wiry, with a searching eye, and keeps one at a distance. I believe in him, and think the division has a competent commander who will make it do famous work. Dr. [Justin] Dwinelle, who has had quasi charge of the corps hospitals, is expected back tomorrow. His position is non est now, as each division hospital is independent of the other. Miss Hancock is doing good work as nurse, and is very much liked by the sick and attendants.

[Thursday] April 7. This is the first pleasant day we have seen for eight days, and it is quite a treat to see the sun once more. General Barlow paid a visit to the hospital today, inspecting it thoroughly, as he does everything, and expressed himself as being well satisfied with its appearance. He is a sharp observer, and nothing escapes his eye. Dr. [Marvin C.] Rowland has not been well for two days, but is better today. He has been appointed surgeon of the 61st New York.

[Sunday] April 10. The bridge over Mountain Run, between here and division headquarters, was carried away last night, and the mail is shut [in] at division headquarters. I have just learned also that two railroad bridges between here and Washington, were swept out by the recent high water. Lieutenant Anderson, commanding ambulance corps, who has been on recruiting service all winter has just returned. I went to the artillery brigade today, and there learned that Captain [William A.] Arnold had gone home to attend the funeral of one of his children, who had died suddenly of croup. The rain fell in torrents all night before last, yesterday, and last night, but it is pleasant today. I met Colonel Francis A. Walker today, and he made pleasant inquiries after my wife whose acquaintance he made last winter.

[Wednesday] April 13. Today it is pleasant, warm, and spring like. I took dinner at division headquarters today, and all the staff, particularly Captain Marlin, made inquiries after Mrs. Potter. The cars are running again to Washington, the bridges having been repaired. Captain Lewis Nolen is appointed inspector general of the 3rd Brigade.

Captain Josiah M. Faville
Company A, 57th New York
(Faville, Diary of a Young Officer)

[Friday] April 15. The weather continues pleasant. I have 85 patients in [the] hospital, and [I] am expecting an order daily to send them away. General [Winfield S.] Hancock will be here tomorrow to inspect the hospital, and we are policing it today with the entire force. Miss [Cornelia] Hancock, the nurse, and Mrs. Lee, the washerwoman, went away today, in accordance with an order from headquarters Army of Potomac clearing away all citizens by [Saturday] the 16th. In consequence of this order all citizens and sutlers are moving away from Brandy Station. By tomorrow it will look quite deserted there.

[Sunday] April 17. The days drag wearily along, and I am almost tempted to wish for active service to dispel the ennui. Yesterday being rainy, General Hancock did not inspect the hospital as was anticipated. Captain [Josiah M.] Faville has sent Mrs. Potter a programme of the hops we had last winter. They came rather too late for use, but will be an interesting souvenir of those delightful times. There is a rumor in the 2nd Division hospital that no more letters will be sent away from the army after today. I don't place much reliance upon it, for they are rather gossipy and a little given to the sensational over there.

[Tuesday] April 19. This is a beautiful day, and I am momentarily expecting General Hancock to inspect the hospital, as he is already inspecting the troops, and will come here next, having sent word to that effect. The pontoon train has just passed along the corduroy toward the Rapidan, which is ominous of "business" in that direction in the course of the next few days. The artillery has been practicing at a target on the plain towards the Fitzhugh house all morning. General Grant is expected to review the 2nd Corps tomorrow. I shall attend with the division staff, as I am desirous of seeing the distinguished lieutenant general.

[Thursday] April 21. The day is delightful and inspection by General Hancock, which did not take place Tuesday, has just been completed. We had quite a galaxy of "stars" present. Major General Hancock, and Brigade Generals [Francis] Barlow and [John] Gibbon, with their several staffs were in my quarters after the inspection was over. I served them a light luncheon with sherry. General Hancock pronounced the hospital perfect in every respect. Indeed, it never looked nicer than now, but [the] sick have all been sent away, Dr. [Marvin C.] Rowland accompanying them to Washington, and to return on Saturday [April 23]. I am now preparing for the anticipated march, filling up my Autenreith wagons with stores, dressings, and medicines, and equipping two army wagons with my own supplies. I think we shall start about the 1st of May. I have received the photographs of the hospital which were taken by [Alexander] Gardner, of Washington, and they are very correct pictures. I shall send two of them home in a day or two.

[Saturday] April 23. The headquarters is all there is left, of that once grand institution, the First Division hospital. All the tents were taken down this morning, and we are now busy packing all the property we cannot take with us in the active campaign approaching. The day is hot and windy, and I should not be surprised if we start most any day, as the ground is drying fast. Yesterday I attended a grand review of the 2nd Corps by General Grant, and it was by far the [best] one I ever saw. The corps never looked finer nor marched better, every officer and man seeming anxious to show the lieutenant general how well they could do. After the review Generals Grant, Meade, Sheridan, and about 20 brigadier generals were entertained by General Hancock at his headquarters. An exhibition drill of the 19th and 20th Massachusetts regiments was also given at General [Alexander S.] Webb's. Dr. [Marvin C.] Rowland has just returned from Washington, where he went with the sick two days ago.

[Monday] April 25. Though division hospitals are among the things that were [moved], I am still in the same place occupying the wall tent for quarters, which stands just where it did all winter. Dr. Rowland has gone to his regiment, which leaves me quite alone, except [for] the steward and nurses. Today has been the warmest of the season thus far, though it rained all last night. There is a rumor that no mails from the army are sent beyond Washington, but we continue to receive our mails regularly. [First] Lieutenant C. [Charles] H. H. Broom [Company K] of "ours" has been detached for duty in the War Department.[5] The lucky and handsome Broom will thus escape the dangers of the campaign. An order was issued yesterday from division headquarters assigning me to the charge of the field hospital during the campaign, and detailing Dr. [Philip M.] Plunkett, 2nd Delaware, to report to me as assistant; also naming the hospital stewards and nurses for the campaign, all to report for duty and instructions the 26th, tomorrow.[6]

**First Lieutenant
Charles H. H. Broom
Company K, 57th New York**
(Faville, Diary of a Young Officer)

[Wednesday] April 27. Measles has appeared among the troops, and the cases are sent to me for isolation as fast as recognized. I have 3 tents full already. Colonel F. [Francis] A. Walker [Adjutant General, Second Corps] is down with a mild varioloid, and is in the quarters lately occupied by Dr. [Frederick A.] Dudley. Dr. [Nelson] Neeley is sick and goes home for 20 days, so he will escape the next fight. Dr. [Marvin C.] Rowland's place will be supplied by Dr. [Philip M.] Plunkett tomorrow.

April 29. Friday. We had a fine dinner today, consisting of beefsteak, pork stew, baked potatoes, coffee, porter, and custard, which is good enough fare, even for a soldier. It is warm and summer like, and I am moving my tent up into the old street, to get rid of the mice that infest the old location. Snakes, too, are beginning to appear. [Patrick] Corbley killed one in his tent a day or two ago. I expect my remaining patients will be sent to Washington tomorrow, and we may move by Monday [May 2]. I understand that all mail will be stopped except for [the] general and staff officers, but I am included in the excepted list. Dr. [Marvin C.] Rowland called today, and Dr. [Alexander N.] Dougherty yesterday.

Sunday, May 1. I sent the remainder of my sick away yesterday. So the decks are clear for action. I have a small white mare that Corbley traded his "joe" horse for a few days ago, which will fit us out very nicely for the campaign. Old Mr. Fitzhugh called upon me this morning to say goodbye, having heard we were to move soon. Dr. [Marvin C.] Rowland was mustered as surgeon yesterday.

May 3, Tuesday. I have just written the last letter home that I shall send from this camp, for we shall, no doubt, be off tonight. This, at any rate, is the import of the orders we are receiving. I visited the 6th Corps on Sunday [May 1], and saw Dr. [James A.] Hall, Colonel [Daniel D.] Bidwell, and others. All sent a kind word to Mrs. Potter. It is now 3 o'clock P. M., and everything is packed up and ready for the start. After supper I shall go over to division headquarters, and remain there until the final order is issued.

GRANT'S OVERLAND CAMPAIGN

1ST THE WILDERNESS

Wednesday, May 4. We sat around [the] music hall at headquarters last night until midnight, then started on the grand Overland Campaign.[7] By the arrival of daylight we had reached the Rapidan at Ely's Ford and soon crossed without opposition, taking the road to Chancellorsville, where the head of the column halted at 9:30 A. M. By noon the entire corps was up, and we bivouacked for the night near Hooker's old battlefield of a year ago. During the afternoon I rode over the field, [which is] still, to quite an extent, marked by the wreckage of that unlucky fight. I examined the various points of interest where I had spent four unhappy days the previous May.

The morning of [Thursday] the 5th, bright and early, we were under way again, but by 10 o'clock A. M. our advance was arrested in its progress, and the ambulance and hospital train halted for some hours in a heavy wood. We finally got under way sometime after noon and moved slowly along, establishing our hospital toward night near the Carpenter house. The division became engaged late in the afternoon, and Lieutenant Colonel [Alfred] Chapman, 57th New York, commanding the skirmish line, was the first officer killed in the division. His body was brought in during the evening, and laid alongside my tent carefully covered with waterproof blankets. [The] next morning it was embalmed by Dr. [Justin] Dwinelle, and afterwards sent to Fredericksburg for shipment north.

For the next two days [Friday and Saturday], the 6th and 7th of May, we heard the rattling of musketry almost constantly, but rarely the sound of artillery, as cannon could be of little service in the dense chaparral. Several hundred wounded were cared for in my hospital during these three days, and on the afternoon of the 7th I was ordered to send them to Fredericksburg, supplied with nurses and three days rations. Dr. C. [Charles] S. Hoyt, surgeon 39th New York, was officer of the day on the 7th and I liked his zeal and method so well that I subsequently had him appointed executive officer of the hospital.[8]

During our stay in the Wilderness we had a supply of ice, that General [Francis] Barlow was kind enough to send from a house near the line of battle. On the night of the 7th we moved toward the left, were at Todd's Tavern on [Sunday and Monday] the 8th and 9th, and at Po River on [Tuesday] the 10th. In the withdrawal of the division from across the Po, some of our wounded were left behind falling in to the enemy's hands. We established ourselves at Cossin's on [Wednesday] the 11th, where we were destined to have the hospital taxed to its utmost capacity.

2ND SPOTSYLVANIA

We have been almost constantly fighting for the past 7 days, and are now confronting the enemy with a prospect of renewing the contest [at] almost any moment, our lines being near Spotsylvania Court House. General [John] Sedgwick, the commander of the 6th Corps, was killed on the 9th near Todd's Tavern by a sharpshooter while he was reconnoitering the enemy position from a redoubt. I saw Colonel [Martin T.] McMahon, of Sedgwick's staff, very soon afterwards, and he told me the general was expiring almost instantly.[9] The 57th regiment has been sent to Fredericksburg to do provost guard duty for the present.

May 13. Friday. [We are] still at Cossin's. Yesterday morning, May 12th, at 4 o'clock the 2nd Corps, after marching all night from our position on the right, attacked the enemy near his center and went over the works with a rush. The First Division [was] in the lead in two columns of masses, each regiment doubled on the center, [with] General [Francis] Barlow leading the charge in his shirt sleeves. We had 45 cannon in our possession at one time during the charge, and brought off 22 of them, also capturing 4,000 prisoners including Generals Edward Johnson and George H. Steuart, besides some colors. Our loss was heavy, and I had 1200 wounded in my hospital before noon.

I have 950 in the hospital today, after sending 450 to Fredericksburg yesterday. Colonel Francis A. Walker was injured by a fall from his horse on the 10th, and is now in my tent. General [Francis] Barlow has sent the division band to play for the wounded in [the] hospital, which is the first music we have been allowed since crossing the Rapidan.

May 15. Sunday. I worked all night last night shipping the wounded to Fredericksburg. [We] used 250 army wagons, all the ambulances and spring wagons of the division, 50 in number, and besides [we] sent a large number on foot. After all the transportation was exhausted, about 200 were still unprovided for and these I was ordered to leave behind, as the corps was moving to the left thus uncovering the hospital. So it must be broken up. Nurses and rations were provided and everything possible was done for their comfort. I was the last authorized person to leave, which I did about 8 o'clock A.M., and within 15 minutes after [General Thomas] Rosser [C. S. A.] came in with a light brigade, capturing the place, paroling the men, and taking the extra rations for his hungry horde. We are not fighting today, but shall probably resume business in a day or two. Lieutenant Colonel [David L.] Stricker, 2nd Delaware, was killed on the 12th, and Colonel [Paul] Frank has been relieved of the command of the 3rd Brigade, reason not known to me. The charge of the 2nd Corps on the 12th is regarded as one of the most brilliant and effective of the war.

May 17. Tuesday. The 49th [New York] has suffered severely in the recent battles, ten officers being reported killed and six wounded. Colonel [Daniel D.] Bidwell is safe. I saw Dr. [James A.] Hall yesterday, who gave me these particulars. I notice all the papers speak of General Grant as though he commanded the Army of the Potomac. General Meade is in immediate command and directs the movements, but of course under Grant's advice and guidance as to the general plan.

[Thursday] May 19. Yesterday morning we had a fight losing about 500 men, [First] Lieutenant [William E.] Hall [Company F], 57th, on Colonel [Paul] Frank's staff among the number.[10] I have had no rest for two nights past from the fact that we have moved our hospital during both nights. The papers speak of the flying enemy, conveying the idea that they are going so fast that we can hardly overtake the routed columns. The truth is we are not 10 miles from Fredericksburg yet, and the 2nd Corps has not yet passed Spotsylvania Court House. We have sent all our wounded to the rear and are under orders to move at 2 o'clock A.M. tomorrow. [We are] prepared for a long march. Dr. [David H.] Houston is on my right writing a letter home.[11] He keeps up good spirits and is in excellent health, enduring the fatigues well for a man of his years. General Grant's headquarters are very near us just now, and I saw him this P.M. The enemy is strongly fortified on this line, and it is doubtful if we can drive him out, though there is a rumor today that he is falling back toward Richmond.

[Friday] May 20. Our mails are very irregular and infrequent, though today I received home papers to the 12th. Miss [Cornelia] Hancock is at Fredericksburg attending to the wounded of the 1st Division, and is reported as performing excellent service. Last night 2 brigades of [General Richard] Ewell's Corps made an attack upon our communications with Fredericksburg, but was handsomely repulsed by the new troops of [Robert O.] Tyler's Division from the defenses of Washington. Today it is very warm and a move seems on the tapis.

3RD THE NORTH ANNA

May 24. Tuesday. For the past 3 or 4 days and nights we have been almost constantly on the move. On the night of [Friday] the 20th, at 11 o'clock, the corps started for the Mattapony River, by a detour around the right flank of the enemy, and in the early morning of [Saturday] the 21st we passed through Bowling Green, a beautiful little village hitherto untouched by the hand of war. By 10 o'clock A.M. we had reached Milford Station and soon established ourselves about a mile over the Mattapony, where we threw up entrenchments and awaited the enemy who came not. We held the position until the morning of [Monday] the 23rd, having meanwhile been joined by the rest of the army, when we set out for the North Anna, arriving at Chesterfield the same afternoon, and here we are. We are about 4 miles from Hanover Junction, where we heard the Rebel cars whistle when we came up yesterday. We had quite a sharp fight last night, the loss chiefly occurring in Birney's Division. Skirmishing and some cannonading are going on today, but no general engagement. It is again rumored that the Rebels are falling farther back, but I do not credit it.

Thursday, May 26. [We are] still at the North Anna, and it is hot. The division is across the river holding an entrenched line, while the hospital is holding a comfortable farm house on the north bank unentrenched. I sent a pail of lemonade over to General [Winfield S.] Hancock and staff, and one to General [Francis] Barlow and his staff as well to cool their parched throats this hot afternoon. Major [William] Ellis [49th New York] was wounded on [Thursday] the 12th, by a ramrod in the arm, but it is not reported as dangerous. Captain [William A.] Arnold [Company A, 1st Rhode Island] lost one of his guns at the Po River on [Tuesday] the 10th— the first [gun] the 2nd Corps ever lost—through no fault of his, however. The gun became entangled in a small tree when the division retired and, as it could not be extracted readily, it was disabled and left to comfort the enemy. It is reported that Lee will make a big stand here—just the contrary of the rumor yesterday, as will be observed. We shall see which is

Captain Augustus M. Wright Company A, 57th New York
(Faville, Diary of a Young Officer)

correct. The 57th is still at Fredericksburg doing provost duty; Captain [Augustus M.] Wright [is] acting as provost marshal.

THE TOTOPOTOMOY

May 30. Monday. We have crossed the Pamunkey River and are again on the Peninsula, our front line of battle being, it is stated, not more than 12 miles from Richmond. We left the North Anna on [Friday] the 27th, bivouacking that night within three miles of the Pamunkey. The 28th and 29th were spent in reconnoitering and skirmishing, and today we are confronting a line of the enemy's works at the Totopotomoy.

May 31. Tuesday. [We are] still at it on the Totopotomoy line. It is a very hot day, and a ration of whiskey has just been issued to the troops. About 2 o'clock P.M. Captain Rose, C.S., 3rd Brigade, came to my quarters in a greatly "demoralized" state, and soon fell fast asleep on the ground inside the tent. At nightfall we were ordered to move, and after loading the wounded into the ambulances and packing up everything, I put Rose into the leading ambulance alone, when we started for Cold Harbor. During the night a wounded man crept in alongside of Rose, and when he awoke in the gray of the morning Rose thought he had been wounded also, and began a self examination with a view to determine as to the fact. He told of this himself afterwards, to the great amusement of all his friends. Colonel [Hiram L.] Brown, 145th Pennsylvania, has not been heard from or of since [Thursday] the 12th, and it is supposed he was captured at the assault at the Salient.[12] I saw his dog "Spot" today at the hospital, looking as though he had lost his last and only friend. I hear Captain R. [Reuben] B. Heacock, of the 49th [New York] was killed at Spotsylvania on [Wednesday] the 18th. Dr. George L. Potter and I made an operation yesterday upon [First] Lieutenant [Peter] Hunt, of Arnold's battery.[13] He was struck in the foot with a piece of shell about noon, and we removed all the fractured bones hoping to save the foot. [Lieutenant Hunt died in Washington a few days afterwards, with lockjaw.]

4TH COLD HARBOR

June 2. Thursday. Today is hot and dusty. The 2nd Corps is now the right of the army, for the first time since we started out, the 6th Corps having been moved from the right toward the left in the night. Yesterday the First Division had 200 wounded, and all were sent away but 35. Thus far today [12 m.] there has been no fighting, only an occasional gun being heard along the lines. We heard a rumor a short time ago that the enemy was preparing to attack our right flank, and that we might be compelled, if he did, to move our hospital to keep it out of danger of probable capture. An officer from General Meade's headquarters just told me that General "Baldy" Smith had joined the Army of the Potomac, on the left, with 20,000 men. Hurrah. Our depot is now at the White House, and our position is very near where we were two years ago under McClellan.

Friday. June 3. We had a severe battle this morning in which the first division lost heavily; I cannot say how many now, but I have already received over 500 in the hospital, and the wounded are being brought in constantly. We are but a short distance from Cold Harbor, yet it seems very difficult to get quite there. The nemesis of the Army of the Potomac appears to be enshrined in that region. Colonel J. [Jeremiah] C. [Clinton] Drake, 112th NY, formerly captain in the 49th New York, was killed [the] day before yesterday. I saw Dr. Hall this morning, and he is well. Colonel Morris, 66th N.Y., Colonel Peter A. Porter, 8th New York Heavy Artillery, and Colonel McKeon, 81st Pennsylvania, were killed this morning, all commanding brigades. Their bodies were brought to my hospital, whence they were sent north. The 57th [New York] has not returned from Fredericksburg yet, though I presume it will join us soon. I have shipped 423 wounded to the White House today.

Saturday. June, 4. [We] sent another consignment of wounded to the White House today numbering 255 and shall probably send more tomorrow. General Grant's headquarters are within 1/4 of a mile of my hospital and I see him quite often. No fighting [occurred] today excepting skirmishing and an occasional gun. The 57th has returned. Captain [Augustus M.] Wright and other officers are looking well, but they will be obliged to take part in the heavy fighting now. I fear the result to the remnant of that once splendid regiment. Dr. [Brower] Gessner is also back again, but he is given to complaining so much that he is no longer an interesting companion. S. B. ("Brain") Butler called on me yesterday and, as he was not feeling well, I gave him a little spirits frumenti, which seemed to brace him up.

Monday. June 6. I sent away 357 more wounded yesterday, making 1035 in the last 3 days. Today we moved the hospital about two miles toward the left and [we] are now at the Tyler House, on the road leading from Cold Harbor to the White House. This estate was formerly owned by Dr. Tyler, a cousin of ex-president [John] Tyler, who died while we were in this vicinity two years ago. We are about two miles from Dr.Gaines' farm, where we camped in May 1862, and where [Fitz John] Porter fought his great battle on the 27th of June, 1862. We are not fighting very heavily these days, but receive about 100 wounded daily into my hospital. We occupy the house for [an] office and mess purposes, and our tents are pitched on the lawn in front. Colonel [John R.] Brooke, commanding the 4th Brigade, was wounded two days ago, and Colonel [James Addams] Beaver [148th Pennsylvania] now commands that brigade. Information has been received that Colonel Brown is in Richmond and unhurt. It is thundering heavily and a rainstorm is imminent. The 57th is in the front line of breastworks doing duty at the post of danger in its accustomed good way. Captain McCuen, provost-marshal at corps headquarters, had one of his legs shot off last evening in front of General Hancock's tent.

Hancock is considered by all as "the right hand" corps commander of this army—one who is always where he is wanted at the critical moment and who punishes the enemy severely when he goes monkeying around with the 2nd Corps. In many respects he is an ideal field commander, and it would be difficult to supply his place should anything happen to render this necessary.

June 8. [Wednesday] [We are] still at the Tyler House. Mrs. General Barlow and Miss [Cornelia] Hancock arrived yesterday morning, and are my guests, Miss Hancock busying herself in caring for the wounded. We have a large ice house on the premises filled with native ice, which is a great comfort to the wounded—and the unwounded. General [Francis] Barlow has just been here to see his wife and found her supplying the wounded with milk punch while we are loading them for shipment to White House.

June 9. Thursday. I have just had orders to send all my wounded to the rear at White House, which looks like a move tonight. Dr. John S. Billings, assistant-surgeon, U.S.A., Medical Inspector, Army of the Potomac, visits the hospital everyday, spending sometime in unofficial intercourse with us, as he finds it a convenient place for obtaining a little rest when he needs it. He has been a frequent guest at odd times during the campaign, and seems to enjoy himself here very much. We always try to make him feel at home and quite welcome, whether for duty or otherwise. Mrs. Barlow and Miss Hancock are with us yet and may remain for sometime. Captain [William A.] Arnold's time has expired, so he has been mustered out, and he went home [the] day before yesterday. I met Captain Elliot on [Tuesday] the 7th. He was well and appeared in good spirits. I should not be surprised if we turned up on the James River next.

Saturday, June 11. The news of the sudden death of James Prince at the mansion house in Buffalo, has just reached me. It was a great shock, as he always appeared the picture of perfect health. Thurlock Weed was at the hospital today, and expressed himself as greatly pleased with the care we give the wounded in our field hospitals, and particularly this one. I am sending away my wounded again today.

Mrs. Barlow and Miss Hancock will return to the White House with this lot. From present appearances I think we shall move tonight.

Sunday, June 12. This is one of the most delightful days we have had since the campaign opened—an ideal summer day in every respect. Religious services were held on the lawn in front of the house this morning, [with] the First Division band furnishing the music [by] playing, among other airs, the doxology at the close. It was [an] impressive and interesting scene to see the soldiers that could get out of the tents gather around, and enter into the spirit of the service, as much as though it were in the finest church. Dr. Aiken expects to start home tomorrow, as his regiment's time expired today.

I am sending away more wounded today, and Dr. [Alexander N.] Dougherty informs me that we shall positively move from here tonight. I suppose there is great anxiety at the North just now as to our operations, but patience, patience. We have more men than McClellan had on the Peninsula, and the rebels are weaker. Yet we need reinforcements, and Grant will have them. Neither [Edwin] Stanton nor [Henry W.] Halleck can prevent it this time. Stanton's principal occupation seems to be, just now, to telegraph bulletins to General [John A.] Dix at Fort Monroe.

5TH PETERSBURG

We left the Tyler House at dark Sunday night. [We] marched all night [Sunday] the 12th [and] all day the 13th, resting at night. [We] marched all day the 14th and [the] 15th until daylight [Thursday] the 16th, when we reached the James River. The troops had already crossed the day before, but as I did not feel well I remained with the main hospital and ambulance train, crossing the James with it about 3 o'clock P.M. of the 16th on a pontoon bridge between Wilcox's Landing and Windmill Point. We pushed on for Petersburg, distant 16 or 17 miles, where the troops were already engaged, reaching there about 10 o'clock P.M., when we immediately set about putting up the hospital and gathering in the wounded, working all night at this business.

June 18. Saturday. We have crossed the Chickahominy and James Rivers and are now fighting a great battle before Petersburg. I have already 850 in my hospital, and the cannonading is terrific. The 57th [New York] is nearly wiped out, [with] all the officers but two being wounded—some of them mortally. Captain [Augustus M.] Wright is wounded in the foot. (It was afterwards amputated and he died.) Captain [Richard S.] Alcoke [(Company A) is wounded] in the chest.[14] (He lost an arm at Fredericksburg). Major [William A.] Kirk [is] mortally [wounded].[15] Captain [Orlando F.] Middleton [is] slightly [wounded]. Adjutant [First Lieutenant George C.] Case [has a] flesh wound in the neck.[16] Lieutenants [Martin V. B.] Brower [Company K] and [Thomas] Britton [Company H] both have flesh wounds and will recover.[17] The regiment had but 45 men for duty yesterday. This is the third day of the battle and the end is not yet. Mrs. General Barlow is here with some members of the Sanitary Commission dispensing luxuries to the wounded. Colonel [James A.] Beaver is slightly wounded in the side, and will go home to recover. The little drummer boy of the 61st, [William H.] Nims, has received a most frightful wound, his face having been nearly torn off by a shell last night.[18]

June 20. [Monday] We did not fight much yesterday, but this morning heavy cannonading on the right is heard, which probably means that the ball has again opened. We appear to be fighting it out on this line and I think it very probable that the contest will continue here, even unto the bitter end. The enemy has certainly reached very nearly, if not quite, his last ditch. The weather is very hot and there is plenty of work to do, but [there is] very little energy [with which] to do it. General Barlow's brother is here and will take a letter for me to Washington, which will enable me to communicate with home.

June 22. Wednesday. Yesterday we moved the hospital about 5 miles toward the left and are now about that distance from Petersburg. We crossed the Railroad leading to Suffolk, and are now located at the Smith House near the Jerusalem Plank Road. General [Winfield S.] Hancock's headquarters are but a few hundred yards away. We are having no fight today with [the] exception of a little cannonading on the right, where the Army of the James holds forth. I traded saddles with Captain Elliot while on the march yesterday and now have a fine English saddle that I like very much better than the one I had before. We are nicely situated again. My tent [is] on a beautiful yard that surrounds a fine house and we have plenty of good shade which is a consideration of importance. In an open, out of door life like this, the difference between good shade and none at all is simply immense. The house is comfortably furnished, with floors carpeted in tapestry, and has such conveniences as we need. I have no idea where the family vanished to, but [I] presume [it has been] to join friends of theirs over in Petersburg. We use the dining room for our mess, and some of the rooms for the sick officers. Colonel [Paul] Frank, commanding [the] 3rd Brigade, is now occupying the parlor, having lost his voice completely, being therefore unable to utter a word of command. Major [William A.] Kirk died [the] day before yesterday at City Point, and it was found necessary to amputate Captain [Augustus M.] Wright's foot. It looks discouraging for him. Captain [Orlando F.] Middleton has returned to duty and is in command of the regiment, being the senior officer present. It seems odd to me that Middleton should be in command, for when I joined the 57th, he was one of the younger lieutenants.

June 25. [Saturday] The weather is very hot, and the roads are dusty, but we have a good supply of ice and plenty of lemons, which serve to make life tolerable. Major [John Gardner] Hazard, Chief of Artillery, 2nd Corps, was just here, and I gave him a glass of lemon punch to cool his parched lips. Captain Lewis Nolen, and Captain [James G.] Derrickson, were both taken prisoners two days ago.

June 27. Monday. Major [William] Ellis has just been to call upon me, having returned from his Spotsylvania wound. He called to see Mrs. Potter while away, and came to report that all was well at home. He has been appointed Inspector General of the 1st Division, 6th Corps, and is now on General [David A.] Russell's staff. Dr. [David H.] Houston, Dr. [Philip M.] Plunkett, and Lieutenant Frank Nolen are preparing to leave, as they will be mustered out on the 30th. Dr. [Alexander N.] Dougherty told me a few days ago, that he would make me Surgeon in Chief of the division if my time did not expire so soon. I informed him that I did not desire the place, as I much preferred my present position. It is more independent, affords me more professional employment, and quite as much honor. Dr. [James A.] Hall is not more than 1/4 of a mile from here with his hospital, and I shall go over and see him this evening. "Brain" Butler was wounded on the 16th or 17th, but I did not see him. However, in response to a note he wrote me saying he was out of money, I sent him $7.00—all the spare funds I had with me at the time.

June 29. Wednesday. We are still at the Smith House and have had 8 days of comparative quietude, which is the longest time we have been in one place since the campaign opened. As Lieutenant Nolen goes out of service tomorrow, I obtained the appointment of Lieutenant [George] Mitchell, of the 57th, in his place as Chief of Ambulances for the division. I called to see Dr. Hall yesterday and found him the same as ever, genial and happy. I met Captain Elliot today at corps headquarters. Captain [James W.] Britt has been mustered as Lieutenant Colonel of the 57th, and is back again for duty, though his knee is not yet sound.[19] Lieutenant Hunt, of the artillery, whose foot George L. Potter and I operated on at the Totopotomoy, died in Washington a few days ago. Miss [Cornelia] Hancock is at City Point, where large base hospitals have been established, caring for the wounded of the 1st Division.

Saturday, July 2. We are still at the Smith House. The weather is insufferably hot and, as we have had no rain to speak of for a month; the air is full of dust. I have moved my quarters into the house because the dust has become so intolerable. Dr. [David H.] Houston will be mustered out today and Dr. Henry A. Martin, U.S. Volunteers, will take his place.

Last evening the medical officers of the division held a meeting here to give expression to their regrets in this separating from our old friend and chief. Appropriate resolutions were passed and a sum of money [was] raised to purchase a suitable testimonial of our regard. Colonel F. A. Walker is again with me, having come over yesterday to have two teeth extracted. He preferred to take chloroform and has not yet recovered from its secondary effects. Major John Hancock is relieved from duty with the First Division and [is] assigned to the 3rd [Division], as he could not agree with General [Francis] Barlow. Walker thinks we will remain here sometime. Quien Sabe? ["Who knows?"]

Monday, July 4. Everything is extremely quiet along the whole line this morning, but 2 or 3 guns having been heard, and they far off to the right. Yesterday Dr. [David H.] Houston, Dr. [Philip M.] Plunkett, and Lieutenant Nolen started for home, going off in fine spirits and great glee. I was very sorry to have them go. They were good and faithful officers, and warm friends of mine. Today is much cooler than common here, though we have had no rain worth mentioning, only a little shower last night. The hospital is in fine condition, containing 170 sick patients but, strange to tell, no wounded. The First Division hospital has the reputation of being one of the best—not to say the very best—in the army. Major [William] Ellis called upon me two days ago and was, as usual, looking well.

[Wednesday] July 6. Our position remains unchanged and I hope will continue so for sometime, as it is too hot to fight. Mrs. Barlow has been up to see the General and I took her to City Point at the request of the General, as he could not go with her himself. We went down in the old family carriage found in the barn on the Smith Estate and I saw her safely on board the steamer bound for Washington. She did not seem well but made no complaint at the time. Dr. [Wallace D.] Martin, and Dr. George L. Potter [145th Pennsylvania] are occupying quarters with me here at the Smith House and they are both very agreeable companions.[20] It appears that the Rebels expected us to attack them on the 4th of July and were in readiness for us [being] under arms all day. We had no idea of making ourselves ridiculous by such nonsense as that on Independence Day. We passed the day very comfortably, while they were sweating with their belts on and their muskets in hand, the hot sun pouring its sweltering rays down upon them. The 3rd Division, 6th Corps moved somewhere today toward the right, and rumor has it that they go to Harper's Ferry. Captain Wilson came over to see me yesterday and is looking well. Dr. George L. Potter and I are each sporting a straw hat, and today in riding to the lines, we met General Barlow coming back, who smilingly returned our salute, but never said a word in criticism of our unmilitary head apparel.

Friday, July 8. Colonel [James W.] Britt is with me now, not having recovered from the injury to his knee, [which he] received last

March. He is applying for leave and will remain here until it comes. Dr. Wilson, brother of Captain Wilson, and late of the 5th corps, committed suicide in Harrisburg a few days ago by cutting his throat. He was a cousin of Dr. George L. Potter, and the news comes through the Philadelphia Inquirer. The doctor and the captain are both very much saddened thereby, as they regarded Dr. Wilson with affection.

July 9. Saturday. I visited the 49th [New York] and took supper with Colonel [Daniel D.] Bidwell and other officers this evening. Major [William] Ellis called while I was there, and we went over to General [David] Russell's headquarters together. Ellis took me out into the woods to show me a carriage that he had "captured," and while we were looking at it orders came for the 6th Corps to start for Maryland to assist in driving out [the] Rebels, who are reported there in force under [Jubal] Early. Ellis was in great glee over the prospect and flew around to make preparations for the transfer of the troops to their new field. I hastily bade him goodbye, but [I] never saw him afterward.

Monday, July 11. We are living in great style at present. Directly across the hall from my parlor is the dining room, where ten officers have their mess, and meet three times a day to enjoy the good things set before them. Dr. George L. Potter occupies one end of the table and I the other. Our white table cloth, white china, [and] silver, together with some glassware we have captured, make our table look very home like and attractive. We have two little Negro waiters in white aprons to serve the table, and the whole get up would do credit to a Broadway restaurant. But it will not last long. Such comforts never do, at least in the army. Captain [Augustus M.] Wright died in Washington from the effects of his wound and the amputation and his remains have been sent on to New York. The officers of the 57th have passed appropriate resolutions expressive of our appreciation of him as an officer and a man, and of our sympathy with his family, that have been sent forward to his sisters.

Wednesday, July 13. [During the] night before last we vacated the Smith House, and found ourselves at daylight in [the] rear of the 5th Corps headquarters, where we proceeded to put up the hospital. Today our whole corps moved back also, and is massed in an open field near by, "in reserve." The siege of Petersburg goes bravely on, that is to say, we are pretty nearly as well off as we were three weeks ago, saving the few hundred men we have lost. The army is greatly delighted at receiving the news of the destruction of the Rebel cruiser "Alabama" by the "Kearsarge", off the coast of France last month.

July 15. Friday. I took a ride this morning, in company with Drs. [Alexander N.] Dougherty and George L. Potter, and Captain Pelton, down to the wagon camp about 5 miles distant, where we saw two men [Daniel Geary and Ransom S. Gordon] hung for an unmentionable crime.[21] It was a very aggravated case and, of course, the punishment was just.

Today it is much cooler than ordinarily, and we are all delighted with the change. An order has been issued authorizing the employment of acting staff surgeons, from among those regimental surgeons of two or more years experience and service, whose terms are now expiring. These medical officers are to have the same pay and allowances as regimental surgeons, and are to be allowed one government horse in addition. This may serve to retain the services of a few who would go out of the field altogether. I do not believe any considerable number will accept the offer. They will really have no actual rank, and will simply be employed as any civil physician under contract.

July 18. Monday. We moved about 1 & 1/2 miles on Saturday and are now occupying the grounds of the Burchard mansion of the Norfolk & Petersburg Stage Road, about a mile east or in rear of General Meade's headquarters. The plantation is owned by a Mr. Burchard, who is the father-in-law of the Rebel General [James] Dearing, of the cavalry service. It is well furnished, has a fine chickering piano with aeolian attachment, and Mrs. Burchard with two daughters, attended by some old servants, are occupying the house. Mr. Burchard went to Petersburg to take Mrs. Dearing the day our forces came up, June 16th, and our lines cut off his return. He did not reach home until the war was over, ten months afterwards. Dr. [Brower] Gessner, who went home on sick leave when we were at the Tyler House, has forwarded an extension of his leave for twenty days more. Dr. [Martin] Rizer, 72nd Pennsylvania, has also been home for 20 days since the campaign opened.[22] Surely, these be fortunate soldiers. Colonel Walker and Captain Pelton spent this evening with us and seemed to enjoy their visit very much. Colonel [James Wallace] Britt goes home tomorrow on 20 days leave. A large number of recruits have been sent to the 57th, which may necessitate my remaining in the service longer than I had anticipated. My time will properly expire on the 16th of September, but if the regiment is filled up to any considerable extent, it is probable that I shall stay a month or two longer. I sent money home early in the month and, as I have not yet heard from it, I am apprehensive [that] the Rebels have captured it in a raid they made on the [Baltimore and Ohio] Railroad in Maryland.

Thursday, July 21. The air is delightfully pure this morning as we had rain yesterday and the day before. I have heard from home today that the money I sent was received in safety. I have, until lately, been hoping to reach home by September 20th, but it looks now as though I would not be able to go until a month later. The government is beginning to appreciate the services of experienced medical officers and will hold on to them as long as possible, the difficulty in replacing them being so very great.

Saturday, July 23. I paid a visit to City Point yesterday and took a look at the hospitals there. They are not in better condition than mine, while their facilities for their preparation and maintenance are far superior. I saw Miss [Cornelia] Hancock there and took dinner with her. We have a new thing in the way of concentrated food called "condensed egg," the eggs being first dried and then put up in hermetically sealed cans, the same as milk. They are very nice indeed, serving the purpose in the preparation of puddings, custards, and many other dishes, nearly or quite as well as fresh eggs. It is thought a general bombardment of Petersburg with a hundred siege guns will take place within the next few days.

Sunday, July 24. We have received orders to move the hospital immediately [with] a part of the train to go to City Point. The weather is very hot and, on that account, I dread the march very much indeed.

Monday, July 25. Last night we were refreshed with a delightful rain, which continued all night long. We did not move today as ordered yesterday, so I took a ride this afternoon, making the tour of the various headquarters—brigade, division, and corps and met Colonel Walker, Captain [Josiah] Faville, and many others of my friends. Captain Faville tells me that his company's time [Company F] will expire on the 12th of August and that he will, therefore, be mustered out on that date. Captain [James C.] Bronson, mustering officer at corps headquarters, informs me that I cannot be mustered out until October 18th.

Considerable heavy firing is heard all along the lines tonight from heavy mortars and rifled cannon and it is expected a terrific bombardment will take place within a day or two.

The organization of the hospital is very complete now. I have one surgeon in charge of food and shelter, whose duty is to superintend putting up the tents and the preparation of the food [and] beds. One surgeon [serves] as executive officer, who promulgates the orders and attends to the registering of names, [the] preparation of reports, and all office details. Three prescribing surgeons look after the treatment of the sick in the wards, and these, together with hospital stewards, wardmaster, clerk, nurses, and cooks constitute quite a staff and corps of assistants. The personnel of the staff is as follows:

Surgeon W. W. Potter, 57th N.Y., in charge of hospital.
Surgeon C. S. Hoyt, 39th N.Y., executive officer.
Surgeon Jas. E. Pomfret, 7th N. Y. H. Artillery, food & shelter.[23]
Assistant Surgeon J. C. Norris, 81st Pa., recorder.[24]
Surgeon M. C. Rowland, 61st N.Y., chief prescriber.
Two assistant surgeons to aid the latter.

Dr. George L. Potter has been appointed surgeon-in-chief of the artillery brigade, and Major John G. Hazard is now chief of artillery of the 2nd corps.[25] Dr. Rowland, who was my assistant all winter at Brandy Station, is back again to take charge of the prescribing department of the hospital, and I was glad to obtain the services of so competent and experienced an officer.

For dinner today we had roast beef, nice broiled potatoes, fresh butter, good bread, and tomatoes, the latter obtained fresh from Norfolk. For dessert [we had] lemon and cranberry pie, watermelon, and ice cream. [Our] hours for meals [are] breakfast at eight o'clock, luncheon at 12:30 P.M., and dinner at six o'clock.

CHAPTER EIGHT —1864

ALONG THE JAMES RIVER

DEEP BOTTOM NO. 1

WE MARCHED ABOUT three o'clock P.M., Tuesday, the 26th, crossing the Appomattox River at Point of Rocks at 11 o'clock at night, and the James before daylight at Jones' Neck, or Deep Bottom. The First Division had a fight early Wednesday morning, the 27th, capturing four 20 pounder Parrott guns and a number of prisoners, losing about 100 men killed and wounded. I rode in the leading ambulance Tuesday night, and was asleep when we crossed the James, the pontoons being muffled so the rumbling over the bridge did not even disturb me. I did not awake until the booming of the guns [the] next morning suddenly aroused me. I took a hasty cup of coffee and began work. It was expected that this movement would be such a surprise to the enemy, that we could push on toward Richmond by this route, and possibly enter the city. It appears the enemy had fortified a line across our path, and as it had become a part of reform policy on the part of Grant not to attack entrenched lines, we were foiled in the one object of the movement. There was another which seemed to be prospering better.

The mine that was constructed in front of Burnside's lines before Petersburg was now completed and ready for firing. We therefore remained over the James River until more than one half of the Confederate force was attracted hither in the belief that our attack in this direction was still real.

116

[Saturday] July, 30. We remained at Deep Bottom until the night of the 29th, when, turning upon our heels, we marched rapidly back, reaching the lines in [the] rear of the 9th Corps in time to witness the explosion of the mine this morning, which occurred soon after daylight. The bombardment and assault soon followed, and the 2nd Corps was massed in reserve, expecting the order every moment to go in to the support of the troops already swallowed up in the seething vortex of destruction. When the mine was exploded, it gave forth a low, rumbling sound, that shook the earth for a considerable distance, and sent up into the air a cloud of red sand and earth that resembled a water spout at sea. In this dusty cloud were men, and guns, and material, mixed in inextricable confusion, all going to their death and destruction. The movement that the 2nd Corps was momentarily expecting was suspended, owing to the failure of the 9th Corps to do its work properly. We are back again at the Burchard House with our hospital, though it is expected that we may be compelled to move yet tonight. I have had no sleep to speak of for the past three nights, and am, therefore, a good deal worn down. I hope we can rest for at least one night.

Monday, August 1. We packed up and started to move Saturday night but had gone only one half of a mile when the orders were countermanded, so we turned around and came back again. Last night, orders were issued for the corps to be ready to move at a moment's notice, and it is the general impression that we shall move somewhere within the next 24 hours. Captain Wilson and Captain Elliot paid me a visit this morning, both in good spirits and handsome as ever. Colonel [James A.] Beaver returned two days ago, but had not fully recovered from the effects of his wound and will, therefore, go back again in a day or two. The weather is very hot again, and we cannot be persuaded to do anything in the daytime that can be postponed until night, or some other good and convenient season.

Wednesday, August 3. The band came to play for the hospital today by order from division headquarters and everybody enjoyed the music, notwithstanding the heat, including Colonel Beaver who is here. Mrs. Barlow died in Washington last week and General Barlow had gone north for 15 days. Poor woman! She contracted her illness in the care of the soldiers and I deeply sympathize with the general in his affliction. I have just learned of the death of paymaster A. C. Winter, U.S. Navy, whose wife was Mollie Raynor, of Lansing, Michigan. Surely, sad news comes in duplicate.

When we were over the James at Deep Bottom the other day, I was within two miles of the ironclad "Canonnicus," on board of which Dr. Adams is serving. I have drawn my pay for July and shall send home $120.00 by Colonel Beaver who goes away tomorrow for 20 days. [He] will deposit it in the express office in Washington for me.

Friday, August 5. Quietude reigns in the camp of the Army of the Potomac today. Indeed it is too hot for anything but quietude. I have invited a little dinner party this evening, among whom are Captain [Josiah] Faville, Captain [James] Bronson, and Captain [Orlando] Middleton, and shall serve a little extra menu, with ice cream and oranges for dessert. The dinner was given in honor of Faville, who goes out of [the] service in a few days.

Monday, August 8. Dr. [Alexander N.] Dougherty expresses himself as anxious for me to return to service as an acting staff surgeon under the new order and promises me the charge of the hospital if I will do so, but I have given no encouragement in that direction. Yesterday Miss [Cornelia] Hancock came up from City Point and spent the day at the hospital and Miss [Helen] Gilson called upon me last evening.[1] Miss Gilson offers to come up and remain a week, caring for some of our bad cases, a kindness which will be duly appreciated. We can give her good quarters in the house and, as she sings well and plays the piano beautifully, it will be quite a cheerful change to have her here, even for a short time.

The failure at the mine explosion of July 30th is still the theme of conversation among the officers, but no one seems to know just where the responsibility therefore rests. A court of inquiry will, I suppose, fix that in due time however. A number of leaves of absence have been granted during the past month, among them one to Dr. [Marvin] Rowland, who goes home sick.

August 10. Wednesday. Everything is going on in the usual daily routine, though there was a little more firing than common on the lines last night and this morning. Yesterday a barge at City Point loaded with ammunition blew up by accident, killing and wounding about a hundred men. The explosion was terrific and could be heard for miles away. We heard it distinctly, and are 6 or 7 miles from the Point. One surgeon going home on leave and awaiting transportation was blown to atoms. Captain Faville will be mustered out tomorrow, together with the greater part of his company. My groom, [Patrick] Corbley, will be mustered out on the 22nd, but will remain until I go, to take care of my horses during transportation.

Friday, August 12. Yesterday I went to City Point to see Captain Faville off. Yes, Faville has gone! I am very sorry, for he was a gentleman in the best sense of the word and a companion who will be very much missed by all his friends. He has invited me to visit him in New York, at his father's, when my time expires. Dr. J. C. Norris, 81st Pennsylvania, my assistant and recorder, went home yesterday for 20 days.

The day is intensely hot, as usual, not even a breath of air stirring. Lieutenant [Sylvester D.] Alvord of General [John] Caldwell's staff, whom we all remember with the kindest feelings, and who was married sometime ago, is saddened by the grievous illness of his wife, who is reported in a dangerous condition. Lieutenant [William E.] Hall was mustered out with Faville, and Captain [George W.] Jones [Company I] goes in a day or two.[2] The 57th is gradually melting away.

DEEP BOTTOM NO. 2

Monday, August 15. Here we are across the James again right where we were before and we are called by the soldiers, "Hancock's Cavalry." The troops moved down to City Point on the afternoon of the 12th, took transports that night, and were sent up here and landed next morning, while the trains went overland and crossed on the bridges as before. We had a fight yesterday and I have 160 wounded in my hospital. I amputated Captain James C. Bronson's right forearm yesterday and he is now in my tent doing well. The day is intensely hot, almost to suffocation.

[Tuesday] August 16. Today the cavalry and the First Brigade [under] General [Nelson] Miles had a fight on the extreme right of our line near Charles City Crossroads, the result of which I have not yet ascertained. I have about 60 additional wounded today, and the heat continues as great as ever. This afternoon a terrific thunder storm burst over us, nearly collapsing the hospital tents. My own tent was in such extreme danger of going down, that I had 4 men hold it up by steadying the ropes at the corners, to keep it from crushing Bronson who is inside with an amputated arm. After the rain I witnessed an artillery duel between 4 or 5 of our gunboats and some land batteries of the enemy. It occurred just at night, and was a splendid sight.

Saturday, August 20. Yesterday I was directed to superintend the shipment of the wounded of the 2nd Corps and the cavalry corps, which made a busy day of it. Two transports, the "Kent" and another, were moored at the wharf opposite my quarters, that are on the bank of the river, and the wounded were carried on board by the ambulance corps. The point where I am located is only 2 or 3 miles below Aiken's Landing, the latter being the place where I was delivered to the U.S. authorities, after being released by the Rebels two years ago. After being in the front of Petersburg so long, where there is nothing but dust and fire—fire of the batteries—it is a delightful change to witness the transports and gunboats sailing up and down the river at night blowing their whistles and displaying their parti-colored lights to avoid collision. It gives the scene a wonderfully commercial aspect, unlike the ordinary surrounding of war. One night I counted 19 vessels from the top of the bank near my tent.

Among the wounded sent away yesterday was Captain Bronson, who will never return to active service, though he could, and probably will, enter the Veteran Reserve Corps. He gave me a fine new saddle cloth, breast strap, and other horse accoutrements. We have had rain for the last three days, and it continued all last night, so, this morning, the roads are not inviting to a long march.

Tuesday, August 23. We left Deep Bottom Saturday evening, marched all night, and next morning found ourselves at the Burchard House again. After a short halt for coffee, we marched to the extreme left to support Warren's 5th Corps in its struggle to take and hold the Weldon Railroad. The Rebels strove desperately to drive Warren off, assaulting his position five times, and were as many times repulsed, with considerable slaughter. We have had much rain during the past week, which has served to make the roads very bad, but has not cooled the air. Indeed, it is about as hot as ever. Dr. [Brower] Gessner is back after his long absence, and Dr. [John] Aiken has returned as an acting staff surgeon, taking charge of the 2nd Division hospital again.

REAMS' STATION

Sunday, August 28. [We are] at the Burchard House. We returned here yesterday morning after a week's absence at Reams' Station and in that direction. After seeing Warren firmly established in his grip on the Weldon Railroad, the 2nd Corps was set to work tearing up the road. On Thursday, the 25th, after having destroyed about 10 miles of the road, we reached Reams' Station, or rather we had already destroyed the track two or three miles farther on, when the enemy attacked us in considerable force. Several different assaults were made, five in all, when we were finally driven out. It pains me to say that the 2nd Corps for the first time in its history behaved disgracefully, some of the men running like sheep. Hancock and his entire staff strove in vain to rally them, exposing themselves to a terrible fire in so doing, even the medical director, commissary of subsistence, and the chief quartermaster were called upon to perform the ordinary duties of aides, which they all did in a gallant manner. Nothing could be done to retrieve the lost fortunes and, with the coming on of darkness, we made preparations to retreat within the Petersburg lines. Captain E. P. Brownson, the corps mustering officer, was killed. Lieutenant Colonel Francis A. Walker, assistant adjutant general, was captured. These were the only casualties to the corps staff. Walker was sent with an order to Miles, commanding the 1st Division, and unconsciously rode into the enemy's lines through a gap in our own. Colonel [James A.] Beaver received a wound in his right thigh that necessitated its amputation through its upper third, which Dr. [J. W.] Wishart and I performed.[3] The colonel was just returning from absence by reason of his Petersburg wound, having arrived only that day, and was going out on foot to take command of the 4th Brigade when he was struck by a rifle ball that shattered his thigh. I had him brought hither from the field on a stretcher, by a detail of 16 men, distance about 10 miles, and he is now inside the Burchard mansion doing well. [He] has, I think, a fair prospect for recovery.

Our loss in killed and wounded was not large, but many were taken prisoners, and our military prestige is gone, though, let it be hoped, only temporarily. We lost 9 guns, including McKnight's 12th New York Battery in which Lieutenant W. [William] S. Bull is serving. This is the second time McKnight has come to grief during the campaign. On the 22nd of June he lost 4 guns. When at Deep Bottom in July, the First Division took 4 thirty-pounders back again, it was regarded by the boys as pretty good interest for the brief loan of McKnight's Napoleons. After all we have passed through during the past week, it seems good to get back here to the Burchard House. Last night the firing continued almost the whole night, and I amused myself [by] watching the shells as they sailed through the air, the spectacle resembling a display of fireworks very much indeed.

Tuesday, August 30. Heavy firing was kept up until a late hour last night, but it amounted to little or nothing in its effects. Colonel [James A.] Beaver is still doing well, though not out of danger yet. He bears his suffering bravely, however, and keeps up good courage, which is half the battle. I hear that Colonel Brown, missing since May 12th, has been exchanged and is at his home in Erie, Pennsylvania. Miss Gilson paid me a call this afternoon, but she did not dismount as she was in some haste to return to City Point. The weather is delightful now, not as hot as it has been and everybody feels more cheerful. General [Winfield Scott] Hancock comes frequently to see Colonel Beaver, and cheers him by saying, nearly every time, "Never mind the leg, Beaver. You'll be a brigadier general now." I took a ride in the country yesterday, and called at a farm house where they served watermelons and peaches in bountiful quantities, so that my appetite in the direction was appeased for the nonce ["for the time"].

Friday, September 2. We are still at the Burchard House which, taken altogether, is the best location for a hospital I have yet seen within all the Petersburg lines. It is near enough to the line of entrenchments to be within easy reach, and far enough away to be out of immediate danger. It is off the main thoroughfare sufficiently far to escape much of the dust, and the ground is well adapted to the proper arrangement of the hospital tents, and to ensure good drainage. The tents are pitched in the peach orchard adjoining the kitchen garden, which latter is well fenced—the only fence anywhere in sight. The family is entirely dependent upon the commissariat of the hospital for daily subsistence, and, in return, Mrs. Burchard gives me such unrestricted use of the house as I may demand. Thus far I have only asked for quarters for Colonel Beaver inside the house, who is occupying the back parlor, looking out upon the garden over a veranda.

I have built a fine brick bake oven near one of the out buildings, that supplies us with fresh bread, pies, and other luxuries. Colonel Beaver seems to be doing well, although I regard his case as still dangerous. Mr. McCallister, his law partner from Bellronte, Pennsylvania arrived late last night, and will remain with the colonel for a day or two. Miss Gilson is here taking care of him, and he seems more cheerful under her considerate and tender ministrations. The weather is now delightful, and the nights cool enough for one to sleep well. We hear that McClellan has been nominated for president by the Democrats at Chicago. It is to be regretted that so good a soldier should be so poor a politician—and that on the wrong side. Dr. Norris has returned from his twenty days leave, having visited Niagara Falls during his absence.

Monday, September 5. I have suffered from neuralgia in my face for a day or two, probably due to an imperfect tooth, which is the first illness I have had for more than a year. Dr. [J. W.] Wishart has extracted the offending tooth, and I have finally obtained relief. Today has been warmer than any day since September came in, the weather of late having been quite fall like in character. Colonel Beaver seems better today, and I have strong hopes of his recovery. Miss Gilson is still here rendering great service to the colonel, frequently entertaining him, and the rest of us I might say as well, with music, both vocal and instrumental, as she sings and plays beautifully. She is a niece of the Honorable Mr. Fay, of Chelsea, Massachusetts, who is a prominent member of the United States Sanitary Commission. Mr. Fay, himself, pays frequent visits to the hospital, and has made many friends among the patients as well as the staff, who all like him very much indeed. He comes up from City Point almost every day while his niece is with us, and takes the tenderest care of her in every way. Colonel Beaver gave me his photograph today, which I sent home at once, and it is now in my military album.

Last night, at midnight, General Grant ordered every gun bearing on the enemy's lines, to fire a shotted national salute [34 guns] in celebration of Sherman's capture of Atlanta. It was a magnificent spectacle, and had not continued long ere the enemy replied with considerable vigor, the fusillade lasting about two hours. A 15 inch mortar [shell landed] near the Appomattox on Butler's front, called "the swamp angel," was particularly noticeable for its share of the work. It can be loaded and fired but four times an hour, owing to the fact that it requires nearly 15 minutes to clean it after each discharge. The fuse, as it goes upward into the heavens, looks like a star, particularly while it poises for a moment, before seceding into the enemy's lines. The air seemed full of shells for a time, and it was a grand pyrotechnic display. Some of the shells burst in the vicinity of the hospital, but did no harm.

A cattle raid has been made in the vicinity of the hospital on the army herd, the whole of which, 2,500 head, was captured and driven off by the enemy, not more than 100 stragglers having been found in the woods afterward. I am told that the scheme was planned and executed by General Dearing, who knew every bridle path in this region where he courted his wife, having, no doubt, rambled over the country many times with her during the happy courtship. The cattle were herded about a mile in rear of the hospital, and when I heard the firing so distinctly as I did, and early in the morning too, I at first thought it something more serious. As it was, however, it simply turned out a clever piece of theft, which every one must concede. It temporarily embarrassed the army for beef, but this was overcome in a few days, while to the enemy it was of inestimable value just at this time, when the Rebel commissariat is at low tide.

Saturday, September 10. Burchard House. We have moved twice during the week, once away from here, and once back again. Colonel [Charles H.] Morgan, chief of staff, [2nd Corps] told Dr. [Alexander N.] Dougherty that the enemy was expected in our rear on the Prince George Road, and the doctor gave us an order on Tuesday the 6th, about 5 o'clock P.M., to move immediately. We obeyed the order promptly although it was in the midst of a driving rain, going out toward the front, where we had our hospital about 200 yards in rear of the line of battle of the 2nd Division for 48 hours. The scare passed over at the end of that time, and we are now back again as good as before.

I have been to City Point today where I ordered a bill of goods, through the medical purveyor, from Baltimore for the hospital, amounting to $1,200. This will give the patients canned fruits, oranges, lemons, and many other luxuries not furnished by the commissary department, which will be paid for out of the hospital fund. This fund accrues from the savings in the rations on the march and in an active campaign, when we cannot use all we are entitled to. Such as are not drawn each day are passed to the hospital as a cash credit, and against this fund we can draw for the purchase of whatever we need not furnished in the supply tables of the several departments, medical, commissary, or quartermasters.

I am beginning to make preparations to leave the service, though I shall not probably be mustered out until the 23rd. Lieutenant [Stephen R.] Snyder, Quarter Master 57th New York, will go at the same time. Dr. [Alexander N.] Dougherty is very anxious for me to say that I will come back after a month spent at home, and take charge of the hospital again, referring to the subject in some way almost every time I see him. Colonel [James A.] Beaver [is] improving day by day and I now have strong hopes of his recovery. Indeed, there is little doubt on the subject. Miss [Helen] Gilson had returned to City Point, and we were all sorry to lose her excellent services, as well as part with her cheerful company. I saw Lieutenant Bull yesterday, who informs me that he expects to go to Buffalo on recruiting service in a few days. So we shall probably meet there before long.

Wednesday, September 14. I have just been informed that I can be mustered out tomorrow if I desire, that being the termination of three years service in my case, the date of my commission being September 16, 1861. In case I accept discharge tomorrow I shall start for home next Monday, the 19th. I will take some time to settle my accounts with the government, and to transport my horses, so I shall be kept in Washington for a few days, and shall not reach home probably until the 25th, or thereabouts. The weather has been cooler again for a few days past, so much so that overcoats have been comfortable morning and evening. Miss [Helen] Gilson paid me a visit yesterday, remaining to dinner. Colonel [James A.] Beaver is continuing to improve and I am confident he will recover.

The Rebels began a furious cannonade on our front about two hours ago, that has not yet ceased though it seems to be dying down somewhat. Some of the shells burst over army headquarters, which are located a short distance to our front. Last evening Dr. [Thomas A.] McParlin, Medical Director of the Army, and Colonel [Thomas] Wilson, Chief Commissary Army of the Potomac, came over on foot and inspected the hospital, after which Colonel Wilson gave us some fine music on the piano in Mrs. Burchard's parlor.

MUSTERED OUT

Thursday, September 15, 1864. Today, being the completion of three years' service with the Army of the Potomac, and the end of the term for which I originally entered [the] service, I have been duly discharged the military service of the United Stated. I have transferred the hospital to Dr. James E. Pomfret, surgeon, 7th New York Heavy

Artillery, who receipts to me for all the property, and for which invoices are now being made out. Dr. Pomfret remained in charge until the following February, when he was succeeded by Dr. Charles S. Hoyt, surgeon, 39th New York, executive officer of the hospital. Dr. Hoyt held the position until the end of the war, and is at present secretary of the State Board of Charities.

From May 3rd, the date of the opening of the campaign, to September 19th, the day of my departure, the register of the hospital showed that we had treated 8,000 patients, of which number over 6,000 had been wounded.

It is safe to say, in concluding this narrative, and as a fitting final remark thereto, that no corps in the army had a greater aggregate of casualties than the 2nd, and that no hospital took better care of its wounded than the First Division hospital, Second Army Corps.

Appendix

After turning over the hospital to my successor, and bidding goodbye to my many friends, I left City Point, the place of embarkation, on the 19th day of September 1864, and arrived in Washington the next day. After some investigation I found it would take weeks, if not months to obtain settlement with the government, so I concluded to go home at once, making my final settlement later. I therefore started my horses in charge of my groom, and took a direct train for Buffalo, where I arrived September 23rd.

Remaining sometime in Lancaster for a rest, and [took] active interest in the presidential campaign then going on. After the election I went to Washington, in company with Dr. Hall, to make my final settlement with the government. It took us about a week to accomplish this. We returned together, and both remained at our respective homes for some weeks. Finally, in February 1865, Governor [Reuben] Fenton appointed me one of the surgeons of New York State troops, to reside in Washington and there look after their interest.

While I was engaged in this duty the war came to an abrupt end and I was in the capital during the stirring events of those final days of warfare, incident to the surrender of all the armies of the Confederacy and the mustering out of our own forces. When the news of Lee's surrender was received in Washington the departments immediately closed and the people thronged the streets, wild with excitement and, in some instances, overcome with emotion. At evening the buildings were illuminated, both public and private, the streets and avenues yet filled with the excited though orderly populace. Alas! In less than a week how changed was the scene.

On the night of April 14th, Good Friday, John Wilkes Booth shot President Lincoln in Ford's Theater, the great statesman and good man dying next morning, at 7 o'clock, in a house opposite the theater, whence he had been conveyed after the shooting. The funeral pageant commenced with the ceremonies in Washington on the 19th and continued until the cortege reached Springfield, Illinois, the final resting place appointed for the remains of the dead president, and lasting altogether about 10 days.

The next great event incident to the period was the Grand Review of the two great armies of the Republic, just prior to their discharge from the military service. This happened on [Tuesday and Wednesday] the 23rd and 24th days of May, [with] the Army of the Potomac marching in review [during] the first named day, and Sherman's western army [during] the second. The reviewing stand was erected in front of the White House, and upon it were congregated the President, cabinet, foreign ministers, and other distinguished citizens, both military and civil. The grand military pageant was witnessed by an immense gathering of citizens from all parts of the country, who welcomed back its defenders with a wild acclaim of joy.

The review ended. The troops were soon mustered out of service and quietly returned to the walks of civil life to resume their duties as citizens of the restored commonwealth. Vernal grasses and flowers had once more come to festoon the graves in battlefields over which the contending hosts of North and South had grappled for four years of deadly war.

There was peace.

ENDNOTES

CHAPTER ONE

1. Daniel Davidson Bidwell, age 42, enrolled on August 1, 1861, at Buffalo to serve three years. He mustered in as the colonel of the 49th New York Volunteers on October 21, 1861. He mustered out on August 18, 1864, at which time he was appointed brigadier general, commanding the 3rd Brigade, 2nd Division, VI. He was killed in action at Cedar Creek, Virginia on October 19, 1864.

   Frederick David Bidwell, comp., *History of the Forty-Ninth New York Volunteers* (Albany: J. B. Lyon Co., 1916), 178.

2. George Washington Johnson, age 39, enrolled on August 1, 1861, at Buffalo to serve three years. He mustered in as the major of the 49th New York on October 21, 1861. He became the lieutenant colonel on January 1, 1863, and was mortally wounded on July 12, 1864, at Fort Stevens, Washington, D.C. He died from his wound on July 29, 1864.

   Henry D. Tillinghast, age 30, enrolled on August 1, 1861, at Buffalo to serve three years. He mustered in as the regimental quartermaster of the 49th New York on October 21, 1861. He died of disease at Fort Monroe, Virginia during May 1862.

   William Bullymore, age 19, enrolled on August 1, 1861, at Buffalo to serve three years. He mustered in as the regimental adjutant (1st lieutenant) of the 49th New York on September 15, 1861, and died from disease during May 1862, at Fort Monroe, Virginia.

   Ibid., 184, 224, 280.

3. Charles H. Bidwell, age 20, enrolled on August 1, 1861, at Buffalo to serve three years with the 49th New York. He mustered in as the 2nd lieutenant of Company F on October 21, 1861, and was promoted to 1st lieutenant on October 22, 1861. He was discharged with a disability on June 21, 1862. He had served before this time as a sergeant in Company B, 21st New York Volunteers.

   Ibid., 178.

4. William F. Wheeler, age 26, enrolled on September 6, 1861, at Buffalo to serve three years with the 49th New York. He mustered in as the captain of Company D on October 21, 1861, and was dismissed from the service on October 4, 1862, for being absent without leave.
   Ibid., 288.

5. James A. Hall, age 46, enrolled on August 10, 1861, at Buffalo to serve three years with the 49th New York. He mustered in as the regimental surgeon on September 10, 1861, and mustered out on October 18, 1864, at Buffalo, New York. The doctor returned to Washington, D.C. to treat the wounded and the sick in the hospitals and died from a disease he contracted on April 8, 1865.
   Ibid., 212.

6. The 21st New York Volunteers was recruited largely from Buffalo and was called the First Buffalo Regiment.

7. William Clendenin Alberger, age 24, enrolled on September 18, 1861, in New York City to serve three years with the 49th New York. He mustered in as the lieutenant colonel on September 20, 1861. Wounded in action on September 17, 1861, at Antietam, Maryland, he was discharged for a disability on December 10, 1862. His father, Franklin A. Alberger, was the mayor of Buffalo.
   Bidwell, *49th N.Y.*, 169.

8. Charles H. Wilcox, age 42, enrolled on May 13, 1861, at Buffalo to serve two years. He mustered in as the surgeon of the 21st New York Volunteers on May 20, 1861, and died of disease on November 6, 1862, at Buffalo, New York.
   Frederick Phisterer, comp., *New York in the War of the Rebellion 1861–1865*, III, 3rd edition (Albany: J. B. Lyon, Co., 1912), 1981.

9. Chandler B. Chapman enrolled at Madison, Wisconsin on June 20, 1861, as the surgeon of the 6th Wisconsin Volunteers and was promoted to brigade surgeon, U.S. Volunteers on October 9, 1861. He resigned on March 24, 1862.
   Adjutant General's Office, *Roster of the Wisconsin Volunteers*, I (Madison: Democratic Printing Co., 1886), 494.

10. A studious check of the roster of the 72nd Pennsylvania did not turn up those casualties. If it did happen, as asserted by the men who were there, the casualties were never reported.

11. Russell, who was sent to the United States expressly to cover the war for his English paper was not allowed to accompany the Federal army on the Peninsula Campaign of 1862. He returned to England shortly thereafter.
    Stewart Sifakis, *Who Was Who in the Civil War* (New York: Oxford University Press, 1988), 563.

12. John Foster, (Company A), Letter to the Fredonia *Censor*, October 23, 1861.

13. Raselas Dickinson, age 52, enrolled on August 6, 1861, at Forestville to serve three years with the 49th New York. He mustered in as the captain of Company I on August 28, 1861. He died from a paralytic stroke on October 12, 1861, at the Union Hospital, Georgetown, D.C.
    Bidwell, *49th N.Y.*, 196.

    Dickinson collapsed with a stroke on October 10, 1861, while on picket duty. The *Censor* published a letter from Dr. James A. Hall, Surgeon, 49th New York and nurse John N. Henry, Company I, on October 30.
    Buffalo *Morning Express*, October 16, 1861. Fredonia *Censor*, October 30, 1861.

14. Buffalo *Morning Express,* October 28, 1861.

15. Ayres, like his colleague, Charles Griffin, made the army a career. Like Griffin, he also saw service during the Mexican War. He was William F. Smith's chief of artillery.
    Sifakis, *Who Was Who,* 23-24.

16. Stevens left the 2nd Brigade, W. F. Smith's Division on October 26, 1861, to assume command of the 2nd Brigade, South Carolina Expeditionary Corps.
    Ibid., 622.

    Robert F. Taylor, former captain in the 13th New York mustered in as the colonel of the 33rd New York on May 2, 1861. He mustered out with his regiment on June 6, 1863, at Geneva, New York. He later saw service with the 1st New York Veteran Cavalry.
    Phisterer, *N.Y. in the War,* III, 2125.

17. Charles Griffin, a professional Regular Army officer, commanded a company of the 5th U.S. Artillery at Henry House Hill in 1861, at the battle of the First Manassas. His flaring temper had earned him some renown by this stage of the war.
    Sifakis, *Who Was Who,* 268-269.

18. Jeremiah P. Washburn, age 32, enrolled on May 9, 1861, at Buffalo to serve two years. He mustered in as the captain of Company C, 21st New York Volunteers on May 20, 1861, and was killed in action at Second Manassas on August 30, 1862.
    Allen M. Adams, age 28, enrolled on May 17, 1861, at Buffalo to serve two years. He mustered in as the first lieutenant of Company C , 21st New York Volunteers on May 20, 1861. He became the captain of Company E on March 1, 1862. He was wounded in action at Fredericksburg on December 15, 1862, and was mustered out with his company on May 18, 1863, at Buffalo, New York.
    Adjutant General's Office, *Annual Report of the Adjutant General of the State of New York for the Year 1900,* vol. 20 (Albany: James B. Lyon, State Printer, 1901), 175 and 301.
    Hereafter cited as NYSAG.

19. The Soldiers' Rest had a terrible reputation for serving food which even the soldiers complained about.

20. Harrison G. Parker, age 44, enlisted on October 11, 1861, at Sheldon and mustered in as a private in Company G, 9th New York Cavalry on the same day to serve three years. He became the battalion quartermaster sergeant on November 8, 1861, and mustered out at Washington, D.C. on September 29, 1862.
    Erastus H. Wilder, age 22, enlisted on September 20, 1861, at Warsaw to serve three years. He mustered in as a private in Company A, 9th New York Cavalry on October 5, 1861, and became a corporal on October 9, 1861. He was promoted to sergeant on July 1, 1862, and became the regimental quartermaster sergeant on December 15, 1862. He reenlisted on December 20, 1863, and was mustered in as a first lieutenant and regimental quartermaster on May 1, 1864. He was captured in action on October 23, 1864, and was discharged for a disability on May 24, 1865.
    NYSAG, 3:246, 350.

21. The two men were never identified by Potter or the regimental historian.

22. August Schweckendick, age 26, enlisted on August 31, 1861, at Buffalo to serve three years with the 49th New York. He mustered in as a private in

Company B on September 2, 1861, and died from typhoid fever on December 7, 1861, at Camp Griffin, Virginia.

Bidwell, *49th N.Y.*, 266.

23. This sketch did not appear in the memoirs.

24. Sydney L. Herrick became a surgeon of U.S. Volunteers on September 4, 1861. He resigned on August 17, 1862, and died on November 22, 1875.

Francis P. Heitman, *Historical Register and Dictionary of the United States Army,* I (Washington, D.C.: U.S. Government Printing Office, 1903), 526.

25. Marcus Carson, age 29, enrolled on October 1, 1861, at North Java to serve three years and mustered in as the first lieutenant of Company G, 9th New York Cavalry on October 11, 1861. He mustered out on May 15, 1862, by the order of the Secretary of War.

NYSAG, III, 57.

26. Doctor Adams remains unidentified.

CHAPTER TWO

1. Reuben E. Heacock, age 40, enrolled at Buffalo to serve three years with the 49th New York on July 30, 1861. He mustered in as the captain of Company E on August 28, 1861, and was killed in action at Spotsylvania Court House, Virginia on May 18, 1864.

Bidwell, *49th N.Y.*, 215.

2. James B. McKean, age 40, enrolled on October 14, 1861, at Saratoga Springs to serve three years. He mustered in as the colonel of the 77th New York on November 23, 1861. He was discharged with a disability on July 27, 1863.

Phisterer, *N.Y. in the War*, IV, 2824.

3. After a great deal of discussion the eight students and I agreed to leave the tense in the memoirs alone. We felt that it would be too time consuming and that it would change the doctor's style too much to alter it.

4. Sylvanus S. Mulford, age 31, enrolled at Elmira to serve two years and was mustered in as the assistant surgeon of the 33rd New York on May 22, 1861. He was promoted to regimental surgeon on August 22, 1861, and resigned on November 25, 1862, to accept an appointment to Assistant Surgeon of U.S. Volunteers.

Phisterer, *N.Y. in the War*, II, 2117.

5. Lewis died outright. Hehr was shot in the face just below the right eye. The surgeons probed four inches into the wound but could not find the ball. They pronounced the wound mortal. Hehr was up and about, walking, eating, and talking by April 11, 1862.

Henry D. Tillinghast, "From the 49th," Buffalo *Morning Express*, April 28, 1862.

Christian Hehr, age 23, enlisted at Buffalo to serve three years with the 49th New York on August 6, 1861. He was mustered in as a private in Company B on August 22, 1861, and was discharged on September 6, 1862.

Milton Lewis, age 22, enlisted on August 26, 1861, at Jamestown to serve three years with the 49th New York. He mustered in as a private in Company K on September 18, 1861, and was killed in action on April 5, 1862, at Lee's Mills, Virginia. He was the first man from Chautauqua County, New York to die during the Civil War.

Bidwell, *49th N.Y.*, 215, 234.

6. Frank Ward, Company D, shot in the leg below the knee, leg shattered; Jerome Spaulding, Company H, flesh wound above the knee; Joseph Weiler, Company F, accidentally shot himself in the foot; Corporal Horace H. Hays, Company D, very slightly wounded in the foot; Walter A. Beach, Company D, accidentally shot two fingers off his right hand.

   Henry D. Tillinghast, "From the 49th," Buffalo *Morning Express*, April 28, 1862.

   Frank Ward, age 19, enlisted on August 9, 1861, at Buffalo to serve three years with the 49th New York. He mustered in as a private in Company D on August 22, 1861, and was wounded in action on April 6, 1862, at Lee's Mills, Virginia (the official report cited April 5). He transferred into the 16th Battalion of the Veteran Reserve Corps some time later.

   Jerome Spaulding, age 22, enlisted on September 7, 1861, at Medina to serve three years with the 49th New York and mustered in as a private in Company H on September 13, 1861. He was wounded on April 6, 1862, at Lee's Mills, Virginia (the official report cited April 5). He was discharged for his wound on October 11, 1862, and later served in Company H, 8th New York Artillery.

   Joseph Weiler, age 35, enlisted at Buffalo to serve three years with the 49th New York and was mustered in as a private in Company F on January 30, 1862. He was discharged with a disability on July 14, 1862, at Philadelphia, Pennsylvania.

   Horace H. Hays, age 21, enlisted on August 15, 1861, at Buffalo to serve three years with the 49th New York. He mustered in as a corporal in Company D on August 22, 1861, and transferred to the Veteran Reserve Corps on September 1, 1863.

   Walter A. Beach, age 21, enlisted on August 12, 1861, at Buffalo to serve three years with the 49th New York. He mustered in as a private in Company E on August 28, 1861, and was discharged with a disability on October 4, 1862, at Bakersville, Maryland.

   Bidwell, *49th N.Y.*, 176, 215, 273–274, 286, 287.

7. Charles H. Hickmott, age 24, enrolled on August 1, 1861, at Buffalo to serve three years with the 49th New York. He mustered in as the 2nd lieutenant in Company F on August 22, 1861, and became the captain of the company on October 17, 1862. He died in action at the Wilderness, Virginia on May 6, 1864.

   Ibid., 217.

8. William P. Russell enrolled and mustered in at Middlebury, Vermont on August 15, 1861, as the surgeon of the 5th Vermont Infantry. Wounded and taken prisoner on June 26, 1862, he was paroled on July 17, 1862. He was discharged from the service on October 11, 1862.

   Theodore S. Peck, comp., *Revised Roster of Vermont Volunteers And List of Vermonters Who Served in the Army and Navy of the U. S. 1861–66* (Montpelier: Watchmen Publishing Co., 1892), 195.

9. William McLean received the rank of 2nd lieutenant in the 2nd U.S. Cavalry on March 27, 1861. He became a 1st lieutenant on May 9, 1861. He transferred to the 5th U.S. Cavalry on August 3, 1861. He was promoted to captain on July 17, 1862, and died on April 13, 1863, from the effects of his war service.

   Heitman, *Historical Register*, I, 625.

10. Sprague served as governor of Rhode Island from 1860–1861.

11. Charles O. Shepard, Jr., age 21, enrolled at Washington, D.C. to serve three years and was mustered in as the 2nd lieutenant of Company B, 82nd New

York on March 1, 1861. He was wounded in action on June 8, 1862, and was mustered in as the 1st lieutenant on July 1, 1862. He was discharged on November 24, 1862.

    NYSAG, 30:456.

12. According to Sergeant John Foster (Company A, 49th New York), the Confederates employed black cavalry against the Federal cavalry. "...Together we all moved forward. Soon the report of artillery was heard in the advance. A regular battery of artillery and quite a numerous body of cavalry, unsupported by infantry, had incautiously advanced too far, and ere they thought of it were pounced upon by a body of infantry, and a force of negro cavalry, followed by a squadron of white cavalry....The negro cavalry, when making their charge, were shouted to by their white allies, 'give no quarter! give no quarter to the damned Yankees.' The negroes are said to have fought better and more desperately than their masters, thereby proving they could be as mean and more valorous than they."

    John Foster, Letter, May 6, 1862, to the *Fredonia Censor*, May 21, 1862.

13. John C. Badham was appointed major of the 5th North Carolina on May 26, 1861. On March 6, 1862, he became the regiment's lieutenant colonel. He was killed in action on May 5, 1862, at Williamsburg, Virginia.

    Weymouth T. Jordan, comp., *North Carolina Troops, 1861-1865*, vol. 4 (1973), 127.

CHAPTER THREE

1. Sanford B. Hunt, age 36, enrolled on August 9, 1862, at Buffalo to serve three years and was mustered in as the surgeon of the 9th New York Cavalry on August 11, 1862. He was discharged on March 31, 1863, for having accepted an appointment as a surgeon in the U.S. Volunteers.

    NYSAG, 34:409.

2. Edward P. Chapin, age 30, enrolled on August 8, 1861, at Buffalo to serve three years and was mustered in as the captain of Company A, 44th New York on August 30, 1861. He was promoted to major on January 2, 1862, and was wounded in action on May 7, 1862, at Hanover Court House, Virginia. He was discharged on July 4, 1862, to accept the colonelcy of the 116th New York.

    Phisterer, *N.Y. in the War*, III, 2296.

3. Orville S. "Tom" Dewey, who was transferred from the 21st New York as a 1st sergeant, mustered in as the 2nd lieutenant of Company A, 49th New York on April 14, 1862, and was discharged on November 26, 1862.

    Thomas Cluney, age 24, enrolled on August 1, 1861, at Fredonia to serve three years with the 49th New York. He mustered in as the 2nd lieutenant of Company A on August 24, 1861, and became the 1st lieutenant on November 2, 1861. He was promoted to captain on April 14, 1862, and was discharged with a disability on May 2, 1864. The disability was removed on March 3, 1865. He mustered out with the regiment on June 27, 1865.

    Bidwell, *49th N.Y.*, 189 and 196.

4. Dr. Gaines was the owner of the Gaines' plantation and Gaines' Mill.

5. Ernst Von Vegesack, age 41, transferred from General Daniel Butterfield's staff and was mustered in as the colonel of the 20th New York on July 19, 1862. He mustered out as an aide de camp at New York City on June 1,

1863. Max Weber became a brigadier general of volunteers and commanded a brigade in the Second Corps at Antietam.

NYSAG, 20:159.

6. The 20th New York, "United Turner Regiment," was a thoroughly drilled regiment which early in its career set a record for not behaving very well under fire. At Antietam, contrary to its previous engagements and several which followed, it did not run while under fire.

7. Charles C. Wheeler, age 26, enrolled on September 8, 1861, at Bath to serve three years with Company E, 1st New York Artillery and mustered in as the 1st lieutenant. He mustered in as captain on January 23, 1862, and was discharged on January 22, 1863.

NYSAG, 8:450.

8. Juan Prim, born in 1814, supported Queen Isabella II in Morocco and in Mexico. He was assassinated in 1870.

[From notes by Benedict Maryniak, Buffalo Civil War Round Table.]

9. Davidson was a former cavalry officer now commanding infantry, a fine point which was not lost upon his "beetle crunchers." The men also thought he was a martinet.

For further comments about Davidson refer to Thomas Hyde, *Following the Greek Cross* (Boston: Houghton Mifflin, 1894).

10. Jeremiah Clinton Drake, age 37, enrolled on August 1, 1861, at Westfield to serve three years with the 49th New York and mustered in as the captain of Company G on August 30, 1861. He mustered out on August 14, 1862, to accept promotion to the colonelcy of the 112th New York. He was mortally wounded at Cold Harbor, Virginia in June 1864.

Bidwell, *49th N.Y.*, 197.

11. The people of Buffalo simply forgot to make a flag for the regiment, a fact which escaped notice until the Buffalo *Morning Express* responded to a letter from the regiment. In the paper's April 23, 1862, edition the editors issued the challenge, "The 49th must have a flag! Who'll be the first in making it ready?"

The following ladies of Buffalo hand stitched a silk regimental flag for the regiment: Mrs. Abbey P. Heacock (mother of Captain Reuben Heacock, Company E), Mrs. Jane Harvey Bidwell (mother of Colonel D. D. Bidwell), Mrs. Esther P. Fox, Mrs. Parnell St. John Sidway, Mrs. Katherine C. Warner, Mrs. Sarah M. Davidson, Mrs. Beulah G. Smith, Mrs. William Hodge, Miss Sarah Hodge, Mrs. Walter M. Stannard, Mrs. Louisa C. Weed, Mrs. Orlando Allen, Mrs. Sarah M. Judson, Mrs. Sophia Pratt, Mrs. Fannie A. Lay, Mrs. Sarah T. Coburn, Mrs. Sarah D. Gilbert, Mrs. Mary P. Burt, and Mrs. Miles Jones. In response, an officer in the regiment wrote a letter describing the presentation to the *Morning Express.*

"Shall the Gallant 49th Be Without a Flag?", Buffalo *Morning Express,* April 23, 1862. "The 49th Regiment—Its New Flag," Buffalo *Morning Express,* June 26, 1862. Bidwell, *49th N.Y.*, 155.

12. A "Tiger" was a loud, rolling growl of approval.

"The 49th Regiment—Its New Flag," Buffalo *Morning Express,* June 26, 1862.

13. On June 13, Jeb Stuart's Confederate cavalry, while making the last leg of its ride around McClellan's army struck two squadrons of the 5th U.S. Cavalry, destroyed 2 forage schooners and a few wagons, then attacked Tunstall's Station. Stuart, who enjoyed his cavalier image, repeated the same "ride" at Gettysburg in 1863, with less "glorious" results.

Stephen W. Sears, ed., *The Civil War Papers of George B. McClellan, Selected Correspondence, 1860-1865* (New York: Ticknor & Fields, 1989), 298.

14. More than likely the men in the 49th New York read about McLean's arrival in the New York *Tribune* which often reported such information quite accurately for the Federal army.

15. Stephen Morris DeFort, age 44, enlisted in Buffalo to serve three years with the 49th New York on August 31, 1861. He mustered in as a private in Company D on September 2, 1861, and was discharged with a disability on August 29, 1863, at Washington, D.C. It was common practice to use enlisted men as orderlies or officers' servants.
    Bidwell, *49th N.Y.*, 195.

16. Edwin Sumner was known as "Bull" or "Bull Head" because he had stopped a spent Mexican musket ball during the Mexican War with his skull and suffered no injury.

17. This is a reference to McClellan's supply base on the James River at White House Landing, Virginia.

18. The other regiment was the 33rd New York.

19. James Kris, age 18, enlisted at Buffalo to serve for three years with the 49th New York and was mustered in as a private in Company F on March 8, 1862. He was killed in action on June 27, 1862. The regiment lost only one man to combat that day. There were at least two others wounded. They were Richard Kigar (Company I) and Felix Viskniskki (Company A).
    Bidwell, *49th N.Y.*, 228, 230, and 284.

    Private Viskniskki's great-granddaughter, Mrs. Benson, related the story of Felix's wounding.

    See Thomas Hyde, *Following the Greek Cross* (Boston: Houghton Mifflin) for a description of this incident.

20. Lucius M. Lamar enrolled as a captain in the 8th Georgia on April 15, 1861. He was elected the major on September 12, 1861. He became the lieutenant colonel on December 24, 1861, and then was elected colonel on January 28, 1862. He was severely wounded and captured on June 28, 1862. He resigned his commission in December 1862, and was appointed colonel of the 18th Georgia Infantry from which he was granted a leave of absence until June 7, 1864.
    Lillian Henderson, comp., *Roster of Confederate Soldiers of Georgia (1861-1865)*, vol. 1 (Hapeville, Ga.: Longino and Porter, Inc., 1955-1958), 934.

21. Theodore B. Hamilton, age 24, enrolled at Elmira, New York to serve two years on May 22, 1861. He mustered in on the same day as the captain of Company G, 33rd New York. He was discharged on December 12, 1862, to accept promotion to the lieutenant colonelcy of the 62nd New York.
    Phisterer, *N.Y. in the War*, III, 2122.

22. Thaddeus P. Mott, age 32, enrolled on May 21, 1861, at New York City for 3 years and mustered in as the captain of Company D, 82nd Infantry. On June 17, 1861, he became a captain in the 19th U.S. Infantry. On October 29, 1861, he was ordered to the 3rd Independent Battery, New York Light Artillery with which he served until July 2, 1862. On February 26, 1863, he enrolled at Albany in the 14th New York Cavalry to serve 3 years. He mustered in as the lieutenant colonel on the same day, and was promoted

to colonel on July 10, 1863. He was honorably discharged on January 18, 1864.

Phisterer, *N.Y. in the War*, II, 1568. Ibid., IV:420.

23. William J. Sawin (Chicopee Falls, Mass.) enlisted December 18, 1861, and mustered in as a private in the 10th Massachusetts Infantry on December 27, 1861. He transferred to Company E, 3rd Vermont Infantry (no date). He was promoted to assistant surgeon, 2nd Vermont on June 21, 1862. He was wounded in action and captured on June 29, 1862. The Confederates paroled him on July 22, 1862. He mustered out on June 29, 1864.

Peck, *Vt. Vols.*, 31.

24. Note. See transactions of the Med. Soc. S.N.Y. for 1863, p. 128, et seq. for Swinburne's report of this hospital. [This is Dr. Potter's notation.]

25. Jacob Bowman Sweitzer was the major of the 62nd Pennsylvania as of July 4, 1861, until he became the lieutenant colonel of the regiment in November 1861. He was promoted to colonel on June 27, 1862, and eventually (March 13, 1865), he received a brevet brigadier generalship for gallantry and meritorious service during the war. He mustered out on July 13, 1864, from the volunteer service November 9, 1888.

Heitman, *Historical Register*, I, 940.

The cartel mentioned by Potter refers to the prisoner exchange program established by McClellan.

26. H. B. Clitz graduated from West Point on July 1, 1841, number 36 in his class. He served as a brevet second lieutenant with the 7th U.S. Infantry from July 1, 1845, until September 21, 1846, when he transferred to the 3rd U.S. Infantry, with which he stayed until May 14, 1861. He was promoted from captain to major of the 12th U.S. Infantry on that day. He became the lieutenant colonel of the 6th U.S. Infantry on November 4, 1863. He was promoted to colonel of the 10th U.S. Infantry on February 22, 1869. He retired on July 1, 1885.

He was breveted first lieutenant on April 18, 1847, for gallantry and meritorious conduct in battle at Cerro Gordo, Mexico. He was promoted lieutenant colonel on June 27, 1862, for gallantry in battle at Gaines' Mill, Virginia. He was promoted to colonel and brigadier general for meritorious service during the war. He is supposed to have drowned on October 30, 1888.

William Parham Chambliss served in the Mexican War from May 23, 1846, through March 23, 1847, with the 1st Tennessee Mounted Volunteers. He then served as a captain in the 3rd Tennessee Infantry from October 7, 1847, through July 24, 1848. He joined the 2nd U.S. Cavalry on March 7, 1855, as a first lieutenant. He rose to the rank of captain on April 6, 1861. He transferred as a captain to the 5th U.S. Cavalry on August 3, 1861, and remained with that regiment until he was promoted to the rank of major with the 4th U.S. Cavalry on March 30, 1864. He was promoted to brevet major on May 4, 1862, for gallantry and meritorious service in action at Warwick Creek, Virginia. He was promoted to brevet colonel on June 28, 1862, for gallantry in action at Gaines' Mill, Virginia. He died on February 22, 1887.

Heitman, *Historical Register*, I, 294, 311.

27. Erasmus W. Haines, age 36, enrolled on August 1, 1861, at Buffalo to serve three years with the 49th New York. He mustered in as the captain of Company F on October 21, 1861, and was discharged on October 16, 1862.

William S. Bull, age 20, enrolled at Buffalo to serve three years with the 49th New York. He mustered in as 2nd lieutenant of Company E on

March 25, 1862. He was mustered as 1st lieutenant and adjutant on October 4, 1862. He was discharged on April 8, 1863.

James A. Boyde, age 25, enrolled on September 16, 1861, at Buffalo to serve three years with the 49th New York. He mustered in as 2nd lieutenant of Company I on October 21, 1861. He mustered in as quartermaster on June 23, 1862. He mustered out on October 18, 1864, at Buffalo.

Bidwell, *49th N.Y.*, 181, 184, 211.

CHAPTER FOUR

1. John A. Jenkins, age 25, enrolled on August 22, 1862, at Washington, D.C. to serve three years with the 49th New York. He mustered in as an assistant surgeon on September 4, 1862. He mustered in as the surgeon on October 19, 1864. He mustered out with his regiment on June 27, 1865, at Washington, D.C.

   Bidwell, *49th N.Y.*, 224.

2. William James Hamilton White, major, surgeon, U.S. Army, April 16, 1862, was killed in action on September 17, 1862, at Antietam.

   Heitman, *Historical Register*, II, 1029.

3. Francis L. Vinton, former captain with the 16th U.S. Infantry, was appointed colonel of the 43rd New York Volunteers on August 3, 1861. He was mustered in as colonel on September 21, 1861. He was discharged September 19, 1862, to accept promotion to brigadier general, U.S. Volunteers.

   Phisterer, *N.Y. in the War*, III, 2288.

4. Martin R. Clark, age 30, enrolled on May 9, 1861, at Buffalo to serve two years with the 21st New York Volunteers. He was mustered in as the 1st sergeant of Company G on May 20, 1861. He was promoted to the 2nd lieutenant on February 17, 1863. He was discharged on March 2, 1863.

   NYSAG, 20:196.

5. Alger M. Wheeler, age 20, enrolled at Buffalo to serve two years with the 21st New York Volunteers and mustered in as the 1st lieutenant of Company B on May 10, 1861. He was promoted to captain on August 9, 1862, and was wounded in action on August 30, 1862, at Bull Run, Virginia. He mustered out with his company on May 18, 1863, at Buffalo, New York.

   He enrolled June 4, 1863, at Buffalo to serve three years with the 33rd Battery, New York Artillery, and he mustered in as the captain on September 4, 1863. He mustered out with the battery on June 25, 1865, at Petersburg, Virginia with the rank of brevet major, New York Volunteers.

   Phisterer, *N.Y. in the War*, III:1981 and II:1630.

6. William T. Bliss, age 32, enrolled at Buffalo to serve three years with the 49th New York. He mustered in as a private in Company E on August 28, 1861, and was promoted to sergeant later on. He mustered in as the 2nd lieutenant of Company F on October 9, 1862. He was dismissed on June 16, 1863.

   Bidwell, *49th N.Y.*, 179.

7. George W. Gilman, age 36, enrolled on July 30, 1861, at Buffalo to serve three years with the 49th New York. He mustered in as the 1st lieutenant of Company E on August 28, 1861. He was discharged with a disability on May 18, 1863.

   Ibid., 68.

8. Fred C. Barger, age 19, enrolled on August 8, 1861, at Westfield to serve three years with the 49th New York. He mustered in as a sergeant of Com-

pany G on August 30, 1861, and was promoted to 2nd lieutenant on April 29, 1862. He mustered in as the 1st lieutenant on September 2, 1862. He lost his right hand to a shell fragment at Fredericksburg, Virginia on December 13, 1862. He was discharged with a disability by order of Secretary of War on May 11, 1864. President Abraham Lincoln personally appointed him U.S. Postmaster of Westfield New York.

Ibid., 27, 135, 173.

9. Edwin Amsden, age 36, enrolled at Portage, New York to serve three years and mustered in as the assistant surgeon of the 136th New York on September 1, 1862. He became the surgeon on December 17, 1864. He mustered out with the regiment on June 13, 1865.

John Boyd, Jr., age 39, enlisted on September 6, 1862, at Bennington, New York to serve three years with the 136th New York. He mustered in as a corporal in Company H on September 25, 1862. He was promoted to sergeant on March 1, 1863, and was wounded in action sometime that year. He was discharged for his wounds on December 3, 1863.

John McCray, age 27, enlisted on August 13, 1862, at Orangeville, New York to serve three years with the 136th New York. He mustered in as a corporal in Company H on September 25, 1862. He was discharged for paralysis on January 16, 1864, at Lookout Valley, Tennessee.

Gad C. Parker, age 36, enrolled on September 6, 1862, at Sheldon, New York to serve three years with the 136th New York. He mustered in as a sergeant in Company H on September 25, 1862. He was promoted to 1st sergeant on March 1, 1863, and later he became the 2nd lieutenant on August 28, 1863. He was promoted to 1st lieutenant of Company E on May 10, 1863. He mustered out on June 13, 1865, at Washington, D.C.

NYSAG, 27: 752, 761, 825, 838.

10. Bleecker L. Hovey, age 44, enrolled on August 19, 1862, at Albany, New York to serve three years with the 136th New York. He mustered in as the surgeon on September 1, 1862. He mustered out on October 19, 1864, to accept an appointment as an assistant surgeon with the U.S. Volunteers.

Ibid., 807.

Cʜᴀᴘᴛᴇʀ Fɪᴠᴇ

1. Theodore F. Hall, age 18, enlisted on August 22, 1862, at Portland, New York to serve three years with the 154th New York. He mustered in as a private in Company E on September 24, 1862, and died of disease on January 26, 1863, in a hospital in Washington, D.C.

NYSAG, 39:1146.

2. William Ellis, age 21, enrolled on July 30, 1861, at Buffalo to serve three years with the 49th New York. He mustered in as 2nd lieutenant of Company E on August 28, 1861, and was promoted to captain on January 25, 1862. He mustered in as major on December 11, 1862. He was wounded in action on May 12, 1864, at Spotsylvania Court House. He died of his wounds on August 3, 1864, in camp at Monocacy Creek, Maryland.

Bidwell, *49th N.Y.,* 199.

3. Samuel K. Zook was enrolled and authorized as the colonel to recruit the National Guard Rifles or Voltigeurs, no date, at New York City. He was mustered in as the colonel of the 57th New York on October 19, 1861. He was discharged on April 23, 1863, to accept appointment as brigadier general to U.S. Volunteers. He started the war as the lieutenant colonel of the 6th New York State Militia.

Phisterer, *N.Y. in the War,* III, 2502.

4. Alfred (Alford) B. Chapman, age 26, enrolled on April 17, 1861, at New York City to serve one month. He mustered in as private of Company D, 7th New York State on April 26, 1861. He mustered out with company on June 3, 1861, at New York City. He enrolled again on August 20, 1861, at New York City to serve three years. He mustered in as the captain Company A, 57th New York on October 19, 1861. He was promoted to major on February 3, 1862. He was promoted to lieutenant colonel on September 17, 1862. He was wounded in action on December 13, 1862, at Fredericksburg, Virginia. He was killed in action on May 5, 1864, at Wilderness, Virginia.
   Ibid., 2495.

5. Henry C. Dean, age 23, enrolled February 20, 1862, at Rochester to serve an unexpired term of duty. He mustered in as assistant surgeon with the 57th New York on February 24, 1862. He was discharged on April 9, 1863, for a promotion to surgeon of the 140th New York Infantry.
   Ibid., 2496.

6. Nelson Neely, age 28, enrolled in Albany to serve three years to serve with the 57th New York. He mustered in as assistant surgeon on August 25, 1862. He was discharged for disability on June 29, 1864.
   Ibid., 2499.

7. John S. Hammell, age 21, enrolled September 6, 1861, at New York City to serve three years with the 66th New York. He mustered in as 1st lieutenant of Company I and was promoted to adjutant on November 4, 1861. He was made captain of Company B on April 15, 1862. He was wounded in action on December 13, 1862, at Fredericksburg, Virginia. He was mustered in as lieutenant colonel on January 11, 1863. Captured in action on June 17, 1864, at Petersburg, Virginia, he was paroled on November 30, 1864, at Savannah, Georgia. He was mustered out with regiment on August 30, 1865, at New York City.
   Albert Van Der Veer, age 21, enrolled at Washington, D.C. to serve three years with the 66th New York. He mustered in as assistant surgeon on January 3, 1863, and as surgeon on July 29, 1864. He mustered out with the regiment on August 30, 1865, at New York City.
   James G. Derrickson, age 21, enrolled on November 7, 1861, at New York City to serve three years and mustered in as the second lieutenant of Company D of the 66th New York on November 12, 1861. He was appointed first lieutenant and adjutant on August 18, 1862. He mustered in as the captain of Company D on January 1, 1863. On March 8, 1863, he transferred to Company C. Captured in Action on June 22, 1864, at Petersburg, Virginia, he was paroled in March 1865 and mustered out on May 15, 1865.
   Charles S. Wood, age 36, enrolled at Alexandria, Virginia and was appointed to serve for three years as the assistant surgeon of the 66th New York on March 8, 1862. He was mustered in on January 16, 1863, as the surgeon. He mustered out on September 22, 1863, to accept an appointment as a surgeon for the U.S. Volunteers.
   NYSAG, 27:803, 901, 914.

8. Augustus M. Wright, age 25, enrolled on July 24, 1861, at New York City to serve three years with the 57th New York. He mustered in as the first sergeant of Company F on August 12, 1861. He was promoted to second lieutenant on August 15, 1861, and to captain on October 21, 1862. He transferred to Company A on June 30, 1863. He was wounded in action on

June 16, 1864, at Petersburg, Virginia and died of those wounds on July 3, 1864, with rank of lieutenant colonel.

Orlando F. Middleton, age 22, enrolled on September 13, 1861, at New York City to serve three years with the 57th New York. He mustered in as first sergeant of Company D on September 24, 1861, and as first lieutenant on June 1, 1862. He became the captain on September 23, 1863, and mustered out on November 11, 1864.

Ibid., 26:89, 144.

9. Daniel Post appears to have been a visiting civilian. He was not on the roster of the 136th New York.

Levi R. Vincent was commissioned first lieutenant and quartermaster of the 136th New York on January 28, 1863, but was declined. He never served with the regiment.

James Wood, Jr., age 42, enrolled on August 26, 1862, at Genesee Falls, New York to serve three years with the 136th New York. He mustered in as the colonel on September 18, 1862, and mustered out at Washington, D.C. on June 13, 1865.

Ibid., 27:838, 867.

10. Henry Van Aernam, age 45, enrolled at Jamestown to serve three years with the 154th New York and mustered in as the surgeon on August 20, 1862. He was discharged on November 5, 1864.

Phisterer, *N.Y. in the War*, V, 3803.

Dwight W. Day, age 24, enrolled at Jamestown to serve three years with the 154th New York and was mustered in as the assistant surgeon on September 26, 1862. He was promoted to surgeon on November 23, 1864, and he mustered out with the regiment on June 11, 1865, near Bladensburg, Maryland.

NYSAG, 39:1128.

11. Patrick Corbley, age 34, enlisted at New York City to serve three years as a private in Company F of the 57th New York on August 23, 1861. He transferred to Company G on August 11, 1864, and mustered out on August 24, 1864, near Petersburg, Virginia. His name also appears as Corblary.

Ibid., 26:26.

12. Potter recorded the name as Captain DeHart of the 7th New Jersey. He was mistaken. The man he referred to was Captain Daniel Hart.

Daniel Hart enrolled in Company E, 7th New Jersey Volunteers to serve three years on September 18, 1861. He mustered in as the 2nd lieutenant of Company E on the same day. He was promoted to 1st lieutenant on May 27, 1862, and to captain on January 13, 1863. He transferred to Company C by March 1863. Promoted to major on February 23, 1865, he was promoted to lieutenant colonel on April 1, 1865, and mustered out on July 17, 1865.

Stryker, William S., *Record of Officers and Men of New Jersey in the Civil War, 1861–1865*, vol. 1 (Trenton: John L. Murphy, 1876), 300, 317, 328.

13. William McLean, Captain, Company H, 5th U.S. Cavalry.

On June 13, 1862, at Hanover, Virginia, Captain McLean received 2 or 3 saber cuts on the posterior portion of his scalp and was taken prisoner. After spending a few weeks in Libby Prison, Richmond, he was paroled. He died from inflammation of the brain on April 13, 1863.

The Medical and Surgical History of the Civil War, vol. 8 (Wilmington, N.C.: Broadfoot Publishing Co., 1991), 10.

14. Nelson Miles, age 23, enrolled in the 61st New York to serve three years and was mustered in as the lieutenant colonel on May 31, 1862. He was promoted to colonel on September 30, 1862. He was wounded in action on December 13, 1862, at Fredericksburg, Virginia. He was wounded again on May 2, 1863, at Chancellorsville, Virginia. He was discharged on June 26, 1864, for promotion to brigadier general of volunteers.

    NYSAG, 26:1000. Charles A. Fuller, *Personal Recollections of the War of 1861*, (Hamilton, N.Y.: Edmonston Publishing, 1990), 81.

    George S. Joyce, age 18, enrolled on September 2, 1861, at Hamilton to serve three years with the 61st New York. He mustered in as a private in Company C on September 6, 1861. He was promoted to first sergeant of Company F on July 20, 1862, and was reduced to sergeant in January 1863. He transferred to Company C on March 4, 1864, and was wounded in action at Reams' Station, Virginia on August 25, 1864. He mustered in as the second lieutenant of Company D on November 17, 1864. He transferred to Company B as the first lieutenant on December 29, 1864, and mustered out with the company on July 14, 1865, near Alexandria, Virginia.

    Phisterer, *N.Y. in the War*, III, 2566.

15. Marvin C. Rowland, age 30, enrolled at Washington, D.C. to serve three years with the 61st New York and mustered in as the assistant surgeon on October 2, 1862. He became the surgeon on March 6, 1864, and mustered out with the regiment on July 14, 1865, near Alexandria, Virginia.

    NYSAG, 26:1044.

16. John H. Bell, age 23, enrolled on September 28, 1861, at New York City to serve three years in the 57th New York. He mustered in as the 1st lieutenant of Company C on November 12, 1861, and was promoted to captain on June 14, 1862. He became the major on January 12, 1863, and he transferred to the 10th Regiment, Veteran Reserve Corps on June 18, 1863.

    James D. Hewett enrolled at Stafford Court House, Virginia to serve three years and mustered in as the surgeon of the 119th New York on March 16, 1863. He was dismissed on June 14, 1863. Before this he had served as the assistant surgeon of the 66th New York.

    Ibid., 26:8 and 35:916.

17. Josiah M. Faville, age 21, enrolled on September 21, 1861, at New York City to serve three years with the 57th New York. He mustered in as the 2nd lieutenant of Company E on November 12, 1861. On March 7, 1862, he became a 1st lieutenant and the adjutant. He transferred to Company H on April 14, 1863, and on November 14, 1863, he transferred to Company A as the captain. He transferred to Company F on June 30, 1864, and mustered out with the company on August 11, 1864. He became a colonel of U.S. Volunteers by brevet on March 13, 1865.

    Phisterer, *N.Y. in the War*, III, 2496-2497.

CHAPTER SIX

1. Robert Corry, age 28, enrolled at Falmouth, Virginia to serve three years with the 57th New York and mustered in as assistant surgeon on May 16, 1863. He was discharged on September 5, 1863. In January 1863, he had attempted to join the 43rd New York, but was declined.

    Phisterer, *New York in the War,* III, 2279, 2496.

2. Stephen R. Snyder, age 24, enrolled in the 57th New York on October 25, 1861, at Constableville to serve three years and mustered in as a sergeant

in Company C on October 26, 1861. He became the 1st lieutenant of Company H on August 1, 1862, and was promoted to quartermaster on April 14, 1863. He was wounded in action (no date) and mustered out on October 14, 1864, near Petersburg, Virginia.

Ibid., 2501.

3. Stewart L. Woodford, age 27, enrolled on August 22, 1862, at New York City to serve three years with the 127th New York. He mustered in as the lieutenant colonel on September 8, 1862. He was discharged on March 5, 1865, to become the colonel of the 103rd U.S. Colored Troops.

NYSAG, 36:1160.

4. James C. Bronson, age 24, enrolled on September 12, 1861, at Utica to serve three years with the 57th New York. He mustered in as a private in Company B on September 24, 1861. He was promoted to 1st lieutenant on September 27, 1861. He transferred to Company C as the captain on August 4, 1863. Wounded in action on August 14, 1864, near Deep Bottom, Virginia, he was discharged for his wounds on December 17, 1864. His discharge was revoked on the same day and he was transferred to the 61st New York.

Phisterer, *N.Y. in the War*, III, 2495.

5. Elisha L. Palmer, age 21, enrolled on July 1, 1861, at Dobbs Ferry to serve three years with the 57th New York. He mustered in as a sergeant in Company I on August 14, 1861. He was promoted commissary sergeant on November 1, 1862, and became quartermaster sergeant May 1, 1863. He mustered in as the 2nd lieutenant of Company A on June 17, 1863, and was captured on picket near Morrisville, Virginia on August 1, 1863. While a prisoner of war, he was transferred to Company G on September 9, 1864, and later was transferred to Company G, 61st New York on December 20, 1864.

Ibid., 2500.

6. George L. Potter mustered in as the surgeon of the 145th Pennsylvania on September 12, 1862. He mustered out with the regiment on May 31, 1865.

Samuel P. Bates, comp., *History of Pennsylvania Volunteers*, vol. 4 (Harrisburg: B. Singerly, State Printers, 1870) 524.

7. George Mitchell, age 18, enrolled on September 26, 1861, at Utica to serve three years with the 57th New York. He mustered in as a private in Company B on October 31, 1861, and was promoted to 1st sergeant on the same day. He was promoted to 2nd lieutenant of Company D on January 2, 1862, and was wounded in action on June 1, 1862, at Fair Oaks, Virginia. He was mustered in as 1st lieutenant of Company G on November 1, 1862. He mustered out on November 1, 1864, near Petersburg, Virginia. He later served with the U.S. Veteran Volunteers.

Phisterer, *N.Y. in the War*, III, 2499.

8. William F. Hill, age 21, who enlisted in Company K of the 20th Massachusetts on August 6, 1862, at Camp Massasoit, Readville, Massachusetts, deserted from the regiment at Antietam on September 17, 1862. He was turned in by Hiram Bingham, the recruiting officer, in New Brookfield, Massachusetts. Listed as a bounty jumper, he was court-martialed and executed by firing squad on August 28, 1863.

John Smith, age 35, a mechanic from Philadelphia, Pennsylvania, who joined the 1st Company, Massachusetts Sharpshooters, 15th Massachusetts Infantry, was shot on the same day. He had been arrested on August 15, 1863, at Morrisville, Virginia for desertion from his camp near Falmouth, Virginia on January 11, 1863.

Robert I. Alotta, *Civil War Justice, Union Army Executions under Lincoln* (Shippensburg, Pa.: White Mane Publishing Co. Inc., 1989), 76–77.

9. Dr. Mary Walker won the Medal of Honor for being the only female army surgeon during the Civil War.

10. Adam Schmalz, age 18, Company E, 66th New York, enlisted on October 23, 1861. He deserted at Gettysburg on or about July 1, 1863. He was arrested at Hanover, Pennsylvania on July 27 and was court-martialed on September 1. On September 27, General Order 92, Army of the Potomac, sentenced him to death by execution with one William Smitz, Company F, 90th Pennsylvania. A firing squad executed them on October 2, 1863.

Alotta, *C.W. Justice*, 84.

11. Frank Rose, age 20, enlisted on September 13, 1861, at New York City to serve three years with the 57th New York. He mustered in as a private in Company D on September 23, 1861. He was wounded in action on October 14, 1863, at Auburn, Virginia and was discharged with a disability on October 3, 1864.

NYSAG, 26:112.

Case No. 54, Rose, F., Pt., D, 57th N.Y., age 20. Injured October 14, 1863, by a shell, resulting in a compound comminuted fractures of the left humerus and the right knee joint. Operated upon by W. W. Potter, 57th N.Y., surgeon on October 14, 1863. Circular amputations of the left arm one inch from the shoulder and of the right thigh at the lower third. Results: August 9, 1864, removal of the sequestrum. Discharged October 13, 1864.

Medical and Surgical History, XII, 883.

12. Alexander N. Dougherty enrolled on August 17, 1861, and mustered in the same day as a surgeon with the United States Volunteers and was assigned to the 1st New Jersey Volunteers. He mustered out July 9, 1865.

William S. Stryker, *Record of Officers and Men of New Jersey in the Civil War, 1861–1865*, vol. 1 (Trenton: John L. Murphy, 1876), 183.

13. Brower Gessner, age 27, enrolled in Alexandria, Virginia to serve two years with the 38th New York and mustered in on September 14, 1861. He was discharged on November 14, 1862, and enrolled at Falmouth, Virginia and mustered in to serve two years with the 10th New York on April 9, 1863. He mustered out on February 9, 1865, near Petersburg, Virginia.

NYSAG, 22:838 and 18:883.

CHAPTER SEVEN

1. James Addams Beaver enrolled as 1st lieutenant, Company H, 2nd Pennsylvania Volunteers for three months service from April 21 to July 26, 1861. He was appointed lieutenant colonel of the 45th Pennsylvania on July 22, 1861, and was assigned to Camp Curtin. He resigned on September 4, 1862, to command the 148th Pennsylvania which he joined on September 6, 1862.

He was wounded through the body at Chancellorsville on May 3, 1863, and was wounded in the right hip at Cold Harbor on June 3, 1864. On June 16, 1864, he was wounded in the left side by a shell fragment at Petersburg and he was hit in the right thigh at Reams' Station on August 25, 1864, which cost him his leg.

He was breveted brigadier general of United States Volunteers before the end of the war. He mustered out on December 22, 1864, at his own request because of his wounds.

Joseph W. Muffly, ed., *The Story of Our Regiment, A History of the 148th Pennsylvania Vols.* (Des Moines: Kenyon Printing and Mfg., 1904), 921.

2. Frederick A. Dudley enrolled August 11, 1862, and mustered in on August 23, 1862, as the assistant surgeon of the 14th Connecticut. He was promoted to surgeon on April 2, 1863. He was wounded and captured on July 3, 1863, at Gettysburg. He was paroled on January 14, 1864. He mustered out on May 31, 1865.

   Charles D. Page, *History of the 14th Regiment Connecticut Vol. Infantry* (Meriden, Conn.: Horton Printing Co., 1906), 374.

3. Justin Dwinelle enrolled as assistant surgeon of the 71st Pennsylvania. He was promoted to surgeon on September 11, 1861, on division level. He mustered out September 10, 1864.

   Bates, *Pa. Vols.*, III, 833.

4. William A. Arnold enrolled September 28, 1861, as captain of Company A, 1st Rhode Island Light Artillery. He transferred to Company E on December 6, 1862, and was promoted brevet lieutenant colonel. He mustered out on June 17, 1864.

   George Lewis, *The History of Battery E, 1st Regiment Rhode Island Light Artillery* (Providence: Snow and Farnham, 1892), 484.

5. Charles H. H. Broom, age 23, enrolled August 1, 1861, at Poughkeepsie to serve three years with the 57th New York. He was mustered in as the 2nd lieutenant of Company K on September 4, 1861. He became 1st lieutenant and quartermaster on May 17, 1862. He transferred to Company K as 1st lieutenant on April 14, 1863, and he mustered out with the company on September 3, 1864.

   Phisterer, *N.Y. in the War*, III, 2495.

6. Philip M. Plunkett, assistant surgeon, 2nd Delaware.

   Roster of Regimental Surgeons and Assistant Surgeons (Gaithersburg, Md.: Old Soldier Books), 8.

7. The Overland Campaign refers to U.S. Grant's drive across the Rapidan River in May of 1864. It lasted from May 4 through June 6, 1864, and included the battles of the Wilderness, Spotsylvania Court House, the North Anna, the Totopotomoy, and Cold Harbor.

8. Charles S. Hoyt, formerly assistant surgeon of the 126th New York, he mustered in as surgeon of the 66th New York on May 11, 1864. He mustered out with this regiment on July 1, 1865, at Alexandria, Virginia.

   Phisterer, *N.Y. in the War*, III, 2203.

9. Martin T. McMahon, born in Canada, served as chief of staff for the VI Corps from 1862, to 1865.

   Mark M. Boatner, III, *The Civil War Dictionary* (N.Y.: David McKay Co., Inc., 1966), 537.

10. William E. Hall, age 21, enrolled at Hoboken, New Jersey to serve three years with the 57th New York. He mustered in as the 1st sergeant of Company I on August 14, 1861. He became the 1st lieutenant of Company F on November 6, 1862. Wounded in action, at Gettysburg on July 3, 1863, and at Spotsylvania on May 18, 1864, he mustered out with the company on August 11, 1864.

    Phisterer, *N.Y. in the War*, III, 2497.

11. David H. Houston was surgeon of the 2nd Delaware.

    Regimental Surgeons, 8.

12. Hiram L. Brown, mustered in on September 5, 1862, he was brevetted brigadier general on September 3, 1864. He was discharged by special order on February 1, 1865.

     Bates, III, 524.

13. Peter Hunt, sergeant, Company C, 1st Rhode Island Artillery was promoted to 2nd lieutenant of Company A, and then to 1st lieutenant of Company A by November 5, 1862. He died of wounds on June 14, 1864, in Washington, D.C.

     Thomas M. Aldrich, *The History of Battery A, First Rhode Island Light Artillery in the War to Preserve the Union* (Providence: Snow and Farnham, Printers), 390.

14. Richard S. Alcoke, age 26, enrolled on April 17, 1861, at New York City to serve one month. He mustered in as a private of Company G, 7th New York Militia, on April 26, 1861. He mustered out with company on June 3, 1861, at New York City. He enrolled again at New York City to serve three years as a private of Company K, 57th New York, on November 20, 1861. He was promoted to sergeant then 1st sergeant before September 18, 1862, on which date he became the 2nd lieutenant of Company I. He became 1st lieutenant on September 19, 1862. He was wounded in action on December 16, 1862, at Fredericksburg. He mustered in as captain on January 1, 1864. Transferred to Company H on May 7, 1864, he was wounded in action on June 16, 1864, near Petersburg and was discharged for disability from his wounds on October 15, 1864.

     Phisterer, *N.Y. in the War*, III, 2494.

15. William A. Kirk, age 44, enrolled as 1st lieutenant of Company F on July 1, 1861, at New York City to serve three years with the 57th New York. He mustered in as captain of Company G on August 12, 1861, and as major on April 7, 1864. He was wounded in action on June 16, 1864, near Petersburg and died of his wounds on June 17, 1864.

     Ibid., 2498.

16. George C. Case, age 23, enrolled on November 1, 1861, at Brooklyn to serve three years with the 57th New York. He mustered in as a private of Company C on November 2, 1861, and was promoted to commissary sergeant on February 5, 1862. He mustered in as 2nd lieutenant of Company G on February 3, 1862, and as 1st lieutenant and adjutant on June 14, 1863. He was wounded in action on June 16, 1864, at Petersburg and was discharged on September 6, 1864.

     Ibid., 2494.

17. Martin V. B. Brower, age 25, enrolled August 29, 1861, at Poughkeepsie to serve three years with the 57th New York. He mustered in as sergeant of Company K on September 4, 1861, and was promoted sergeant major on January 1, 1863. He mustered in as 2nd lieutenant of Company K on March 13, 1863. He was wounded in action on June 16, 1864, before Petersburg and mustered out with his company on September 3, 1864.

     Thomas Britton, age 23, enrolled on June 27, 1861, at Riverhead to serve three years with the 57th New York. He mustered in as a private of Company I on August 14, 1861. He was promoted to corporal, sergeant, and 1st sergeant by May 1862. He mustered in as 2nd lieutenant on May 29, 1862, and was wounded in action on June 30, 1862, at White Oak Swamp. He was wounded in action at Fredericksburg on December 11, 1862. He mustered in as 1st lieutenant of Company H on November 14, 1863. Wounded in action on June 16, 1864, at Petersburg, he mustered out on October 5, 1864.

     Ibid., 2494, 2495.

18. Dr. Potter in his memoirs said that the boy's name was George Nims. He erred. The boy was William Nims.

     William H. Nims, age 17, enlisted on November 4, 1861, at New York City to serve three years with the 61st New York. He mustered in as a musician of Company I on November 6, 1861. Transferred to Company F on September 12, 1862, no further service record of him exists.
     NYSAG, 26:1014.

     William H. Nims, Company D, 61st New York, was wounded on June 17, 1864, at Petersburg and was admitted into the First Division, Second Corps Hospital before being transferred to Columbian College Hospital at Washington, D.C. on June 22, 1864. A shell fragment struck him in the face, destroying the right eye, fracturing the nasal bone and the right superior matilla. Treatment consisted of removal of all of the bone fragments and adjustment of the lacerated soft parts.

     On April 25, 1865, the doctors found a small fistula communicating with a necrosis of the spongy bones. Surgeon Thomas R. Crosby, U.S.V., had all of the accessible bone removed to keep the nasal canal open and to prevent as much deformity as possible around the orbits. The patient was discharged on April 26, 1865. In 1867, examiner G. W. Avery reported that Nims continued to suffer excessively and that his very unpleasant deformity made it impossible for him to obtain work.
     Medical and Surgical History, VIII, 329–330.

19. James Wallace Britt, age 23, enrolled on September 13, 1861, at New York City to serve three years with the 57th New York. He mustered in as the captain of Company D on November 12, 1861. He was wounded in action at Antietam on September 17, 1862, at Fredericksburg on December 13, 1862, and at Chancellorsville on May 2, 1863. He mustered in as lieutenant colonel on July 23, 1863, and mustered out on January 5, 1865.
     Ibid., 2494.

20. Wallace D. Martin served as the assistant surgeon of the 62nd Pennsylvania from March 17, 1863, through October 9, 1863, when he resigned.
     Bates, vol. III, 461.

21. Private Daniel Geary and Ransom S. Gordon, Company E, 72nd New York raped a camp follower named Mrs. Stiles on June 18, 1864. Gordon apparently was the rapist and Geary was his accomplice.
     Alotta 1989, 117 and 120–121.

22. Martin Rizer mustered in on October 10, 1861, to serve three years with the 72nd Pennsylvania as assistant surgeon. He was promoted to surgeon on August 4, 1862, and was mustered out on August 24, 1864.
     Bates II, 1869, 834.

23. James E. Pomfret, age 36, enrolled July 22, 1862, at Albany to serve three years. He mustered in as surgeon of the 113th New York Infantry on July 24, 1862. He was reassigned on February 7, 1865.
     Phisterer, *N.Y. in the War*, II, 1392.

24. John C. Norris mustered in on March 21, 1863, to serve three years as assistant surgeon. He was promoted to surgeon on October 23, 1864, and mustered out on June 29, 1865.
     Bates, II:1173.

25. John Gardner Hazard began the war as a 1st lieutenant, 1st Rhode Island Artillery on August 25, 1861. Promoted to captain on August 18, 1862, he

remained with the company and became the major on April 19, 1864. He mustered out July 1, 1865, and died in 1897.
Boatner, *Civil War Dictionary*, 390.

CHAPTER EIGHT

1. Helen Gilson worked for the U.S. Sanitary Commission from the time of the Peninsula through 1864. She specialized in training contrabands and freedmen in running efficient kitchen operations. She also served as a nurse among black troops.
Boatner, *Civil War Dictionary*, 344.

2. George W. Jones, age 21, enrolled on September 15, 1861, at New York City to serve three years with the 57th New York. He mustered in as the 1st lieutenant of Company G on September 25, 1861, and as the captain of Company H on November 1, 1862. He transferred to Company I on May 7, 1864, and mustered in as the major on July 4, 1864. He mustered out on August 13, 1864.

   Sylvester D. Alvord, age 25, enrolled at Fondas Bush to serve for three years with the 93rd New York and he mustered in as a private in Company D on October 14, 1861. He was promoted to commissary sergeant on July 22, 1862, and quartermaster sergeant on January 13, 1863. He mustered in as 2nd lieutenant of Company H on October 8, 1863. He was transferred to Company F on May 18, 1864, and was promoted to 1st lieutenant on July 4, 1864. He was discharged on October 17, 1864.
Phisterer, *N.Y. in the War*, III:2498 and IV:3047.

3. J. W. Wishart was the surgeon of the 140th Pennsylvania.
Regimental Surgeons, 206.

BIBLIOGRAPHY

Adjutant General's Office. *Annual Report of the Adjutant General's Office of the State of New York for the Year 1900.* Albany: J. B. Lyon, 1901.

Adjutant General's Office. *Roster of Wisconsin Volunteers.* Vol. 1. Madison: Democratic Printing Co., 1886.

Alotta, Robert I. *Civil War Justice Union Army Executions.* Shippensburg, Pa.: White Mane Publishing Co., Inc., 1989.

Bates, Samuel P., comp. *History of Pennsylvania Volunteers.* Vols. 3 and 4. Harrisburg: B. Singerly, State Printers, 1870.

Bidwell, Frederick David., comp. *History of the Forty-Ninth New York Volunteers.* Albany: J. B. Lyon Co., 1916.

Boatner, Mark Mayo, III. *The Civil War Dictionary.* N.Y.: David McKay Co., Inc., 1966.

Buffalo *Morning Express.* October 1861, April 1862, and June 1862.

Foster, John. Letters to the Fredonia *Censor,* October and May 1862.

Fuller, Charles A. *Personal Recollections of the War of 1861.* Hamilton, N.Y.: Edmontson Publishing Co., 1990.

Heitman, Francis P. *Historical Register and Dictionary of the United States Army.* Vol. 1, 11. Washington, D.C.: U.S. Government Printing Office, 1903.

Henderson, Lillian, comp. *Roster of Confederate Soldiers of Georgia (1861-1865).* Vol. 1. Hapeville, Ga.: Longino and Porter, Inc., 1955.

Jordan, Weymouth T., comp. *North Carolina Troops, 1861-1865.* Vol. 4. 1973.

148

The Medical and Surgical History of the Civil War. Vols. 8 and 12. Wilmington, N.C.: Broadfoot Publishing Co., 1991.

Muffly, Joseph W., ed. *The Story of Our Regiment, A History of the 148th Pennsylvania Volunteers.* Des Moines: Kenyon Printing and Mfg., 1904.

Page, Charles D. *History of the 14th Regiment Connecticut Volunteer Infantry.* Meriden, Conn.: Horton Printing Co., 1906.

Peck, Theodore S., comp. *Revised Roster of Vermont Volunteers Who Served in the Army and Navy of the U.S. 1861–1866.* Montpelier: Watchman Publishing Co., 1892.

Phisterer, Frederick, comp. *New York in the War of the Rebellion 1861–1865.* 3rd edition. Albany: J. B. Lyon Co., 1912.

Roster of Regimental Surgeons and Assistant Surgeons. Gaithersburg, Md.: Old Soldier Books.

Sears, Stephen W., ed. *The Civil War Papers of George B. McClellan, Selected Correspondence, 1860–1865.* N.Y.: Ticknor and Fields, 1989.

Sifakis, Stewart. *Who Was Who in the Civil War.* N.Y.: Oxford University Press, 1988.

Stryker, William S., Record of Officers and Men of New Jersey in the Civil War, 1861–1865. Vol. 1. Trenton: John L. Murphy, 1876.

INDEX